The Bottlenose Dolphin

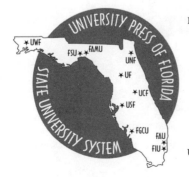

Florida A&M University, Tallahassee
Florida Atlantic University, Boca Raton
Florida Gulf Coast University, Fort Myers
Florida International University, Miami
Florida State University, Tallahassee
University of Central Florida, Orlando
University of Florida, Gainesville
University of North Florida, Jacksonville
University of South Florida, Tampa
University of West Florida, Pensacola

University Press of Florida

GAINESVILLE · TALLAHASSEE · TAMPA · BOCA RATON

PENSACOLA · ORLANDO · MIAMI · JACKSONVILLE · FT. MYERS

The Bottlenose Dolphin

BIOLOGY AND CONSERVATION

JOHN E. REYNOLDS III

RANDALL S. WELLS

SAMANTHA D. EIDE

05 04 03 02 01 00   6 5 4 3 2 1

LIBRARY OF CONGRESS CATALOGING-IN-PUBLICATION DATA
Reynolds, John Elliott, 1952-
The bottlenose dolphin: biology and conservation / John E. Reynolds
III, Randall S. Wells, Samantha D. Eide.
p. cm.
Includes bibliographical references (p.).
ISBN 0-8130-1775-0 (alk. paper)
1. Bottlenose dolphin. 2. Wildlife conservation. I. Wells, Randall S.
II. Eide, Samantha D. III. Title.
QL 737.C432 R49 2000
599.53's—DC21 00-029899

The University Press of Florida is the scholarly publishing agency
for the State University System of Florida, comprising Florida A&M
University, Florida Atlantic University, Florida Gulf Coast University,
Florida International University, Florida State University, University
of Central Florida, University of Florida, University of North Florida,
University of South Florida, and University of West Florida.

University Press of Florida
15 Northwest 15th Street
Gainesville, FL 32611–2079
http://www.upf.com

To all those individuals, living and deceased,
who have helped us understand and appreciate
bottlenose dolphins. As we wrote this book,
our recently departed mentors and friends,
David and Melba Caldwell, Steve Leatherwood,
Ken Norris, and John Prescott, were on our minds.

Contents

Figures and Tables

Color Plates (following page 176)

Tables

Acknowledgments

A great many people contributed time or resources to this book. Although these individuals are not responsible for any deficiencies, they have contributed to any success the book may enjoy. We are very grateful to them all, but especially to Meta Osborn, who has helped the Eckerd College Dolphin Project in many ways. In addition, we thank John and Rosemary Galbraith, who have provided unbelievable support of marine science at Eckerd College; the Disney Wildlife Conservation Fund and the National Marine Fisheries Service for helping us expand our research horizons; the McGarry Student Research Fund; and Eckerd College colleagues, Lloyd Chapin, Gregg Brooks, and Rick Haskins, who, together with the National Marine Fisheries Service, have provided funds to help defray the costs of putting this volume together. The interest and assistance of staff at the University Press of Florida is also much appreciated; in particular we thank Chris Hofgren and Gillian Hillis. Finally, we note, with gratitude, the logistic help provided by students involved in the Eckerd College Dolphin Project: most recently these included Jason Allen, Jonathan Birnbaum, Rebecca Goodnight, Kristin Harrison, and Kari Higgs.

Randy Wells thanks the Chicago Zoological Society, and especially Director George B. Rabb and Chairman Edward McCormick Blair, Jr., for crucial ongoing support of the Sarasota Dolphin Research Program. Mote Marine Laboratory provided initial support for this program in 1970–1971, and today provides a base of operations in Sarasota for the ongoing research. Earthwatch Institute has provided funds and volunteers since 1982 that have maintained essential continuity for the program. We have received much-needed and much appreciated support from the Disney Wildlife Conservation Fund, Dolphin Quest, the National Marine Fisheries Service, Ronnie and John Enander, and Don and Lee Hamilton. The quality of research in Sarasota Bay has benefited greatly from the dedicated efforts of colleagues Sue Hofmann, Kim Hull, Howard Rhinehart, and Kim Urian.

Several people, with different backgrounds, read parts or all of the text and provided helpful comments. We deliberately sought breadth of comment because we hope the book appeals to people with a wide range of interests in dolphins. Folks who commented include Beth Forys, Tessa Hill, Alison Kirk-Long, and Dana Wetzel. We are especially grateful to the following three colleagues who carefully read the entire text and provided comments: Dan Odell, Sentiel (Butch) Rommel, and John Twiss. In addition, we thank Danielle Ponsolle for editorial assistance and the two individuals (Charles Potter and Laela Sayigh) who provided reviews to the editors of the University Press of Florida; both did an incredibly careful job and provided a number of important comments about content and format of the book.

Similarly, a number of individuals provided illustrations or photographs to support the text. Flip Nicklin and Minden Pictures provided unique and beautiful images of dolphins in the wild. Butch Rommel used his mastery of anatomy and his creative abilities to provide illustrations that clarify the unusual adaptations that make dolphins what they are. Sam Ridgway and Michelle Reddy of the U.S. Navy provided some wonderful photographs of dolphins and dolphin scientists, including the historic views of Tuffy; Marya Willis-Glowka provided artistic flair to interpret how dolphins appear; Dan Odell and Sea World of Florida provided a range of images that help illustrate both education and science; Laela Sayigh kindly allowed us to use a spectrogram of dolphin whistles; the Johns Hopkins University Archeological Collection and the Staatliche Antiken Sammlungen und Glyptothek in Munich allowed us to use beautiful images depicting ancient Greek perspectives on dolphins; very useful, and even unique, photographs were provided by colleagues Jason Allen, Bill Carr, Jay Gorzelany, Denise Herzing, Sue Hofmann, Megan Stolen, and Kim Urian; and Beth Forys used her GIS and other skills to assist with graphs and maps, and specifically to assist Kris Herrington to provide a general distribution map.

Mostly, we thank our various colleagues and friends who have helped us learn about and love bottlenose dolphins. In Randy Wells's case, such associations go back nearly three decades to his pioneering work with Blair Irvine and Michael Scott, and they extend through his work with Ken Norris and the multitude of colleagues with whom he has worked to understand dolphins in Sarasota Bay. In John Reynolds's case, his work with Dan Odell in the mid-1970s and beyond stimulated questions and collaborative projects to last a lifetime, and his subsequent work with the Marine Mammal Commission and with his many students and colleagues at Eckerd College and elsewhere has kept him excited, informed, and humbled. For Samantha Eide, the world of dolphin science is newer, but she is grateful to her friends involved with the Eckerd College Dolphin Project with whom she has spent many hours on a boat, just watching dolphins.

We are grateful to colleagues who provided unpublished information on dolphins or other organisms or who assisted our search for certain information. These people include Peter Best, Robert Hueter, Alison Kirk-Long, Frances Michaelis, Bill Perrin, Simon Northridge, and Ben Wilson.

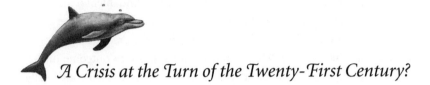

A Crisis at the Turn of the Twenty-First Century?

"Wildlife management actually is largely a matter of human management, an ordering of wildlife-related institutions. . . . How we behave in relation to natural populations . . . is a human affair tightly interwoven with the needs, competition, and frivolities of humans—and with the social institutions they build. There is, it seems to me, a typical touch of human arrogance in this cant of mind that tells us we are managing animals when we are really trying to manage ourselves."[1] In this simple but articulate statement, the late Ken Norris captures the essence of dealing with bottlenose dolphins and other animals with which we share space and other resources on this planet. Few species have captured the human imagination the way dolphins have, and a few people have devoted lifetimes to understanding and conserving dolphins. But ultimately, the well-being of dolphins and other wildlife is tied closely with human activities and human perceptions.

The focus of this book is the bottlenose dolphin (*Tursiops truncatus*); we describe how the species is built to swim fast and dive deep; we discuss its ability to communicate and to exhibit extraordinary cognitive abilities; we provide insights into how dolphins live and breed and raise their young. But throughout the book, superimposed on the dolphins and their habitat, are interactions with humans. We hope readers will come to understand both the bottlenose and effects of human activities a little better—and to understand that solutions to issues come hard.

To the layperson reading a newspaper on a Sunday morning, bottlenose dolphins are sometimes portrayed as free-spirited creatures of near-human intelligence being held against their will in captivity. However, when it comes to dolphins, few portraits are unambiguous. For example, Nancy Klingener's article in the June 7, 1995, issue of the Miami Herald, entitled "Activist Tries to Free Dolphins, but the Mammals Choose to Stay," suggests that, even in the animal rights community, there are fundamental disagreements about the proper use and treatment of dolphins. Certainly the question of maintaining dolphins, or indeed any other wild creatures, in captivity is a topic which merits debate. To date, one important outcome of this debate is the maintenance of animals in zoos and aquaria under continually improving conditions, where they reproduce successfully and often approximate natural life spans.[2] For example, survival in modern oceanaria of dolphins,[3] killer whales (*Orcinus orca*), and other species of marine mammals is similar to survival estimated for those same species in the wild.[4] However, even evidence of longevity and apparent well-being of captive marine mammals does not solve the dilemma for some people.

For example, some members of the animal rights community feel strongly that nearly all of the approximately 650 bottlenose dolphins currently (as of 1998) held in captivity worldwide should be released into the wild.[5] The underlying assumption is that this is what is best for the animals themselves. On the other hand, many marine mammal scientists suggest that, unless there are compelling reasons to do so,[6] such as endangered status of the species, release of captives may not be in the best interest of either the wild population (due, for example, to introduction of diseases and subsequent deaths of many animals or to artificial genetic mixing) or the released individuals (due to their inability to capture live prey, inability to successfully join appropriate social groups, etc.). Such studies raise the question of whether people want to release captive dolphins into the wild to make themselves feel virtuous or to really do what is most humane for the captives or the wild populations.

In those few studies in which some monitoring has occurred, long-term captive dolphins released into the wild rarely fare well, if they survive at all. For example, seven Indian Ocean bottlenose dolphins were released from Atlantis Marine Park near Perth, Western Australia.[7] The seven included both captive-born and wild-born animals that had been maintained at the park for a decade. The release occurred because the facility was shut down for financial reasons; since the impending closure was known for some time, efforts were made to prepare the dolphins for life in the wild. The results were not promising. Three of the dolphins were recaptured due to their very apparent and rapid loss of body condition (up to 15 percent of the prerelease body weight); of the remaining animals, one (a calf) was lost and presumed dead, and the status of the others was uncertain, although confirmed and unconfirmed sightings occurred for some time. The scientists who assessed the success of the release effort concluded that "[r]eleases of dolphins from other facilities in the world will likely occur. However, it may not be the most humane approach for those dolphins, and if undertaken, should be run as a careful scientific experiment with realistic alternatives for those animals that do not manage the transition."[8]

At least some of the dolphins released from the Atlantis Marine Park turned to begging for fish from passing boaters, but they were still unable to maintain adequate body condition. This circumstance has also occurred when impromptu (and illegal) releases have occurred. In one infamous incident in 1996, two captive dolphins were released illegally from a facility in the Florida Keys.[9] These two animals had not been adequately prepared for survival in the wild. When they were ultimately rescued by the National Marine Fisheries Service, they were in poor condition and would almost certainly have perished without intervention.[10] In such cases, we expect that even the most ardent supporter of release programs for dolphins and other marine mammals would admit that living in captivity is better than a slow death by starvation.

On the other hand, scientific, carefully controlled release programs can be quite successful.[11] Two young male dolphins, Misha and Echo, were captured in Tampa Bay, Florida, in 1988, held for a period of two years in captivity, carefully reconditioned to permit them to feed on living food and to otherwise not require human attendants, and released in 1990 into their native waters. Careful monitoring showed that the two males reacclimated beautifully to life in the wild. Within five weeks of their release, the two separated from one another, with each reoccupying his original home range in the bay. Through 1993, both appeared to be doing well, although one of the animals (Echo) has not been spotted since 1993.[12] Possible keys to the success of this release include the relatively short time the animals were maintained in captivity, the careful extinction of dependence of the dolphins on humans, release into waters and social groups with which the animals were very familiar, and the young age of the animals.

So return to the wild may, in some isolated instances, be a viable and humane option for particular dolphins, but few releases have been as well conceived or executed as Misha's and Echo's. Nor are the release candidates generally as suitable. However, the question of whether the potential costs of release of captive dolphins in terms of disease transmission to wild animal populations (not necessarily confined just to bottlenose dolphins) outweigh the potential benefits for individual animals is still important. Finally, people considering release of animals should, but often do not, consider whether such animals can become threats to human health and welfare by becoming nuisance animals used to accepting food from people.

But there is an insidious and unresolved additional question regarding what is best for dolphins that plagues the coastal waters of the world as the twenty-first century begins: Is the natural world a healthier place to live than the captive environment? Stated otherwise, have humans so altered the coastal and marine environments that the well-being of some wild dolphins may paradoxically be in greater jeopardy than the well-being of captives? There is evidence that at least some dolphin habitats may be so modified that they are heading in this unfortunate direction. Thus, unbeknownst to most people, by far the most serious issues for dolphins today concern the future of wild populations, not well-being of captives. The focus of the news media noted at the outset of this chapter has often been somewhat misplaced.

For example, the questions of the health of dolphins and the relationship of health and habitat quality have become rather pressing for the 130 animals occupying the Moray Firth, Scotland, where 95 percent have skin lesions (up to seven different types) and 6 percent possess evident anatomical abnormalities.[13] Adult females and calves appear to display lesions more frequently than adult males and subadults. At this time, the reasons for the apparent health problems in this small, isolated group of dolphins are unknown, but deleterious effects of anthropogenic pollutants can certainly not be ruled out. However, the role of cold water temperatures pushing the limits of the species' tolerance must also be considered.

A recent study of bottlenose dolphins in Sarasota Bay[14] indicates that males may exhibit impaired immune function, possibly related to bioaccumulation of anthropogenic toxicants[15] (for example, PCBs and DDTs) during the life span of the animals. Inasmuch as older males are more successful sires of calves than younger males, what do such health problems and possible effects on reproduction mean in terms of dolphin population genetics and social systems? All that can be said with certainty is that the "natural and normal" reproductive biology may have been disrupted, possibly due to contaminants created and released by humans.

Interestingly, female dolphins (like many other female marine mammals) are able to unload a lot of their lipid-soluble toxicants (for example, organochlorine pesticides) in the rich, fatty milk they provide to their calves.[16] First-time mother dolphins in Sarasota Bay have on only one occasion successfully raised a calf in the nearly thirty years in which dolphins there have been studied. One wonders whether first-time mothers, which have accumulated toxicants over a period of five to twelve years (a figure that applies to age of onset of sexual maturity for female dolphins in Sarasota Bay, but not necessarily elsewhere),[17] may be giving their newborns such a hefty dose of poison that they cannot survive. There are other data that reinforce the need for concern that health of firstborn dolphin calves may be compromised by the heavy toxicant burdens they acquire from their mothers. For example, milk produced by female dolphins in Sarasota can contain high levels of toxicants,[18] and one firstborn calf had the highest total pesticide levels of any Sarasota Bay dolphins that were tested. The organochlorine levels in this animal were as much as five times higher than those in a similarly aged fourth-born calf.[19] In dolphins located off South Africa, approximately 80 percent of the total DDT and PCBs in the bodies of females was transferred via lactation to their offspring.[20] On the other hand, sexually mature female dolphins may reproduce every three or more years;[21] so after their first calves, mothers may never have the time to accumulate as many toxicants as they did prior to their firstborn. A study of five captive female dolphins showed that age, reproductive history, and lipid content of the milk were related to the concentrations of organochlorines present; interestingly, the highest concentrations were present in a thirty-four-year-old animal during what was apparently its first (orphan-induced) lactation.[22] Likewise, the amount of toxicant transferred to a beluga whale (*Delphinapterus leucas*) calf appears to be related to a variety of factors, including age of the mother, her own toxicant levels, the lipid content of the milk, and the duration of lactation.[23]

In many regards, studies of the effects of anthropogenic toxicants on individual marine mammals and on population dynamics still are in their infancy.[24] However, experimental studies[25] on harbor seals (*Phoca vitulina*), which also live many years and which eat the same sorts of foods humans and dolphins do, have indicated impairment of immune function following consumption of contaminated fish. The magnitude of the immune response was inversely correlated with toxicant levels (especially PCBs) in blubber. Scientists have demonstrated in nonmarine mammals that the PCBs and PBBs (polychlorinated biphenyls and polybrominated biphenyls, respectively) are strong agents of immunosuppression.[26]

In all likelihood, in waters or food webs where toxicant levels are high, all bottlenose dolphins, not just the old males in which bioaccumulation is greatest, are affected. In fact, some of the highest concentrations of total DDTs for any cetacean were found in bottlenose dolphins off California.[27] Reproductive success may be impaired in a number of ways. For example, firstborn calves may receive and perhaps become debilitated from doses of toxic chemicals they cannot successfully combat (see discussion above). In California sea lions (*Zalophus californianus*), high levels of organochlorines in the late 1960s were thought to have led to premature births of pups,[28] although other factors, such as disease agents, may also have played an important role.[29] Other ways by which toxicants could impair reproduction have also been suggested in marine mammals. For example, a correlation exists between high levels of organochlorines and lowered testosterone levels in Dall's porpoises (*Phocoenoides dalli*).[30] In common, or harbor, seals, implantation of the embryo in the uterus of the mother was hindered in animals fed a diet high in organochlorines.[31] Even though no incidence of such problems has been reported for bottlenose dolphins, the possibility of physiological dysfunctions as a result of excessive exposure to toxicants certainly exists.

In addition, a number of studies of marine mammals suggest a tie between toxicant levels and susceptibility to disease.[32] Perhaps the most noteworthy example of this relationship involves beluga whales in the St. Lawrence estuary. These animals, long known to carry extremely high toxicant loads, also had a higher prevalence of cancer than has been reported in any other group of free-ranging cetaceans.[33] In fact, 37 percent of all tumors that have ever been reported from all cetacean species *worldwide* were found in this single small population of belugas, suggesting "an influence of contami-

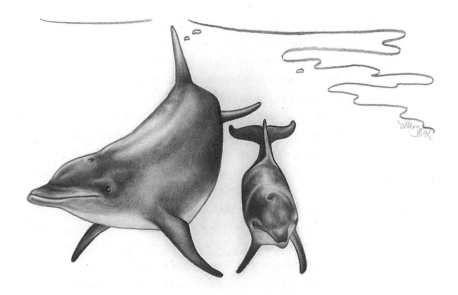

Fig. 1. A mother and calf swimming. Marya Willis-Glowka.

nants through a direct carcinogenic effect and/or a decreased resistance to the development of tumors."[34]

Altogether, it is abundantly clear that, due to the introduction of anthropogenic toxicants, the chemical makeup of dolphin habitat is not what it once was. And the change does not bode well for the animals.

Nor are anthropogenic toxicants the only chemical threats to marine mammals. Certain algae called dinoflagellates produce natural toxins, such as lipid-soluble brevetoxin and water-soluble saxitoxin. Brevetoxin, produced by the dinoflagellate (*Gymnodinium breve*) responsible for "red tides," has been identified as the cause of two die-offs of endangered Florida manatees (*Trichechus manatus latirostris*) in 1982 and 1996.[35] The latter event killed almost 150 individuals along the southwest coast of the state and made headlines internationally; less well advertised were the deaths of at least thirty dolphins, as well as countless fish, seabirds, and other marine organisms in the same area at the same time, and possibly from the same cause.

Brevetoxin was found in tissues and in the gut contents (primarily menhaden, *Brevoortia* spp.) of a few (eight out of seventeen tested) bottlenose dolphins that died as part of a massive die-off in 1987–88 of at least 750 animals along the Atlantic coast of the southeastern United States. Based on this finding, as well as lack of other compelling evidence as to the cause of the die-off, some scientists suggested that indirect effects of red tides were to blame.[36] However, to confuse the issue of cause of death, very high tissue concentrations of a variety of anthropogenic toxicants (including immuno-suppressive substances) were found in the dead dolphins.[37] Scientists stated: "Although the impact of these contaminants is not fully known, their role as causative agents in this recent mass mortality must be considered."[38] Pa-thologists subsequently examined archived tissues and ultimately suggested that a distemper-like virus called morbillivirus accounted for the deaths of these animals.[39] The precise interplay between the natural toxins, the an-thropogenic toxicants, the virus, immune dysfunction, opportunistic infec-tions, and death are still unclear,[40] but the morbillivirus infection alone could certainly have led directly to some immunosuppression, thereby opening the door to secondary infections of various types.[41]

Serological evidence, in the form of antibodies, of past morbillivirus in-fections has been found in living, apparently healthy bottlenose dolphins in coastal waters of the Gulf of Mexico and the western Atlantic. Thus, recur-rent epizootics (that is, diseases attacking a large number of animals simul-taneously)[42] appear to have occurred in the animals since at least the early 1980s.[43] Offshore bottlenose dolphins appear to have even higher prevalence of morbillivirus antibodies, possibly because they may associate at sea with pilot whales (*Globicephala* spp.), in which the disease may be indigenous to a specific locality[44] (such diseases are said to be enzootic).[45] Why do some dolphins survive this deadly infection, whereas others perish? Possibly the latter have been compromised by heavy body burdens of toxicants, as has been suggested for striped dolphins (*Stenella coeruleoalba*) during a 1990–92 epizootic event in the Mediterranean Sea.[46] In fact, the experimental studies of harbor seal immunology noted above leave open the possibility that ex-posure to high levels of organochlorines could increase susceptibility to vi-ral infections seen in a number of marine mammal species.

Saxitoxin was implicated in the deaths of fourteen humpback whales (*Megaptera novaeangliae*) off New England in 1987.[47] In addition, possibly over 70 percent of the three hundred or so Mediterranean monk seals (*Monachus monachus*) living off the western Sahara-Mauritanian coast may have succumbed to saxitoxin poisoning in 1997.[48] However, it is possible that a newly discovered morbillivirus caused the monk seal mortality.[49] Possibly scientists will discover, as they did with the 1987–88 die-off of bottlenose dolphins mentioned above, that synergistic effects of several factors may have been responsible for the monk seal die-off.[50] To date, no dolphin deaths have been attributed to saxitoxin exposure, but the incidence of saxitoxin-related die-offs in other marine mammals indicates that dolphins may be at risk.

One may notice that the older literature contains few records of die-offs of marine mammals due to exposure to biotoxins (brevetoxin or saxitoxin). Certainly, scientists are becoming more aware of, and better at detecting, biotoxins in marine mammals; that fact alone could account for the more recent diagnoses. However, the increase in frequency of reports may actually reflect developing conditions. For example, on a global basis (not necessarily in particular regions), it appears that outbreaks of toxic dinoflagellates have increased.[51] In fact, "the number of toxic blooms, the economic losses from them, the types of resources affected and the kinds of toxins and toxic species have all increased."[52] The changes in incidence probably have multiple causes, but they suggest a link, in at least some cases, with discharge of anthropogenic chemicals, including nutrients such as fertilizers used for agriculture. If this is the case, once again we face a situation where humans have modified natural systems to the great detriment of the inhabitants.

Other aspects of bottlenose dolphin habitat and lifestyle may jeopardize particular dolphin populations as well. Dolphins have the misfortune to seek for their food many of the same species people like to eat. The resulting competition can manifest itself in ways that harm dolphins directly or indirectly. For example, it has long been recognized that coastal netting along the North and South Carolina coasts kills a number of dolphins (possibly on the order of two to three dozen mortalities annually), and in one case even led to overharvest and commercial extinction of the target species, the sturgeon (*Acipenser oxyrhynchus*).[53] As the fisheries continued operating in the 1990s, dolphins continued to die. In 1993, seventy-four bottlenose dolphins were reported dead off the coast of North Carolina; of those, twenty-six (35.1 percent) showed evidence that human activities, including netting, caused death, and twenty-eight (37.8 percent) were not examined or were too decomposed to determine whether human interactions had occurred.[54] Most dolphin strandings in that region in 1993 took place during the spring (when ocean gill netting occurs) and fall (when stop nets receive heavy use). Depending on the status of particular stocks of dolphins, such mortality may or may not be sustainable.

The situation is by no means confined to coastal Carolina waters—the same scenario occurs with a great variety of fisheries and marine mammals all over the world, and new examples of such "incidental take" are reported regularly. Perhaps the most publicized example involved the "take"[55] of several species of dolphins (of which the bottlenose was not a primary target) in yellowfin tuna (*Thunnus albacares*) purse seines at a level that historically reached more than 400,000 dolphins a year in the eastern tropical Pacific Ocean![56]

One should not conclude that commercial fishing gear alone entangles and kills dolphins. For example, recreational fishing gear has been implicated in injury and mortality of dolphins in Florida and elsewhere, but this factor is rarely acknowledged and factored into conservation efforts.[57]

Fishing effort can affect dolphins in other ways. Environmental factors such as the availability and quality of food can affect reproductive potential (termed fecundity), age at sexual maturity, birth size, and body condition.[58] In the wake of a ban on coastal commercial netting operations, habitat use patterns of bottlenose dolphins near Tampa Bay, Florida, changed dramatically.[59] "New" locations were used heavily, often for feeding, after the ban. Concurrently, at least in the short term, dolphin reproductive success boomed, as measured by frequency with which calves were sighted in the area.[60] These changes in dolphin habitat use, behavior, and productivity coincided with dramatic increases in abundance, school size, and size of individual mullet (*Mugil* spp.), a favorite dolphin prey.[61] Standing stocks of other dolphin prey increased as well in that area.[62] Although cause and effect cannot be determined, the coincidence suggests that regulation of human fishing can apparently benefit dolphins, just as unregulated or poorly regulated fishing can be detrimental.

Although the relationship may seem intuitive, there are no hard data to prove that bottlenose dolphin populations may be limited by food availability. There is, however, at least some circumstantial evidence to relate size of other marine mammal populations and availability of prey. Perhaps the most striking example involves the precipitous (over 80 percent) decline of Steller sea lion (*Eumetopias jubatus*) stocks occupying the Bering Sea, Gulf of Alaska, and waters around the Aleutian Islands.[63] Some scientists suggest that the drop may relate to human competition for walleye pollock (*Theragra chalcogramma*),[64] although the relationship between pollock stocks and local sea lion abundance is not entirely clear.

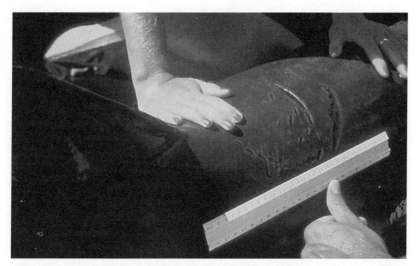

Fig. 2. Scars on Ms. Mayhem resulting from an attack by a large shark. Randall S. Wells, Chicago Zoological Society.

In a similar way, the number (as suggested by beach counts) of endangered Hawaiian monk seals (*Monachus schauinslandi*) occupying the species' largest rookery at French Frigate Shoals has dropped by nearly 50 percent in the past decade,[65] possibly due in large part to changing oceanographic patterns and a subsequent drop of 30 to 50 percent in productivity in that area since the early 1980s.[66] It should also be noted that overfishing by commercial fishing operations likely played at least some role in the reduction of both monk seal prey and the monk seals themselves.

There are other ways by which fishing effort may indirectly affect dolphins. In Florida, populations of large coastal species of sharks have been depleted by about 80 percent since 1970.[67] The elimination of large numbers of predators has to have great consequences, some subtle and some overt, in coastal ecosystems. One likely direct effect would be a reduction in shark predation on dolphins. Scars resulting from shark bites occur on 36 percent of the bottlenose dolphins in Moreton Bay, Australia,[68] and on over 30 percent of the bottlenose dolphins in Sarasota Bay.[69] One would expect those percentages to drop over time if there were fewer and fewer sharks. A possible but unproven consequence of the reduction in predatory sharks could be an increase in populations of certain prey species such as rays. Scientists recently have documented several cases where bottlenose dolphins have died due to broken stingray spines embedded in their heads or bodies.[70]

Thus, greater numbers of rays could create more encounters with dolphins, encounters that may prove lethal for the latter. Whatever the effects of diminished shark populations may be, two things are certain: (1) those effects will be long lasting, because shark populations, like those of dolphins and other species with low fecundity, do not recover quickly; and (2) neither scientists nor managers really know what those effects are or will be.

Although uncertainty exists about cause and effect and about the future of marine ecosystems, some interesting speculation has occurred that suggests plausible links between overfishing and major ecosystem change. One especially fascinating scenario attempts to explain why sea otter (*Enhydra lutris*) populations and kelp forests around the Aleutian Islands have crashed. The otter is a "keystone species," the presence of which promotes a productive kelp forest ecosystem; lack of otters has led to kelp deforestation and to a significant reduction in inshore productivity in that area. Scientists suggest that killer whales (*Orcinus orca*) have recently begun to prey heavily on otters because their normal prey, Steller sea lions, have become so rare. As noted above, the decline in the sea lion populations may be due to human overfishing. Thus, it is suggested that overfishing has contributed to decimation of Steller sea lions, causing killer whales to shift to eating otters, which has caused deforestation of local kelp beds.[71]

Along the same lines, noted marine ecologist Paul K. Dayton and his colleagues have spent decades studying kelp ecosystems. They worry that nature, even of ecosystems that seem pristine, is presently far removed from what is "normal"; lacking appropriate benchmarks, we are really incapable of understanding what the natural ecosystem in a particular location is or the extent to which changes we observe are caused by natural or anthropogenic factors.[72] Lacking such knowledge, what should be the goals of ecosystem restoration and conservation? More germane to dolphins, what role do they play in the revamped ecosystems they now occupy? Can the dolphins survive and remain healthy as the habitats they require degrade further? What are the limits of dolphin adaptability?

These and other questions suggest that it may not be an entirely humane act to return captive animals to the wild. Their enclosures may not be natural, but neither is nature! Let us hasten to add that the solution is not to turn our backs on nature and focus on creating the best possible captive environments. For the good of all wild species, and of humans as well, people must focus on preserving those areas and resources that are still in good shape

Fig. 3. Five dolphins swimming in a close formation. Flip Nicklin and Minden Pictures.

while attempting to reverse trends of habitat degradation elsewhere. Ultimately, the fate of bottlenose dolphins and of other species on this earth rests in the wild, not in captivity.

A potential, but avoidable, crisis exists for bottlenose dolphins and many other species as we enter the twenty-first century. To help people understand the dolphins and the issues, we wrote this book. We have attempted to create a reference to inform people of what dolphins really are and do; what dolphin habitat needs are; what threats exist to dolphins and habitat; how people have interacted with dolphins through history; and how we may conserve dolphins, along with our own and other species. This book is not designed to perpetuate myths or to further mystical views of dolphins. Rather, it attempts to provide information that may help people understand these remarkable animals and their world.

Bottlenose Dolphins

SPECIAL OR NOT?

Certain terms evoke rather clear images in the mind. The imposing mountain Denali (meaning "The Great One") creates an image of grandeur, spirituality, and danger as it looms over the landscape of central Alaska. Rolls Royce is synonymous with wealth and luxury. Typhoons represent the destructive force of an angry nature. A perfect red rose provides transient beauty. A person looking at a helpless, naked baby cannot help thinking of purity and innocence.

But what about the term *bottlenose dolphin*? The words, like those mentioned above, certainly evoke a clear image for most people. However, people do not agree on what the proper image is or should be.

Fundamentally, the bottlenose dolphin is a member of the mammalian order Cetacea (whales, dolphins, and porpoises), and the suborder Odontoceti (whales that possess at least one pair of teeth as adults). The many types of toothed whales stand in contrast to the members of the suborder Mysticeti, which use baleen plates suspended from the upper jaw to feed.[1] The scientific name of the bottlenose dolphin is *Tursiops truncatus. Tursiops* means dolphinlike, and *truncatus* refers to the worn (that is, truncated) teeth of a presumably old specimen from the River Dart in England[2] described nearly two hundred years ago by Montagu.[3]

Fig. 4. Open-mouthed posture shows the dolphin's teeth. Flip Nicklin and Minden Pictures.

Fig. 5. Five dolphins swimming in shallows. Flip Nicklin and Minden Pictures.

As placental mammals, dolphins share certain attributes with humans, dogs, cows, mice, and most other mammals with which people are familiar. For example, all mammal species have mammary glands that produce milk to nourish the young; virtually all mammals give birth to live young; all species have hair at some point in their lives; all have generally similar hearts and circulatory systems; and mammals typically maintain a constant body temperature and are warm blooded.[4] These are just a few of the many attributes dolphins share with other mammals. Thus, it would, perhaps, be reasonable to consider dolphins as no more special than the other 4,000-plus species of mammals that occupy the earth.

This is not to say that dolphins and other cetaceans are ordinary or mundane. Like all species, bottlenose dolphins are exquisitely adapted for their particular niche. Like all the marine mammals, they are large in size (for heat conservation, among other things), streamlined, and powerful. Structures that could cause drag as they swim (for example, hind limbs, hair, external ears) have been lost, and propulsion occurs by movements of flukes. They employ unusual structures to communicate and navigate underwater, and they possess abilities such as deep and prolonged diving, seawater ingestion, and staying warm in cold water, which leave humans shaking their heads in admiration and wonder. These and other attributes are considered in detail

Fig. 6. A dolphin underwater. Marya Willis-Glowka.

It appears that even thousands of years ago people felt some sort of kinship with these aquatic creatures.[9] Ancient myths originating from points around the world involve the transmutation of humans into dolphins and vice versa.[10] Perhaps dolphin behavior, in which individuals may appear to care for one another or even place themselves in positions where their own well-being is compromised for the sake of another individual,[11] reminds people of acts of human kindness. Amazingly, dolphins have assisted drowning people, and in some parts of the world, dolphins team up with human fishermen, to the mutual benefit of both.

Fig. 8. An ancient Greek bowl depicting the god of wine, Dionysus, and the origin of dolphins. The myth states that Dionysus was kidnapped by pirates, but he retaliated by turning them into dolphins. Note the bunches of grapes and the vines in the sail. Attic Black Figure Kylix, made by Exekias, circa 550–530 B.C.E. Courtesy of Staatliche Antikensammlungen und Glyptothek, Munich.

Fig. 7. Swimming dolphins. Marya Willis-Glowka.

in chapter 4. For now, let it suffice that bottlenose dolphins and their
tives do, indeed, have some special attributes that cause their human a
ers to consider them to be beautiful and remarkable.

Thus, many people are not content to consider dolphins as quali
equivalent to, say, a field mouse. Dolphins possess qualities that so
make people perceive them as deserving of special attention. T
people, the bottlenose dolphin represents free-spirited life in a prist
ocean. Whether they generally enjoy watching wildlife or not, boat
ages may stop to observe a group of dolphins cavort and leap, f
or simply swim synchronously along a channel. The experience
leaves many people feeling cleansed and happy; the word *therapeu*
used.

Why do such people relate to dolphins so much? The answer
back in our own roots; for example, the ancient Greeks, Cretar
mans included dolphins prominently in their mythology, art,
ture.[5] There is an interesting relationship between the Greek wo
meaning dolphin, and *Delphis*, referring to womb, and the
viewed in some Greek creation myths as "the living womb of th
ation."[6] Other myths included gods and goddesses assuming
dolphins; in some cases, dolphins even served as escorts of
general, the use in art of a "dolphin by itself is an allegory of
spired in the ancient legends which show it as a friend of ma

Fig. 9. Dolphin riding by humans, especially children, is commonly reported in ancient legends and modern anecdotes from around the world. This ancient Greek vase, made by The Athena Painter about 490 B.C.E., depicts the phenomenon well. Courtesy of Johns Hopkins Archeological Collection.

Lockyer describes stories from ancient history, as well as modern times, regarding a variety of close ties between dolphins and humans.[12] In particular, she focuses on the recurring theme of people (reported from the time of Pliny the Younger, two thousand years ago, to the present) developing a close association with and even riding on dolphins. One ancient story recounts how a boy and a dolphin near Naples, Italy, became close friends, with the dolphin giving the boy a ride across the water to school every day. When the boy tragically died, the dolphin is said to have mourned and tragically died as well. Such stories may "have a fanciful tone to them," but in at least some regards "do seem plausible" in light of well-documented modern interactions.[13] For example, at Opononi, New Zealand, a female bottlenose dolphin named "Opo" was renowned for allowing children to ride on her back in the mid-1950s.[14] Most wild sociable dolphins have been solitary animals "which seemingly chose, even if temporarily, human company, either in the absence of or in addition to the company of conspecifics."[15] The recurring phenomenon of dolphins apparently seeking human interaction defies easy explanation.

The coordination of dolphin behavior to accomplish goals (for example, food acquisition, rearing of offspring) suggests to some an "intelligence" and a degree of sociality that we egocentrically tend to reserve for our own, but virtually no other species. Certainly, the discovery that dolphins have large, complex brains has done nothing to reduce the feeling that people, dolphins, and relatively few other mammals are special due to their intelligence.

The movement to demonstrate that dolphins possess a level of intelligence comparable to our own began with the work of Dr. John Lilly in 1960. Despite a general lack of scientific evidence to support his claims, Lilly boldly painted a picture of dolphins being "more intelligent than any man or woman," and as keepers of oral histories that "go back thirty million years, passed on by the traditions taught by cetacea to one another."[16] Lilly predicted that humans and dolphins might hold conversations by 1980.[17]

The romantic image created by Lilly's books caught the general public's imagination, and lack of hard evidence did little to sway opinions. In 1972

Fig. 10. A dolphin underwater. Marya Willis-Glowka.

Fig. 11. Dolphins swimming toward viewer. Marya Willis-Glowka.

noted cetacean researchers David and Melba Caldwell published a paper with the suggestive title "Dolphins Communicate—But They Don't Talk," in which they noted that dolphins produced stereotyped acoustic signals that communicate general information about situations, rather than specific instructions or solutions. To the Caldwells' chagrin, their results were greeted with outright hostility—in their own words: "The surprise that we felt in finding that individual dolphin whistles are largely stereotyped has been nothing compared to the surprise felt at the unbridled anger that we evoke when forced to state this conclusion. It is an unpleasant experience, for we too want to be loved by our fellow man, to evoke social approval rather than anger. To have been cast in the role of destroyers of one of the few myths remaining to our own benighted species was forced upon us, not sought."[18]

Scientists continue to battle public opinion that dolphins and humans may one day converse. According to the late Frank Awbry, "Actually human-dolphin communication is mostly a fantasy, like Hugh Lofting's Dr. Dolittle. People want so much to be able to talk to animals that they cannot believe that noisy animals are not talking to each other and even trying to talk to us. . . . the myth of linguistic communication between humans and animals seems no more likely to go away than do other pseudo-scientific myths."[19]

Twenty-five years after the Caldwells were castigated, there continues to be a gulf between what the majority of scientists considers to be dolphin "intelligence" and what the general public believes. The fact that dolphins continue to evoke, for some people, an image of a nonhuman, near-human intelligence has contributed to protests by animal rights groups regarding the humanity of maintaining dolphins in captivity. If dolphins represent a marine equivalent to ourselves, shouldn't ideas of ethical treatment of humans be extended to the dolphins? Of course, a logical but rarely taken next step would extend the courtesy to even those poor, lowly species that are not fortunate enough to share those human traits we so admire in ourselves!

Being brainy isn't always a good thing. Clever dolphins effectively compete against human fishermen, occasionally even stealing the catch before the eyes of a frustrated fisherman. In addition, dolphins and other marine mammals may damage fishing gear or even injure fishermen.[20] For example, in the twelve-month period starting July 1973, bottlenose dolphins in the Indian and Banana Rivers in Florida caused about $441,000 worth of damage to gill nets and trammel nets used to harvest a variety of finfish.[21] Bottlenose dolphins off Louisiana damaged beach seine nets by attempting to take fish captured in the nets.[22] The image dolphins create in the eyes of people whose gear is damaged or whose ability to earn a living is threatened by dolphin foraging or other behavior is likely to be that of an expensive and aggravating pest, one which the world could well do without. As a consequence, both commercial and recreational fishermen have been reported to deliberately shoot dolphins.[23]

On the other hand, we have learned that dolphins may be good indicators of human and environmental health problems. Bottlenose dolphins may occasionally live more than five decades,[24] a decent approximation of a human life span prior to the advent of modern medicine. They eat many of the same aquatic prey we do.[25] As mammals, many aspects of their physiology, reproduction, and health are generally similar to our own. If dolphin populations dwindle or suffer reduced reproductive success or longevity, isn't that a warning to us? As mentioned above, the image of the dolphin as a large, aquatic coal miner's canary has entered many scientists' minds.

In reality, the bottlenose dolphin embodies all the images noted above, inconsistent as those images may seem to be. Dolphins are beautiful swimmers, exquisitely adapted to their habitat. They are also large, effective predators who kill and consume prey we desire for ourselves. They symbolize freedom, but some of the environments they occupy are becoming less and less conducive to their health and well-being. They appear in some cases to seek and enjoy people, yet some people do them harm. Their large brains and elaborate behaviors cause people to see in dolphins something of ourselves. Whatever people see, the bottlenose dolphin is, for most of us, not simply another species of mammal.

Dolphin Evolution

ORIGINS AND OUTCOMES

Many biologists consider that the modern era of biology began in 1859 with the publication of Charles Darwin's *The Origin of Species*. Bearing in mind the fundamental importance of the evolutionary perspective, we include early in this book a review of the ancestry of bottlenose dolphins, in particular, and of cetaceans, in general.

Scientists use a variety of tools to assess phylogenetic relationships. Historically, the two primary approaches involved comparative anatomy/physiology and paleontology, both of which provided Darwin with considerable insight. However, anatomical or other phenotypic similarities can result from evolutionary convergence, as well as from common ancestry. The fossil record for many taxa remains incomplete, even though it is growing. Thus, traditional methods for the assessment of relationships are still extremely valuable but could usefully be augmented.

The primary, but not the only, augmentation has occurred with the development and easy application of molecular techniques. With the availability of low-cost, user-friendly approaches such as polymerase chain reaction (PCR) to amplify genes, both the mitochondrial and nuclear genomes of many species have been examined to assess both evolutionary patterns and relationships among living forms.

Fig. 12. Two dolphins swimming side by side. Flip Nicklin and Minden Pictures.

Altogether, evidence based on anatomical patterns, molecular similarities, and the fossil record contributes to our understanding of the phylogeny of whales. Interestingly, not all of the scientific evidence supports exactly the same conclusions, making evolutionary biology of cetaceans an exciting and dynamic field.[1]

There are three suborders of the order Cetacea:[2] the Archeoceti (primitive, extinct forms), the Mysticeti (baleen whales), and the Odontoceti (the toothed whales).[3] The latter two suborders probably evolved from the archeocetes.[4]

Although scientists agree that cetaceans arose from four-legged terrestrial mammals, the ancestral group(s) to which cetaceans are most closely allied has been debated. In fact, scientists have questioned whether cetaceans were all derived from a single ancestral group (that is, they are monophyletic) or from more than one (that is, they are polyphyletic).

The eminent anatomist William Henry Flower was one of the first scientists to suggest, in 1883, that cetaceans were closely related to ungulates (hoofed animals), especially members of the order Artiodactyla (the even-toed ungulates, including cows).[5] Flower based his assessment on comparative gross anatomy. Since that time, information regarding blood chemistry, insulin, fetal blood sugar, chromosomes, uterine structure, and tooth-

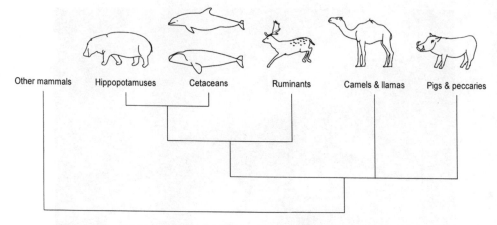

Fig. 13. This cladogram illustrates relationships among groups of organisms such as marine mammals. Here, the close evolutionary relationship of cetaceans to various artiodactyl groups is shown, as well as the particularly close relationship between hippopotamids and cetaceans. Based on M. C. Milinkovitch et al., "Cetaceans Are Highly Derived Artiodactyls," 114. Sentiel A. Rommel.

enamel structure has reinforced Flower's hypothesis.[6] Paleontological evidence suggested that primitive whales evolved from a long-extinct group called the mesonychid condylarths, which were terrestrial precursors of later ungulates.[7] Thus, cetaceans and artiodactyls may have shared a common condylarth ancestral stock.[8]

Most scientists today appear to support a closer relationship between cetaceans and artiodactyls than between cetaceans and perissodactyls (the odd-toed ungulates, such as horses) or other mammalian groups.[9] Some scientists feel, however, that the question is still quite unresolved when one examines all of the fossil, morphological, and molecular evidence.[10]

Since the early 1990s the molecular approach has both supported traditional interpretations of cetacean evolution and added some intriguing new possibilities. As noted above, most molecular results confirm that the cetaceans are more closely related to the artiodactyls than they are to other terrestrial mammals.[11] However, there are a number of interesting hypotheses that have emerged from molecular studies of cetaceans. For example, there is some evidence that cetaceans are more closely related to one group of artiodactyls (the Ruminantia—for example, cows, sheep, deer) than either ruminants or cetaceans are to other artiodactyls (the Suiformes—pigs, peccaries, and hippopotamids; and the Tylopoda—camels and llamas), and

Fig. 14. A dolphin resting at the surface. Marya Willis-Glowka.

that the order Cetacea might be more appropriately designated as a suborder of the Artiodactyla rather than as a separate, distinctive order.[12] In a
somewhat similar vein, experimental evidence based on analysis of proteins
and DNA has led to the assertion that cetaceans and the hippopotamids are
most closely related (that is, they are sister taxa, somewhat separate from
other artiodactyls).[13] Many molecular studies focus on comparisons of mitochondrial DNA. However, comparisons of a highly conserved region of
the nuclear genome (the interleukin-2 gene) of a number of placental mammals showed more similarity between dolphin and pig gene sequences than
between dolphin and the other artiodactyl species for which interleukin-2
sequence data are available.[14] Thus, some recent mitochondrial and nuclear
DNA analyses both support the contention that cetaceans are most closely
related to hippopotamids and pigs (that is, the Suiformes).

Fig. 15. A group of dolphins. Marya Willis-Glowka.

The use of molecular biology has, thus, generally supported what scientists have thought about relationships of cetaceans with other mammals, although molecular techniques have provided answers that have greater resolution by suggesting the specific group of artiodactyls to which the whales are most closely related. Molecular techniques have also been used to make the rather counter-intuitive finding that sperm whales (family Physeteridae), which are odontocetes, are more closely related to the baleen whales than either group is to the remaining odontocetes.[15] However, given the relatively few studies of whale DNA that have been done, it is clear that a lot more molecular data are needed to accurately assess whale phylogeny, because "an argument based on a small data set with respect to relevant species may be unstable."[16] In other words, the story may change as more data are collected.

The oldest known cetacean is the archeocete *Pakicetus,* fossils of which are 52 million years old, from the early Eocene epoch.[17] However, there are a number of different archeocetes represented in Eocene deposits, which are approximately 36–55 million years old.[18] The most primitive family, to which *Pakicetus* belongs, is the Protocetidae, which included relatively small animals (less than three meters long). Characteristics of the family included several features: (1) skulls that are not very streamlined (and are, therefore, said to be "non-telescoped"; see chapter 4 for discussion of telescoping of the dolphin skull); (2) nostrils located at the tip of the snout, rather than atop the head as blowholes; (3) the normal mammalian pattern of having different types of specialized teeth, such as the incisors, canines, premolars, and molars that humans possess (a condition referred to as *heterodont*), rather than homodont dentition (that is, all the teeth being of the same type) or a lack of teeth altogether; and (4) at least in some cases, presence of hind limbs.[19]

An interesting intermediate fossil form, *Ambulocetus,* existed during the early-mid Eocene.[20] *Ambulocetus* was clearly an archeocete, but it possessed hind limbs and could move about on land, probably in a manner similar to that of modern sea lions. Its aquatic locomotion was probably most like that of a modern otter, involving undulations of the spine up and down, together with paddling of the pelvic appendage.[21]

The other family of archeocetes is the Basilosauridae, which includes the medium-sized, dolphinlike members of the subfamily Dorudontinae and the gigantic, snakelike whales of the subfamily Basilosaurinae. Both groups

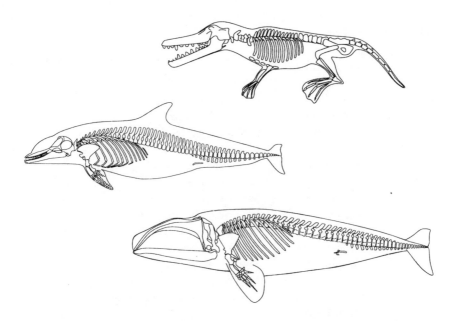

Fig. 16. Ancestral whales, such as *Ambulocetus (top)*, did not resemble their modern relatives, the odontocetes *(middle)*, and mysticetes *(bottom)*. *Ambulocetus* still possessed attributes we associate with terrestrial mammals—features such as hind legs, for example. Sentiel A. Rommel.

possessed a more telescoped skull and more derived dentition than the protocetids.[22] Hind limbs were also reduced in size. The dorudontines were probably the ancestors of both modern odontocetes and mysticetes.[23]

The true odontocetes first appeared around the start of the Oligocene epoch, about 36 million years ago and became widespread and diverse during that geologic period (36 to 25 million years ago). There are five odontocete superfamilies: Squalodontoidea (all extinct), Platanistoidea (river dolphins), Physeteroidea (sperm whales), Ziphioidea (beaked and bottlenose whales), and Delphinoidea (dolphins, porpoises).[24] Two families within the superfamily Squalodontoidea bear mentioning here due to their relevance to dolphins. The members of the family Agorophiidae represent the most primitive true odontocetes, dating from the Oligocene, and possess morphological attributes intermediate between those of the archeocetes and modern odontocetes. The family Squalodontidae evolved from the agorophiids and, in turn, are ancestral to later odontocetes, including delphinids such as the bottlenose dolphin.[25]

Table 1. Families of Cetaceans

Suborder	Family	Common name	Number of species
Mysticeti		Baleen whales	11
	Balaenidae	Right, bowhead whales	3
	Neobalaenidae	Pygmy right whales	1
	Balaenopteridae	Rorquals (e.g., blue, fin, humpback whales)	6
	Eschrichtiidae	Gray whale	1
Odontoceti		Toothed whales	67
	Physeteridae	Sperm whale	1
	Kogiidae	Pygmy/dwarf sperm whales	2
	Ziphiidae	Beaked and bottlenose whales	19
	Monodontidae	Beluga and narwhal	2
	Platanistidae	River dolphins (susu)	2
	Iniidae	River dolphin (boutu)	1
	Pontoporiidae	River dolphins (baiji, franciscana)	2
	Phocoenidae	True porpoises	6
	Delphinidae	True dolphins (including killer whale, pilot whales, and the bottlenose dolphin)	32

Source: J. E. Reynolds et al., "Marine Mammals of the World," 9–10.

The superfamily Delphinoidea includes a number of families.[26] All members of the families Kentriodontidae and Albireonidae are extinct, whereas the families Delphinidae (true dolphins, including killer whales, pilot whales, and numerous smaller species), Phocoenidae (true porpoises), and Monodontidae (belugas and narwhals) include living representatives. Members of all three living families possess asymmetrical, highly modified, streamlined telescoped skulls,[27] which may have been acquired independently in each.[28]

Based on similarities in features of the skulls, kentriodontids from the middle Miocene epoch (approximately 15 to 20 million years ago) may have led to the family Delphinidae. Although the delphinids first appeared in the fossil record in more recent sediments dating from the Miocene epoch, about 11 million years ago, fossils designated as representing the genus *Tursiops* are much more recent. Fossil remains of several species of *Tursiops* have been found in Pliocene epoch deposits, 2 to 5 million years old, and fossils identified as *Tursiops truncatus*[29] have been found in Pleistocene epoch (less than 2 million years old) deposits from both the Atlantic (Maryland) and Pacific (China). It has been suggested that the species originated in the Mediterranean region,[30] but such an interpretation may be premature.[31] A recent and detailed account of *Tursiops* fossils appears in Barnes.[32]

The preceding assessment is based primarily on analysis of fossil bones, especially crania (skulls) and teeth. As noted at the outset of this chapter, molecular techniques now provide high resolution insights to some systematic questions. Bottlenose dolphins, all of which, as noted above, have been generally considered to be a single species, *Tursiops truncatus,* are found throughout temperate and tropical waters around the world. The species generally occupies waters with surface temperatures between 10 and 32 degrees Celsius, perhaps because dolphins themselves prefer this temperature range, or perhaps because favored prey occupy this range.[33] Possibly to avoid stressful temperatures, dolphins in some areas such as the Atlantic coast of the United States seasonally migrate. In support of dolphins' ability to occupy different habitats as environmental temperatures shift, scientists documented a northward shift in the species' range during warm-water incursion associated with El Niño events off California.[34]

Water that is too cold seems more restrictive to bottlenose dolphins than is warm water. Although body size influences the ability of a marine mammal to retain body heat, with larger bodies possessing a more favorable surface area to volume ratio for heat conservation, many small cetaceans oc-

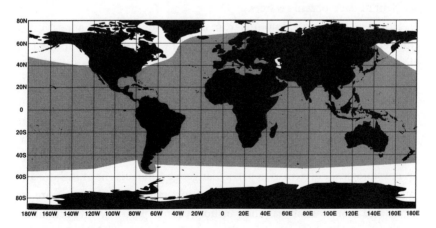

Fig. 17. Distribution of bottlenose dolphins worldwide. Elizabeth A. Forys and Kristine L. Herrington.

Fig. 18. A dolphin leaping from the water. Marya Willis-Glowka.

cupy more polar waters than *Tursiops*. In the North Pacific, for example, Washington state[35] on the east and the southern Sea of Okhotsk and Kuril Islands on the west represent the limits to bottlenose dolphin range. However, harbor porpoises (*Phocoena phocoena*) and Dall's porpoises, both of which are smaller than bottlenose dolphins, occupy more northern waters with impunity. The same holds true in the North Atlantic, where bottlenose dolphins are occasional visitors to New England in the summer[36] and to coastal waters of Norway. In the southern hemisphere, *Tursiops* is found as far south as Tierra del Fuego in South America, as well as off the coasts of South Africa, Australia, and New Zealand.[37] Nor is dolphin distribution limited to coastal waters. It is well documented that the bottlenose is a common resident of deep oceanic waters.[38]

However, bottlenose dolphins from different locations can appear quite different morphologically. This polymorphism has contributed to the fact that scientists at different times have suggested the existence of twenty different species![39] Depending on their geographic location (specifically whether they occupy high or low latitudes), adult bottlenose dolphins range in size from two meters to nearly twice that length;[40] not unlike what occurs with other mammals, the larger individuals tend to be found in colder latitudes. Several studies have documented and detailed anatomical, ecological, or physiological differences in particular geographic regions of inshore and offshore stocks of bottlenose dolphins; most noticeably, the latter are far larger and more robust than their inshore counterparts.[41] With such differences in mind, the question has arisen: are all bottlenose dolphins really the same species?

Scientists have examined the mitochondrial genome, including the cyto-chrome B sequences, of bottlenose dolphin specimens from all parts of the species' range worldwide.[42] Using a technique called a bootstrap analysis to determine the most likely relationships among groups, the authors have suggested that (1) animals from the Indian Ocean and tropical western Pacific Ocean indeed constitute a different species, tentatively called *Tursiops aduncus;* (2) there is support for considering *T. aduncus* to be more closely related to the species of the genus *Stenella* (for example, spinner/spotted/striped dolphins) and two species of *Delphinus* (common dolphins) than to *T. truncatus;* (3) in the Atlantic, inshore and offshore *T. truncatus* could be distinguished genetically; (4) inshore bottlenose dolphins in the Atlantic Ocean and Gulf of Mexico appear to be monophyletic; and (5) non-*T. aduncus* Pacific specimens of *T. truncatus* were most closely related to the inshore, Atlantic group. Thus, the very nature of what constitutes a bottle-nose dolphin is currently under critical review. Practical implications of this topic are considered further in chapter 9, dealing with stock identification; at this point, however, we note that the question of what constitutes a species or stock is not simply an academic one. The answers have serious conse-

Fig. 19. A close-knit group of dolphins. Marya Willis-Glowka.

quences, for example, for both management and conservation of wild dolphins and for the potential reintroduction to the wild of captive or rehabilitated dolphins.

Far from being a static discipline, the evolutionary biology of cetaceans is dynamic and exciting. Not only are relationships with other mammalian groups still debatable, but relationships within suborders and even at the presumed species level appear to be very uncertain. This uncertainty and the excitement associated with new discoveries and new syntheses actually permeate scientific inquiry of cetaceans, both living and dead.

Function and Structure

"Structure without function is a corpse; function *sans* structure is a ghost."[1] Biologists agree that an assessment of function and structure together permits an exciting encounter with species adaptations.

Young children sometimes play a game where they look at objects (structures) and imagine what those objects actually do (function). Biologists often play the same game when they study species. What is the function of the tusk of the narwhal *(Monodon monoceros)*? Why do certain species of toothed whales (odontocetes) actually lack functional teeth? How do whales that are primarily adapted to maintaining heat in their bodies keep certain heat-sensitive internal structures (testes, spinal cord, fetuses) from overheating during times of extreme muscular activity? Why do dolphins and other toothed whales only have a single external nostril (that is, the blowhole) whereas other mammals, including baleen whales, have two? Creatively pondering the relationship between form and function can sometimes lead to marvelous insights into species biology.

One of the best examples of creative reflection leading to insight is recounted in *The Porpoise Watcher* by the late Kenneth Norris, one of the "fathers" of modern marine mammal science. In his chapter entitled "The Jaw-Hearing Porpoise,"[2] Norris describes how he found a dolphin's lower jaw bone.[3] To be sure, Norris had already seen a lot of dolphin jaws, both in living animals and during dissections. But much like Hamlet with poor

Yorick's skull, Norris contemplated the dolphin bone he found on the shore. Noting that it was hollow, that the hollow region would be filled in the living dolphin with a fat body, and that the jaw would articulate (form a joint) with the skull near where the ear bones were positioned, Norris hypothesized that the fat-filled jaw might serve as a conduit for sound to reach each ear. If this unusual pathway permitted sounds to reach one ear before the other, this might help answer the question of how dolphins hear directionally underwater, something humans and other terrestrial mammals cannot do. Norris's synthesis turned out to be right.

Like all species, the bottlenose dolphin is exquisitely adapted to its particular niche. Those adaptations include anatomical and physiological attributes (considered in this chapter and chapter 7) and behavioral features (elaborated in chapter 6). Although some traits may be similar to those of terrestrial mammals, some reflect changes to accommodate living in a marine environment. Simply existing in water has certain consequences.

For example, the thermal conductivity of water is about twenty-five times greater than that of air of the same temperature,[4] a physical principle that a person can easily test by sitting for an hour in a 70°F room and in a bathtub filled with 70°F water. The latter induces a chill due to excessive loss of body heat, whereas the former is comfortable. Other constraints that exist

Fig. 20. Four dolphins swimming toward camera. Flip Nicklin and Minden Pictures.

for a mammal in a marine environment include considerable drag (since seawater has a density almost three orders of magnitude greater than that of air), impairment of vision due to lack of light below depths of just a few meters even in very clear water, and the need to surface to breathe.

Some of the "solutions" for living in a marine environment are fairly obvious. For example, all marine mammals are large.[5] Large size alone is a vital prerequisite for sea mammals because large size reduces the surface area-to-volume ratio, thereby reducing the relative area over which heat can be lost from the body.[6] Since marine mammals have body temperatures similar to our own, and since they almost always occupy waters considerably colder than their body temperature, there is an enormous tendency for marine mammals to lose body heat and thereby to suffer some stress or even to die of hypothermia. Large size alone helps reduce those possibilities.

Large size may confer other benefits to species that occupy environments in which food resources are patchily distributed temporally or spatially. Large animals have a lower weight-specific metabolic rate than do smaller ones.[7] This means that a large animal may eat absolutely more food than a small one, but that each unit of body weight (each gram, for example) in the large individual consumes less energy in a given time period. One benefit of this is that the larger animal may fast for longer periods. People certainly understand this principle since we, as large mammals, can fast for days (even if we prefer not to!), whereas small pets such as hamsters need a nearly constant supply of food to survive. Large animals also have the potential to store considerably more energy in the form of blubber than smaller animals can. Thus, large size is an admirable trait for species, like many of the marine mammals, that may not have constant access to food. This adaptation is taken to its limit by the large baleen whales (such as the fin whale, *Balaenoptera physalus*), which may only feed for half of each year or less.

In this chapter, we take two primary approaches: First we consider dolphin general morphology—how the animals are built.[8] Concurrently, we discuss how particular anatomical systems or structures (for example, the muscles or the skeleton) help the animal to function properly. We then consider some complex adaptations (such as for diving and thermoregulation)[9] that involve a number of systems. At the end of this chapter, we ask readers to ponder the question: Are dolphins basically similar to humans, but with some interesting variations, or are dolphins fundamentally different from us?

External Anatomy

Like all other cetaceans, the bottlenose dolphin possesses external features that allow it to move easily in an aquatic environment. The body is spindle shaped (that is, fusiform) and lacks most of the external protuberances characteristic of terrestrial mammals. For example, dolphins lack hair, external ears, and hind limbs, although vestigial pelvic bones are embedded deep in dolphin muscles. The only features that do protrude from the body of a dolphin are its front flippers (called pectoral appendages), dorsal fin, and the flukes with which it propels itself.

Even the head of the dolphin appears streamlined. In an arrangement termed telescoping, the bones of the skull have become modified through the lengthy process of evolution in a way that provides a tapered rostrum (anterior portion of the skull) and that moves the nostrils dorsally (as a blowhole) to permit the animal to breathe easily while swimming. The specific skull modifications involved in telescoping are discussed below.

The extreme streamlining, together with other traits described later in this chapter, allow dolphins to swim very quickly. The fastest human swimmer in the 1996 Olympic Games was Aleksandr Popov, who won the men's 50-meter freestyle sprint by swimming 2.3 meters per second (equivalent to nearly 5.2 miles per hour).[10] By contrast, dolphins routinely cruise at speeds of 1.4 to 3.1 meters per second (3.1 to 6.9 miles per hour), and have been clocked at an impressive 8.3 meters per second (18.5 miles per hour) for a

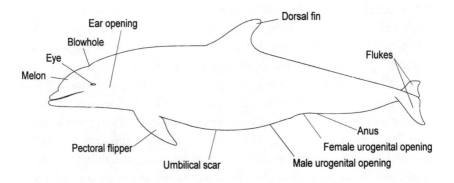

Fig. 21. Drawing showing the general body form and external features of a bottlenose dolphin. Note the different positions of the male and female urogenital openings. Sentiel A. Rommel.

very short distance.[11] In addition, dolphins swimming at 2.0 meters per second (approximately the maximum speed of Olympic swimmers) show little elevation of metabolic, heart, or respiration rates relative to what they experience in a resting state.[12] What represents peak output for a human apparently does not faze a dolphin in the least.

At least some populations of bottlenose dolphins are sexually dimorphic, meaning that adult males and females appear different. The main difference for these *Tursiops* is that males grow to be larger than females.[13] One should note, however, that this is not always the case. Male and female dolphins in the Indian and Banana Rivers of Florida, for example, show no statistical differences in body or skull lengths.[14] Interestingly enough, at least in dolphins occupying Sarasota Bay, Florida, females tend to be larger than males through age six, but growth of females slows after that point, such that they reach essentially their full body mass by age ten. In contrast, ten-year-old males possess only about 70 percent of their maximum potential body mass.[15] Ultimately, sexually mature male dolphins in Sarasota Bay are, on average, about 26 percent heavier than adult females (approximately 260 kilograms for males versus slightly more than 190 kilograms for the females).[16] Although very large body size of an individual may suggest that it is a male (the reproductive organs of both sexes are internal) one can verify the sex of a living individual only by examining the ventral body openings, or in the case of males, when the penis is extruded from the body.

Despite the high regard in which many people hold bottlenose dolphins, a verbal portrait of the external appearance of the species, relative to other delphinids, represents an exercise in moderation in virtually all regards. *Tursiops truncatus* is of moderate size, with adult males reaching a length of between 2 and 3.9 meters, depending on their geographic range.[17] The maximum body weight reported in the literature for the species is 275 kilograms,[18] although males weighing 284 kilograms have been measured in Sarasota Bay. The body is generally rather robust (although relatively slender individuals are reported in groups with more typical, husky animals),[19] with a somewhat tall, falcate dorsal fin and moderately long pectoral (front) flippers, which are pointed at the tips. The species has relatively few obvious markings against a gray background hue; various shades of gray, and even some brownish shades, are common on different animals. Even the number of teeth present (eighteen to twenty-six per tooth row) is intermediate among the delphinids. For example, long-snouted spinner dolphins, *Sten-*

Fig. 22. Among the true dolphins (family Delphinidae), the bottlenose is intermediate in body size and shape, as well as in some life history attributes (see chapter 5). Here the bottlenose is compared to the much smaller spinner dolphin (*Stenella longirostris*) and the larger Risso's dolphin (*Grampus griseus*). Note that the dorsal fin of the spinner dolphin is angled forward in some, but not all, forms of that species. Sentiel A. Rommel.

ella longirostris, may have more than sixty-five teeth per row, whereas at the other end of the scale, Risso's dolphins (*Grampus griseus*) lack teeth in the upper jaw (called maxillary teeth) altogether and have only about four to six (never more than seven) teeth per side of the lower jaw or mandible.[20] Typical of many marine animals, countershading occurs, with the back being darker than the belly, an adaptation that presumably allows animals to blend in better with their surroundings, thereby both facilitating the capture of prey by dolphins and reducing the chances of dolphins becoming prey themselves. Sometimes a light blaze occurs on the sides of the animal, and some *Tursiops* may develop spots on the ventral side.

A couple of features do stand out. Bottlenose dolphins tend to have a relatively short rostrum, and the melon (a rounded, fat-filled region located atop the skull between the rostrum and the blowhole) is well demarcated. In some instances these features may be the only strong evidence that distinguishes the species from some others.[21]

The generalist morphology of *Tursiops* reflects its generalist ecology (in other words, form and function really *do* go hand in hand).[22] The species occupies a wider range of habitats and consumes a wider variety of prey (for example, about fifty different prey species found in stomachs of dolphins in the southeastern United States alone) than does virtually any other odontocete.[23]

The Integument

The outermost layers of a dolphin form the integument, composed of both the skin and associated structures. Although we may view our skin as a relatively stable and uninteresting layer that merely separates us from our environment, the integument should be viewed as "a multifunctional organ system that sculpts the animal's boundary with its aquatic environment. It forms a protective and dynamically insulative layer, adds buoyancy and forms propulsive structures, such as the flukes."[24] Functions such as preventing loss or gain of water are so fundamental that we often tend to forget the skin's role in keeping our bodies functioning normally. However, to accomplish its varied functions, the integument must have a lot of components. And although we may take it for granted, the integument represents the largest organ system of the body of both humans and dolphins.

The general structure of the dolphin integument is not significantly different from our own, although lack of hair and sweat glands in the dolphin represent a couple of obvious adaptations in the latter. A general text or atlas of veterinary anatomy[25] provides a good overview of the general arrangement of cell layers in the "typical" mammalian integument.

The most superficial layer of the integument is called the epidermis and is composed of many layers of flattened (squamous) epithelial cells, the outer layers of which have lost their nuclei and contain a water-resistant protein called keratin. As in humans, dolphin epithelial cells are constantly lost and replaced, a feature that whale population biologists find useful as they attempt to acquire tissues noninvasively for genetic research.[26] In the bottlenose dolphin, the outermost epidermal layer may be completely replaced at the astounding rate of every two hours.[27] Such a high rate of turnover probably helps keep the surface of the animal smooth (that is, by reducing the possibility of attachment of fouling organisms) and thereby minimizes drag as the animal swims.[28] This suggests that the energy spent to constantly pro-

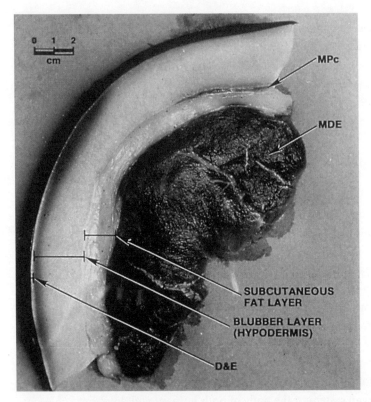

Fig. 23. A cross section through dolphin skin and underlying tissue reveals several layers: D&E represent dermis and epidermis, respectively; MPc is a dermal muscle, and MDE is the large back (epaxial) musculature. Note the very dark color of the muscle, due to the presence of myoglobin, a respiratory pigment that binds oxygen and prolongs diving. From Ridgway and Fenner, "Weight-Length Relationships of Bottlenose Dolphins," with permission of Sam H. Ridgway.

duce new epithelial cells is less than that gained by reducing drag that would result from a rougher outer body surface.

Proceeding inward, the next layer is the dermis, in which there exist blood vessels, nerves, and connective tissue, including a matrix of fibers. Beneath the dermis lies the hypodermis, which is the site of a dolphin's blubber layer, described as a "continuous sheet of adipose tissue, reinforced by a network of collagen and elastic fibers."[29]

Associated with the dolphin integument, beneath the blubber, there exists a fibrous subdermal connective tissue sheath that may act as a "peripheral skeletal element"[30] for the locomotory muscles. The dolphin may, in fact, be considered as living tissue wound tightly in a thin-walled, pressurized cylinder. The structure and likely function of the subdermal sheath lend insight into both dolphin locomotion and how dolphins maintain their hydrodynamically favorable shape. The nature of the fibers and the angles at which they crisscross provide resilience so that the dense subdermal connective tissue actually seems to function like a spring when it is bent in any particular direction—the elastic recoil may provide an extremely valuable energy-saving adaptation.[31]

The dolphin integument, as noted above, functions in a number of important ways. One of the more obvious roles of the integument involves thermoregulation. There are several possible avenues by which a species could adjust to the high thermal conductivity of water. One is to become large and to reduce the size of limbs and other external protuberances; this reduces the surface area-to-volume ratio, as described above. Another solution is to develop better insulation, something that the integument accomplishes admirably. Although blubber is not as effective for insulation as thick, dry fur, the best-adapted marine mammals have evolved thick blubber layers because fur could become wet and lose most of its insulating ability.

One should not assume that blubber is the same in all species; it varies in both thickness and in composition. For example, the blubber of a small tropical cetacean (the pan-tropical spotted dolphin, *Stenella attenuata*) is

Fig. 24. Two dolphins swimming on their sides. Flip Nicklin and Minden Pictures.

thinner and contains less lipid than the blubber from a comparably sized cetacean (the harbor porpoise) that occupies colder, temperate waters; these differences lead to nearly a fourfold increase in conduction of heat from the body of the spotted dolphin.[32] In addition, blubber composition is not necessarily the same in the body of a particular individual. The chemical composition of harbor porpoise blubber is not homogeneous in individual animals, suggesting that its efficacy for insulation may also vary. In fact, blubber in some regions of the porpoise body is metabolized to meet energy demands of the animal far more quickly than is blubber from other regions, reinforcing the idea that what scientists term "blubber" actually includes a chemically heterogeneous tissue that serves different functions.[33] Specifically, there are two general functional types of harbor porpoise blubber: thoracic-abdominal blubber is used for insulation and energy storage, and posterior blubber helps maintain the hydrodynamic shape of the animal.[34]

In bottlenose dolphins, blubber thickness varies seasonally and with the body size, reproductive state, and nutritional status of the individual. No analyses have been done to assess blubber composition (and efficacy for insulation) throughout the dolphin's body, but it seems likely that the heterogeneous composition and diverse functions described for harbor porpoise blubber would also be found in dolphins.

Insulation helps keep body heat inside the dolphin, a necessity to prevent excessive heat loss and hypothermia. However, there are conditions, such as times of prolonged fast swimming or during summer months in the subtropics when ambient water temperatures may approach dolphin body temperature, in which it is important for a dolphin to be able to dump excess body heat, just as we do when we sweat. In the dolphin, this requires a means by which to bypass the insulation, which is accomplished by changes in blood flow through the peripheral circulatory system (to be discussed later in this chapter).

Another obvious role of the integument, which has been briefly mentioned above, involves reduction of drag on the animal. Scientists typically consider two types of drag that hinder progress through the water. Viscous, or frictional drag occurs when a viscous medium, such as water, creates friction with a body moving through that medium. Viscous drag varies directly with the amount of surface area with which the fluid interacts. Thus, a smooth-skinned dolphin, possessing few external protuberances, minimizes the viscous drag it experiences.

Fig. 25. Two dolphins swimming. Official U.S. Navy photograph.

Pressure, or inertial drag, is caused by pressure differences around a moving body and the effects of pressure on the flow of the medium. As a result of forward movement, the surrounding fluid separates from the posterior surface of the body, creating a wake of turbulence behind the body (as anyone who has driven a small car and attempted to pass a large, fast-moving truck can testify!). To minimize the wake, and subsequently pressure drag, animals evolved fusiform body shapes that postpone the separation point.

Although the relationship of integumentary structure and reduction of viscous drag is evident, reduction of pressure drag may seem to be unrelated to function of the integument. This is not the case. The distribution of blubber helps to sculpt the body contours of marine mammals, including dolphins. By helping create the most hydrodynamically efficient shape, blubber actually decreases pressure drag. In fact, the primary attribute that reduces the total drag in swimming dolphins is having a streamlined body form.[35]

A third type of drag, called wave drag, is also experienced by air-breathing swimming animals.[36] Wave drag results when a swimmer is at or near the surface of the water, thereby generating surface waves that interact with the body and slow forward progress. One scientist towed a model shaped like a dolphin at a constant speed and measured drag induced at different depths, with dramatic results: drag was as much as five times as high when the model was at the surface as when it was totally submerged.[37] Not until the model was submerged to a depth equivalent to three body diameters did the wave drag cease being a factor. Of course viscous and pressure drag continued to affect swimming at any depth.

Blubber can also serve as a kind of protection against predation.[38] The frequent occurrence of healed shark bite scars on bottlenose dolphins in Sarasota Bay, and the apparently low mortality due to shark attack, attest to the fact that dolphins are often successful in escaping from sharks when they are bitten.[39] This success may be due, in part, to the fact that in order for a shark to reach any vital organs, it must first bite through a fairly thick integument, providing a dolphin with the opportunity to break free of the bite.

Another possible function of blubber involves its use for buoyancy. Although several authors have suggested that blubber serves this function,[40] data do not exist to thoroughly substantiate the idea.

On the downside in terms of cetacean health, in recent years blubber has also begun to serve as a compartment for storage of lipophilic[41] environ-

Fig. 26. As a dolphin cruises through the water, drag holds the animal back. This illustration shows the position of the dermal ridges in the skin, which parallel the pathway that water flows smoothly over the surface of a dolphin. The fusiform body of the animal reduces the amount of drag it experiences. Based on Sokolov and Surtaine. Sentiel A. Rommel.

muscles (termed epaxial) cause the vertebral column to flex dorsally in the upstroke, whereas the ventral muscles (hypaxial muscles) cause flexion in the opposite direction to produce a downstroke.[46]

As might be expected in a fast and powerful swimmer such as the bottlenose dolphin, the axial muscles possess a large functional cross-sectional area, which provides a great deal of force.[47] Similarly, it comes as no surprise to find that dolphin vertebrae have long spines (also called spinous processes) for muscle attachment to increase leverage and thus force output. Finally, as noted earlier, the presence of a subdermal connective tissue sheath not only allows the epaxial muscles to insert in a unique fashion that provides a mechanical advantage, but also provides an internal spring that increases efficiency.

When humans and most other mammals swim, the motion they use produces thrust some of the time, but the limbs must be repositioned (a recovery phase), during which time no thrust occurs. Thus, thrust is generated only about half the time for swimmers that use a paddle motion. Efficiency of swimming increases tremendously in species that can generate thrust during the entire stroke. This is precisely the case in dolphins. Their lunate flukes, powered by the axial muscles, function as extremely efficient hydrofoils that produce lift-based thrust and increase efficiency of swimming.[48] However, it has been observed that even though dolphins are well adapted for efficient swimming, they "show no unusual hydrodynamic performance" relative to similarly shaped swimmers.[49]

Swimming efficiency is also related to avoidance of situations in which drag is increased. For example, as noted above, wave drag creates an enormous impediment to fast-swimming dolphins at or near the surface. Dolphins and other marine mammals can avoid having to expend considerable energy to overcome wave drag by doing two things: (1) avoiding high velocity movements when they are at the surface to breathe or do other activities; and (2) maintaining whenever possible a position at least three body diameters deep when swimming fast.[50] In addition, some scientists have theorized that "porpoising" (leaping clear of the water) represents an energy-saving behavior of swimming dolphins.[51] The authors calculate that the energetic cost of leaping clear of the water by a fast-swimming dolphin is less than the cost of combating wave drag; conversely, it would cost a slow-swimming animal more to propel itself clear of the water than to experience wave drag.[52]

Fig. 28. Freeway, who was rehabilitated (see chapter 8) at the Dolphin and Whale Hospital at Mote Marine Laboratory, leaps clear of the water immediately upon release. Randall S. Wells, Chicago Zoological Society.

A final behavior that is energetically beneficial to dolphins is wave riding. In tests conducted with dolphins maintained by the U.S. Navy, scientists[53] found that wave riding in the wake of a boat permitted dolphins to go twice as fast for the same energetic cost. In addition, heart and respiratory rates and post-exercise lactate levels[54] in blood were reduced in wave riding animals. Wave riding, incidentally, is not only associated with wakes of boats; dolphins have also been observed riding wakes of large, fast swimming whales.[55]

In summary, dolphins are fast, efficient swimmers due to several adaptations: fusiform body shape; axial muscles with large cross-sectional areas; skeletal features that enhance leverage; unusual patterns of muscle insertion via a subdermal sheath; propulsion using flukes, which function to promote lift and thrust; and behaviors that minimize expenditure of energy while swimming.

We turn our attention at this point to the structures to which the muscles attach—the skull and skeleton, the most complete description of which appears in a chapter by Rommel.[56] Modifications to suit an aquatic existence occur throughout the skeletal system.

Anyone who has ever lifted a cetacean bone has probably been impressed with its relative lightness. Cetacean bones are less dense than those of many other species, and they are permeated with oil (another feature that people may notice with some dismay when they examine a cetacean bone that has not been fully cleaned!). It has been speculated that this is an adaptation to promote buoyancy, an attribute that saves energy when an animal is at the surface, but which would be energetically costly as an animal dives. The function of light bones in cetaceans is not well understood. In fact, the vast majority of aquatic (marine and freshwater) mammals possess heavier bones than their terrestrial counterparts (quite apparent in the bones of manatees and dugongs, order Sirenia). Only cetaceans and some pinnipeds (seals, sea lions, and walruses) are exceptions to this rule.[57] Possibly the exceptions occur as an adaptation to facilitate diving.[58]

Telescoping of the skull has already been mentioned as a modification to enhance streamlining and facilitate breathing while swimming.[59] First described more than seventy-five years ago by Miller, telescoping in odontocetes most noticeably involves elongation of the bones that precede the orbits or eye sockets.[60] These include the tooth-bearing bones of the upper jaw called the premaxillae and maxillae. In addition, but perhaps less obviously, the bones that lie behind (caudal to) the orbits tend to be compressed (shortened and/or overlapping). This is especially true of the frontal, parietal, and occipital bones. The nasal bones, which in terrestrial mammals typically provide a roof over the nostrils or nares, lie caudal to and do not form a roof over the nares in the dolphin and other odontocetes. In fact, dolphin bony nares point vertically so that they open directly toward the blowhole, on the dorsal side of the animal.

There are other skull features that do not relate to telescoping. The simple, peglike, homodont teeth, which are not replaced, are located in the maxillae.[61] In some odontocetes, the right and left halves of the skull look very different (that is, the skull is said to be strongly bilaterally asymmetric). This feature is less obvious in the bottlenose dolphin than in many other species (for example, sperm whales). Finally, the zygomatic arch, a ridge of bones below the orbit to which strong chewing (masseter) muscles typically attach in most animals, is minute in the dolphin. The small size of this bone probably is a reflection of additional streamlining, as well as of dolphin feeding behavior, which involves swallowing prey whole rather than chewing it.

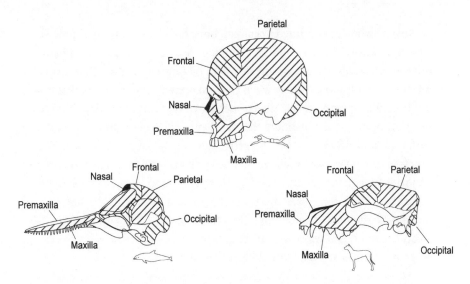

Fig. 29. Although a human skull may not be representative of the "typical mammal," it is nonetheless more similar to that of most mammals with which we are familiar (for example, a dog) than is the dolphin skull. The dolphin skull has been influenced by a process called telescoping. Sentiel A. Rommel.

To match the dimensions of the upper jaw bones, the lower jaw, or mandible, is equally extended and contains the same number of teeth (eighteen to twenty-six per row) as the upper. A mandible is actually composed of two dentary bones, which join at the "chin" at a what is called the mandibular symphysis. The caudal parts of the dentary bones are hollow and extremely fragile. They contain special fat bodies, called the intramandibular fat bodies, which abut the ear bones (tympanic bullae).

Although the bones of the skull are the same in bottlenose dolphins as they are in humans and other mammals, the proportions and positions of the bones are dramatically different. The consequences of telescoping permit dolphins to move more easily through the water. In addition, the skulls and lower jaws possess features that enhance acoustic communication (to be discussed later in this chapter) and reflect feeding habits.

The axial skeleton (primarily the vertebrae) is also somewhat modified. Extensions of vertebral spines to enhance leverage for the muscles associated with fast swimming have already been noted. In addition, with the exception of the cervical (neck) vertebrae, the dolphin possesses different numbers of the various other types of vertebrae (thoracic: in the chest; lumbar: in the "lower back"; and caudal: associated with the tail) relative to typical terrestrial mammals. Interestingly enough, sacral vertebrae are entirely lacking in dolphins, an observation that may not be surprising when one considers that sacral vertebrae form a joint, or articulate, with the pelvis, which is vestigial in dolphins and other cetaceans.

Like the skull, the skeleton of the limbs (the appendicular skeleton) shows obvious differences relative to that of a typical terrestrial mammal. The most obvious changes in the front (pectoral) flipper involve shortening of the long bones (for example, humerus, radius, and ulna) and extension of the "finger bones" (called phalanges) to form a "paddle," rather than an "arm." The hind (or pelvic) limb, of course, is absent externally except in some very rare cases; all that typically remains is a tiny vestige of the pelvic bones, buried deep in the pelvic region musculature.

Visceral Organs

A student who has taken a course in comparative anatomy could examine the body of a bottlenose dolphin and locate most organs rather easily. As noted above for the integumentary, muscular, and skeletal systems, modifications relative to the typical terrestrial plan have occurred, but most (not all) systems represent variations on general mammalian themes, rather than startling, new structures. Rather than providing a detailed account of each internal organ system, we confine our observations to those features for which structure and function differ from the usual.

In animals such as dolphins, for which diving is an important daily behavior, one would expect to find modifications of the respiratory system. Indeed, they exist but may, at first, seem somewhat counterintuitive. For example, people have sometimes suggested that diving mammals should have large lungs to carry a lot of oxygen. But large lungs filled with air would be energetically quite costly during a dive because they induce buoyancy, and some seals that are proficient divers actually exhale prior to diving.[62] In addition, humid air at sea level contains only about 15 percent oxygen (for dry air, the percentage approaches 20 percent), so an enormous increase in lung volume would be needed to produce a relatively small increase in oxygen-carrying capacity. Therefore, the most proficient diving mammals tend to have relatively small lungs, not large ones; this means, of course, that the lungs are not an important location where oxygen is stored in diving dolphins.

Other features of the respiratory system are also modified. The one that has received the most attention involves the airways that serve as a conduit for air between the lungs and the external environment. As already noted, dolphins possess just a single blowhole, but they have two internal nares on the dorsal surface of the skull. Dissection reveals that the right nasal passage does not reach the outside as a separate opening. Instead it contains a series of blind sacs, which are inflated with air, and a prominent nasal plug. These and associated structures are generally considered to be involved in sound production in odontocetes, although the exact site of sound generation is still debated.[63] Humans and most mammals, of course, produce sounds using taut membranes called vocal cords in the larynx, a region that has been suggested but not demonstrated as the site of sound production in cetaceans as well.[64] The nasal sac system, as a potential producer of a variety of sounds for communication and echolocation, represents one of the few *de novo* anatomical structures one encounters in a dolphin. However, the *physical process* by which sounds are likely produced, which involves passage of a stream of air across structures that vibrate at particular frequencies, is similar in odontocetes and in "typical mammals," like humans, that use vocal cords.

Two other changes in the respiratory system are also worth noting. The first is that even the very small air passages leading to the fragile, thin, alveoli, where oxygen actually diffuses into the bloodstream in the lungs, are reinforced with muscle and/or cartilage so that they remain open even when pressures during a dive effectively collapse the lungs. The collapse of the alveoli prevents oxygen exchange during a dive. However, diving mammals derive a great benefit from the cessation of gas exchange because it also limits the amount of nitrogen that can diffuse out of the lungs and into the blood and tissues during the dive, thereby reducing the possibility of "the bends."[65]

The other obvious modification concerns the larynx. As noted above, the site of sound production in most mammals is the larynx, and there has been speculation that the larynx serves the same function in dolphins and other odontocetes. Most marine mammal scientists feel that the anatomy of the dolphin larynx does not lend itself to sound production; certainly no vocal

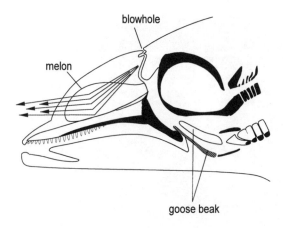

Fig. 30. The production and focusing of sound by dolphins and other odontocetes involves structures unlike those of any other mammals. Sound is produced by various structures associated with the air passageway between the goosebeak (larynx) and the blowhole and focused through the fatty melon. Sentiel S. Rommel.

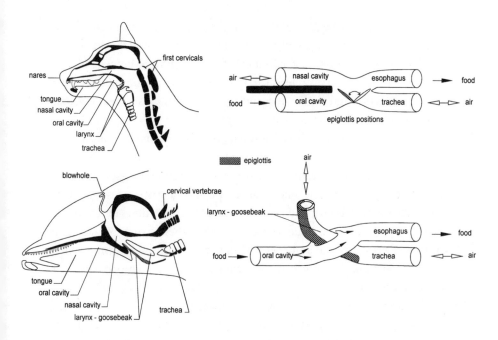

Fig. 31. Due to the unusual morphology of the larynx (called the goosebeak) and the nasal passages, the passages for food (the oral cavity and esophagus) are clearly separated from the air passages (nasal cavity and trachea) in the dolphin. This allows the animal to breathe while swallowing. Sentiel A. Rommel.

Fig. 32. Dolphin showing its teeth. Flip Nicklin and Minden Pictures.

cords are present. Instead, the dolphin larynx is extremely modified into an unusual structure, the shape of which led to the appropriate nickname of the "goosebeak." This odd specialization fits snugly into the bony nasal passage of the skull and serves at least two functions: (1) to permit simultaneous sound production and swallowing; and (2) to clearly separate breathing and ingestion and swallowing of food.

The dolphin digestive system also has some interesting specializations, even though the fundamental components are those one typically finds in mammals. Our own digestive system consists of an oral region (mouth, teeth, a tongue with taste buds), an esophagus, a gastrointestinal tract (stomach and intestines), and accessory organs of digestion (for example, salivary glands, liver, and pancreas). Altogether, these structures facilitate capture of prey, physical and chemical digestion, absorption of nutrients, and transport via rhythmic muscular contractions (termed peristalsis) of digested food and waste.

As noted above, dolphins lack strong masseter (chewing) muscles because they swallow prey whole. Their peglike, homodont teeth are useful for grasping prey, but clearly could not chew as effectively as molars. Just as the teeth are not designed to initiate much physical breakdown of food in the dolphin mouth, neither are there salivary glands present to produce enzymes to initiate chemical breakdown there.[66]

When food passes through the muscular esophagus, it does not simply enter a single stomach compartment as is the case in most mammals, but rather a series of three stomach compartments or chambers.[67] The first chamber, called the forestomach, is muscular and distensible—a receiving chamber somewhat similar to the crop of birds; however, some chemical digestion also occurs in this chamber, presumably due to squirting, or refluxing, of acid and enzymes from the second, or glandular, stomach.[68] Generally, less digestible remains of prey items, such as squid beaks and fish otoliths, are retained in the forestomach for quite awhile.

The second chamber corresponds approximately to our own stomach. It is glandular, producing mucus, as well as digestive enzymes and hydrochloric acid to chemically break down food. Finally, the slurry of partially digested food passes through a connecting channel and enters the third, or pyloric, stomach, a relatively simple sac, where mucus appears to be the main secretion.

The pyloric stomach chamber ends at a strong muscular sphincter, beyond which lies the first section of small intestine, the duodenum. Initially, the dolphin duodenum is expanded into a sac called the duodenal ampulla, the secretory layer (mucosa) of which resembles that of the pyloric stomach.[69] Following the ampulla, the remainder of the small intestine and the large intestine are not remarkable, except that it is especially difficult to determine externally the point at which the small intestine becomes the large. In humans and many other mammals, a cecum (appendix) marks the intersection of the large and small intestines; lack of a cecum in dolphins makes the intersection of small and large intestines difficult to discern. As in most species, absorption of nutrients occurs primarily in the intestines of dolphins.

Bile enters the duodenum to facilitate fat digestion, despite the fact that dolphins lack a gall bladder, a sac that typically holds bile produced by the liver. Similarly, digestive enzymes of various types produced by the pancreas enter the duodenum. It should be noted that, as is typical of other mammals, the cetacean pancreas also serves as an endocrine organ, producing hormones such as insulin in the cells of the islets of Langerhans.[70]

The presence of multiple stomach compartments is superficially reminiscent of what is found in cattle and other herbivorous ruminants (order Artiodactyla). However, the latter possess a four-chambered system adapted for the slow fermentation of cellulose and absorption of nutrients, whereas

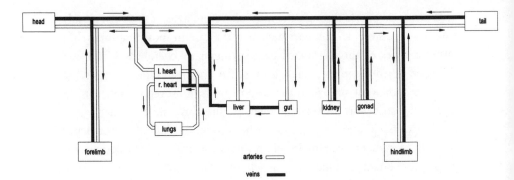

Fig. 33. The general pattern of circulation in a mammal is shown. Sentiel A. Rommel.

the dolphin stomachs provide fast digestion of protein and probably little absorption. The stomach systems of ruminants and cetaceans actually function quite differently, and most aspects of their gross and microscopic anatomy are also very different—oddly enough, there is a close evolutionary relationship between artiodactyls and cetaceans (see chapter 3).

As was the case for the digestive system, the dolphin circulatory system generally corresponds well with those of other mammals. Although the structures associated with the dolphin circulatory system are not out of the ordinary, their arrangements permit certain processes to occur to a greater extent than is the case for most mammals. For example, at least part of the solution for prolonged diving and for thermoregulation in dolphins and other cetaceans lies with the circulatory system (see below).[71]

An example illustrating differences between blood circulation in dolphins and in other mammals involves the blood supply to the brain. Instead of channeling blood directly to the brain via a couple of large discrete arteries (vertebral arteries and internal carotid arteries) as occurs in humans and most other mammals, dolphins use an intricate network of blood vessels which include an epidural and a thoracospinal rete.[72] This highly derived pathway may serve to dampen pressure fluctuations.[73]

Another subtle modification concerns so-called arteriovenous anastomoses (AVA), where blood is shunted directly from an artery to a vein, thereby bypassing capillary beds where exchange of gases and nutrients occurs. In dolphins, AVAs are found superficial to the blubber,[74] where they presumably function, via dilation or constriction of arterial diameters, to regulate heat loss to the environment.

Less subtle are the countercurrent heat exchangers dolphins and other marine mammals use to regulate heat loss to the environment. Although most of the dolphin body is well insulated, parts such as the flippers, dorsal fin, and flukes are not; they serve as so-called thermal windows, through which body heat can easily be lost to the environment. Arteries carry warm blood away from the core of the body toward the periphery; if that warmth were juxtaposed with cold skin, loss of body heat would result. However, the arteries leading outward are surrounded by rings of veins, which carry cold blood back toward the body core. Through the process of diffusion,[75] the blood in the arteries releases its warmth to the blood in the veins. In this way, arterial blood is cool-cold by the time it reaches the peripheral parts of the body, so that heat loss, via diffusion to the environment, is minimized. Just as important, the returning venous blood is generally (see exceptions below) warmed almost to core temperature.

The dolphin can adjust the amount of heat lost by adjusting the diameter of peripheral arteries; this is possible because arteries have walls that contain muscle and elastic fibers, in contrast to veins, which tend to have relatively thin, flaccid walls. Vasoconstriction lets less blood reach the surface, whereas vasodilation permits more blood to flow. Thus, if a dolphin overexerted itself and needed to dump body heat, it would vasodilate its peripheral arteries so that the surrounding veins could not capture all the arteries' heat. In this way, body heat in arterial blood would reach the periphery of the dolphin and diffuse to the environment.

Dolphins and other cetaceans are not unique in their ability to regulate diameters of blood vessels to conserve or dump body heat. Humans can and do vasodilate and vasoconstrict to regulate loss of body heat (consider circulation to your face when you go outside on a cold winter day and when you reenter a warm room). However, we lack extensive vascular countercurrents and conserve heat far less effectively than dolphins.

Some body tissues are especially sensitive to high temperature. These areas require special adjustments in the vascular system. For example, production and storage of viable sperm are impaired even at body temperature in many mammals. The problem is typically solved by placing the testes and epididymides outside the body in a scrotum and by the presence of a vascular countercurrent in the blood supply to the testes.[76] But dolphin testes are located in the abdominal cavity, where core temperature is maintained. How do dolphins maintain sperm viability?

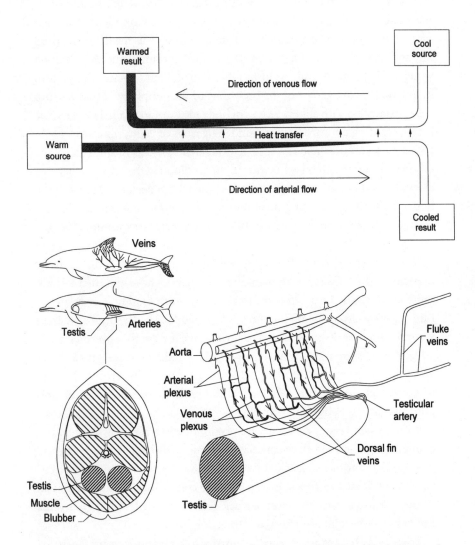

Fig. 34. One of the many amazing attributes of cetaceans involves the development of circulatory adaptations to retain heat in their bodies while they exist in cold water. The presence of countercurrents (top figure) is critical to heat conservation. On the other hand, certain organs (testes, uterus, spinal cord) cannot stand long-term exposure to high temperatures, as might be generated when an animal exercises. For such organs, vascular shunts allow cool blood to reach deep internal organs. Sentiel A. Rommel.

Measurements of testicular temperature suggest that dolphin testes are maintained at subcore temperature.[77] Cetaceans can employ a unique venous system to return cold blood from the superficial regions of the body directly to the caudal regions deep in the abdomen. There, a countercurrent exchanger exists that cools arterial blood leading to the testes.[78]

There are other internal organs and tissues that also need to be kept from overheating. Chief among these are the spinal cord (surrounded by heat-producing—that is, thermiogenic—axial muscles) and a fetus within the uterus. Probably, cooling of these structures occurs in ways similar to that used for the testes with "injection" of cold venous blood deep into the core of the body.[79]

Interesting adaptations to permit the reproductive organs to function well have been described. Although the intra-abdominal position of the testes is not typical of mammals, the reproductive system of the bottlenose dolphin is not terribly unusual. As is the case in some artiodactyls, the non-erect dolphin penis is curved into an S shape in the body wall; upon erection, the penis straightens and becomes turgid, but does not change much in length or diameter.

In female dolphins, the uterus is bicornuate (literally two horned), as is the case for many terrestrial mammals. The placenta resembles that of artiodactyls. The paired ovaries can be found in the usual position at the distal ends of the uterine (fallopian) tubes, with fetal development occurring more often in the left uterine horn.[80] Paired mammary glands are abdominal in position, near the urogenital opening.[81]

Reproduction in females has been studied in captive dolphins using a technique called radioimmunoassay to assess levels of reproductive hormones (for example, estrogen and progesterone) in the blood.[82] These hormone analyses indicated that dolphins are probably spontaneous ovulators (that is, ovulation is not induced by sexual activity); the estrous cycle is quite variable in length—twenty-one to forty-two days long; and there is also considerable variation in number of estrous periods within a given year. Sustained progesterone levels in the blood above 3,000 picograms/milliliter indicate pregnancy in dolphins, and gestation is about one year.

In terms of reproductive tract anatomy of marine mammals, there appear to be few specialized features associated with a marine lifestyle. Rather, reproductive tract anatomy appears to reflect phylogenetic relationships among groups (hence the similarities between dolphin and artiodactyl reproductive organs).

The urinary system may also reflect phylogeny. In all mammals, the fundamental functional unit of the kidney is called a nephron, which is composed of a nest of capillaries called the glomerulus (for blood filtration) and a series of straight and convoluted tubules (for secretion and reabsorption). Mammals possess a metanephric kidney, which in some species (for example, desert rodents) can produce very concentrated urine as a means to conserve water.[83]

As odd as it may seem, marine mammals face the same osmoregulatory problem as desert rodents, namely lack of fresh water to drink. Somehow, both groups must minimize water loss from their bodies. Scientists have speculated that marine mammals might have kidneys that can concentrate salt so effectively (in other words, produce very concentrated urine like a desert rodent) that ingestion of seawater could actually lead to a net gain of fresh water for osmoregulation.

Like other mammals, dolphins and other cetaceans possess metanephric kidneys. However, rather than having a single large organ, these animals, as

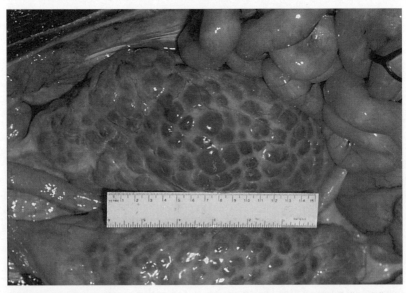

Fig. 35. A dolphin kidney, somewhat resembling a bunch of grapes. Each "grape" is a miniature kidney. SeaWorld, Florida.

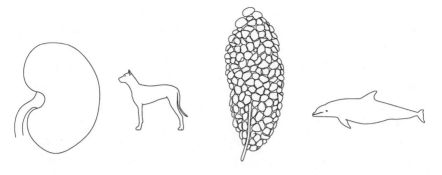

Fig. 36. A dolphin kidney and a dog kidney do not look alike at all, even though both perform the same function and possess similar internal structures. Sentiel A. Rommel.

well as seals and some other marine mammals have so-called reniculate kidneys, consisting of hundreds of small functional kidneys (called reniculi) packed closely together within a connective tissue capsule, and looking much like a bunch of grapes stuffed into a plastic, vacuum sealed bag. Perhaps not surprisingly given their relationship to cetaceans, some artiodactyls also have reniculate kidneys.

The function of reniculate kidneys has been speculated by a number of authors. Some have suggested that the reniculate arrangement permits greater capacity for blood filtration, an adaptation associated with diving.[84] Others have noted that reniculate kidneys are somewhat smaller than one would expect and have suggested that the reniculate kidney may be a space saver that packs as many nephrons as possible into a given volume, a handy adaptation for a species that has optimized its streamlined shape. Yet others feel, instead, that such kidneys may simply be related to large body size,[85] which helps explain why some large hoofed animals, which are neither streamlined nor great divers, also have reniculate kidneys.

The real question is: Do bottlenose dolphins produce urine that is concentrated enough that they could consume seawater and excrete enough salt to have a net gain of fresh water? The answer is that, despite work done to date, we really don't know! Although several studies have addressed the question, the results have not provided clear evidence. Seawater drinking (termed mariposia) was studied in a related small odontocete, the common dolphin (*Delphinus delphis*), and it was suggested that this species drinks enough seawater to facilitate excretion of nitrogenous wastes such as urea, but that common dolphins "do not need to drink seawater to maintain water balance."[86]

If dolphins do not need to drink to obtain water, how do they obtain fresh water for their bodies? Although the answer is not known with certainty, it is likely that water generated by metabolic processes provides what they need; recall that complete oxidation of glucose (glucose plus oxygen) yields carbon dioxide and *water*. Diet also plays a role. Some of the food dolphins consume (such as invertebrates like squid) have the same concentration of salts as seawater, whereas other food (such as marine fishes) is less concentrated than seawater. Thus consumption of fishes introduces less salt to the dolphin than does consumption of invertebrates; eating fishes may permit a net gain of water.

The remaining major anatomical system about which much is known in bottlenose dolphins is the nervous system. We consider some of the cranial nerves later in this chapter, but deal with the structure and function of the brain in chapter 7, when we discuss intelligence, communication, and cognition.[87]

Suites of Adaptations—Diving and Thermoregulation

DIVING

One of the clearest, most comprehensive descriptions of marine mammal diving was created by noted marine mammal physiologist Robert Elsner.[88] His approach involves an exploration of how diving animals overcome what he refers to as the "triad of asphyxia": hypoxia (a decline in available oxygen), hypercapnia (an increase in carbon dioxide), and acidosis (an accumulation of the products—for example, lactic acid—of anaerobic metabolism).

On short dives, dolphins rely on their stores of oxygen to maintain efficient, aerobic metabolism. Those stores include the blood, where hemoglobin binds oxygen to erythrocytes, or red blood corpuscles, and the skeletal muscles, where a related molecule, myoglobin, also binds oxygen. Although the blood volume of bottlenose dolphins is relatively low (representing about 7.4 percent of the body weight),[89] compared to 22 percent in deep-diving southern elephant seals, *Mirounga leonina*,[90] and 8 percent in humans),[91] the high percentage of the body represented by myoglobin-rich

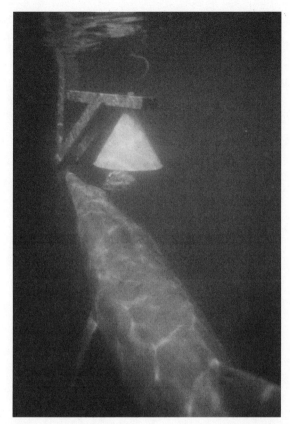

Fig. 37. The U.S. Navy does a great deal of work on dolphin physiology, including studies of how dolphins dive so well. In this photograph, a dolphin exhales into a funnel so that the gas content of its exhaled air can be analyzed. From Kanwisher and Ridgway, "The Physiological Ecology of Whales and Porpoises," with permission of S. H. Ridgway.

skeletal muscle means that overall oxygen carrying capacity in dolphins is quite high relative to terrestrial mammals. Thus, on a short-duration dive, dolphins apparently are able to maintain aerobic metabolism and avoid the triad of asphyxia.

Problems arise, however, during prolonged, deep dives. We have already alluded to some of the solutions dolphins employ: their lungs are rather small, reducing the energetic cost for the dolphin to overcome great buoyancy; and their alveoli collapse due to pressure, thereby preventing gas exchange and facilitating avoidance of the bends.[92] In fact, scientists have demonstrated very low nitrogen levels in the skeletal muscle of a diving dolphin.[93]

But there are more profound adjustments. One of the first physiological responses when a dolphin initiates a deep dive is bradycardia, a slowing of heart rate. For example, dolphins trained to dive for five-minute periods in a pool showed an abrupt drop in heart rate from about 100 to 12 beats per minute, with a gradual leveling off at about 25 beats per minute; on surfacing, the animals experienced a brief period of elevated heart rate.[94] Since decreasing heart rate is often accompanied by a slowing of metabolic rate

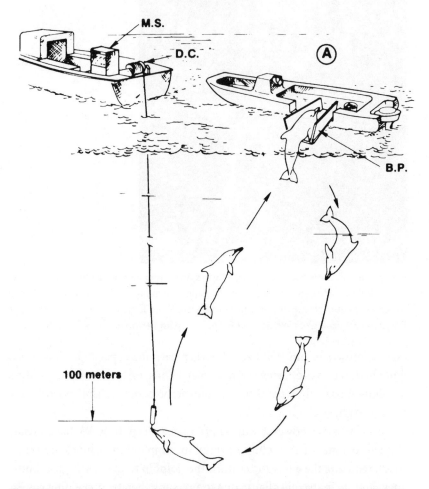

Fig. 38. Dynamics of oxygen and other gas utilization and blood circulation during diving were examined by the U.S. Navy using at-sea analyses following dives by a trained dolphin. From Ridgway and Howard, "Dolphin Lung Collapse and Intramuscular Circulation during Free Diving," with permission of S. H. Ridgway.

(hypometabolism), bradycardia may reflect a reduced need for oxygen. However, the actual presence of hypometabolism during unrestrained dives of free-ranging animals is controversial.

Ischemia (deprivation of tissues and organs of circulating blood) also contributes to increases in dolphin dive time. Ischemia affects many visceral organs, skeletal muscle, and skin. The condition occurs when arteries and arterioles maximally vasoconstrict, and it precipitates two important results. First, the circulating blood, with its oxygen stores, is reserved for the organs that require a constant supply of oxygen: the heart and brain. In addition, the cessation of circulation to the skeletal muscles means that myoglobin, which has a higher affinity for oxygen than does hemoglobin, cannot "steal" all the oxygen from the blood and, therefore, from the vital organs.

The skeletal muscles, of course, have their own oxygen stores bound to myoglobin, so aerobic metabolism can continue for awhile even during ischemia. During a dive, however, that oxygen store may be completely consumed. At that point, anaerobiosis occurs, lactic acid concentrations begin to build, and cellular pH decreases. Scientists have suggested that bottlenose dolphins probably seldom exercise hard for sustained periods of time while diving and, when they must do so, they are able to rely to a large extent on aerobic metabolism in the muscles.[95]

Other attributes possessed by some deep-diving mammals, but not necessarily by dolphins, include high hematocrits (red blood corpuscle concentrations), sequestering of blood cells in the spleen during diving to reduce blood viscosity, and apparent tolerance of heart and brain tissue to low oxygen concentrations. Specifically, unlike the brains of "typical" mammals, the dolphin brain may be capable of some degree of anaerobiosis,[96] although corroborating data do not exist. However, the blood of small odontocetes contains considerable glucose, which would be an important adaptation for the central nervous system under low oxygen conditions such as prolonged dives.[97]

In searching for reasons why some marine mammals are great divers one should not, of course, overlook the obvious. Animals that are as streamlined and as efficient swimmers as dolphins can dive better, in part, because they move through the water with minimal expenditure of energy (and therefore of oxygen). However, in measurements of dolphin swimming and diving energetics, oxygen consumption for deep-diving dolphins was far less than

Fig. 39. Dolphins' unusual hydrodynamic and pressure-sensing capabilities allow them to economize on energy use by riding a bow wave. Randall S. Wells, Chicago Zoological Society.

anticipated.[98] After attaching a camera (appropriately called a critter-cam) to the back of a dolphin, physiologist Terrie Williams discovered why: when the dolphin reached a depth of about 70 meters, its tail stopped moving, but its body kept descending.[99] Williams hypothesized that, once extreme pressure associated with depth collapses the dolphin's lungs and compresses other body tissues, the animal's density causes it to sink with no muscle activity and, more importantly, no unnecessary expenditure of energy. The same process, in reverse, could allow effortless surfacing; once the dolphin's lungs refill and body density lessens as it ascends from depth, its buoyancy alone could cause it to surface without expending any energy to actively swim. In addition, scientists have described a burst-and-glide style of swimming as dolphins descend;[100] introduction of periods of gliding presumably save energy, thereby prolonging the dive.

With all of these adaptations, to what extent is diving in dolphins enhanced, relative to humans? A trained male dolphin named Tuffy was trained to dive *repeatedly* for nearly 5 minutes and to depths of 200 to 300 meters.[101] The maximum voluntary breath hold recorded was 7.25 minutes for a captive female dolphin.[102] The absolute depth and time limits for dolphin diving are not known. By contrast, the deepest human breath-hold dive is 117 meters, and the longest breath hold is just over 6 minutes; one presumes that the individuals accomplishing such remarkable feats would not be able to repeat them without considerable rest. Perhaps a more appropriate comparison of human diving comes from observations of the Ama, a group of Japanese divers who manually harvest benthic invertebrates. To do so, they perform about 100 breath-hold dives a day, with each lasting about 1 minute, and few exceeding 90 seconds, to depths that generally do not exceed 15 meters.[103]

Dolphins can certainly dive better than people, but the difference may not be as impressive as has been imagined. However, it should be kept in mind that coastal bottlenose dolphins do not need to be especially good divers, relative to other marine mammals; offshore forms of bottlenose dolphins may be another story. On the other hand, some marine mammal species such as sperm whales *(Physeter catodon)*, bottlenose whales *(Berardius bairdii)*, and northern elephant seals *(Mirounga angustirostris)* may exceed dive depths of a mile and dive times of an hour—a much more impressive performance.

In summary, dolphins and their relatives possess a suite of respiratory, circulatory, and biochemical adaptations. Coupled with their hydrodynamically favorable shape and very smooth integument (both of which re-

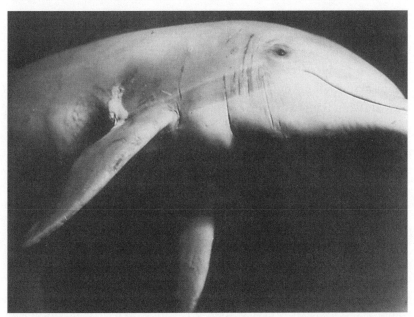

Fig. 40. In this famous photograph, navy dolphin Tuffy takes his own picture after diving to a particular depth. Tuffy was trained to dive repeatedly for nearly five minutes per dive and to depths of up to 300 meters. At such depths, pressure collapsed his rib cage, as shown in this picture. From S. H. Ridgway, "Buoyancy Regulation in Deep Diving Whales," with permission of S. H. Ridgway. Official U.S. Navy photograph.

duce drag), their energetically efficient locomotion, and changes therein, and possibly their ability to change body density, these features permit many species to dive far better than the best human divers.

THERMOREGULATION

Like humans and other mammals, dolphins are homeotherms (they maintain a relatively constant body temperature) and endotherms (they derive heat from internal, metabolic processes). Enzyme structure and activity, necessary for a species' survival, are very sensitive to temperature. For a species to be able to function well over a range of temperature regimes, adaptations are needed to keep heat loss and gain to a minimum. For dolphins, which often occupy water colder than their core temperatures, the problem is almost always to prevent loss of body heat. Only when undergoing strenuous exercise or possibly when ill does a typical dolphin need to unload excess body heat to the environment.

Thermoregulation, like diving, involves a number of adaptations, many of which have been elaborated above. Relatively small surface area due to large body size and reductions in external appendages, the presence of insulation, thermal windows with countercurrent exchangers, and vascular shunts to permit selective cooling of certain organs and tissues all assist dolphins in functioning optimally. Even in cold water, when blood flow to the extremities is limited in order to conserve body heat, scientists have noted that dolphins may periodically allow warm blood to reach the skin.[104] This was suggested by observations of a dolphin that dilated its arteries to flush a lot of blood to its flukes on surfacing after a dive. A general similarity was noted between dolphins and camels in terms of unloading heat at the most opportune times, rather than continuously.[105] Dolphins do so after a dive, when peripheral parts of the body (for example, active muscles) cannot "steal" oxygen critical to certain organs during the dive,[106] and camels do so at night, when water loss accompanying heat loss would be minimized.

Other characteristics associated with living in cold water include special enzymes designed to function in peripheral parts of the animal at reduced temperatures, relative to deep body or core temperature. In addition, during times of thermal stress, animals may increase their metabolic rates.

Mammals are able to maintain a resting metabolic rate when they occupy a particular range of temperatures, called the thermal neutral (or thermoneutral) zone. As ambient environmental temperatures drop below or rise

Fig. 41. Navy scientists conduct heat flow experiments on a bottlenose dolphin. This and other noninvasive techniques have provided considerable insight into dolphin physiology and health. Official U.S. Navy photograph.

above the zone, metabolic rate (and therefore energetic demand on the animal) goes up. The lower and upper limits of the thermal neutral zone are termed the lower and upper critical temperatures, respectively. In a study of captive dolphins, scientists found that the upper critical temperature was around 28°C, which was also ambient temperature for the water in the tank.[107] The lower critical temperature averaged 13°C, with large dolphins or animals with thick blubber having lower critical temperatures that are less than the average value and small animals or those with thinner blubber layers having a higher value for the lower critical temperature. It is important to note that (1) dolphins that are acclimated to different temperature regimes show a somewhat different range for the thermal neutral zone (likened to resetting of a home thermostat depending on seasonal changes in temperature); and (2) wild dolphins change both the quality and quantity of their blubber seasonally.[108] However, a thermal neutral zone of 13–28°C corresponds well to the range of surface temperatures (that is, 10–32°C) normally occupied by the species in the wild.[109] In warmer parts of the species' range, such as Sarasota Bay, Florida, summer water temperatures sometimes approach dolphin body temperatures. In these cases, dolphins have higher metabolic rates than they do during winter, when increased blubber thickness presumably works to the animals' advantage.[110]

Nonetheless, there are times when animals cannot maintain optimal body temperature by changing their metabolic rate or other internal means. For that reason, species complement their anatomical and physiological responses with behavioral ones. For example, along the mid-Atlantic coast of the United States, some dolphins migrate seasonally, perhaps in part as a response to cold. In cold weather, dolphins and other marine mammals may bask at the surface, where their dark skin absorbs solar radiation. Thus, a complete understanding of thermoregulation must take into account a suite of behavioral, anatomical, physiological, and biochemical adaptations.

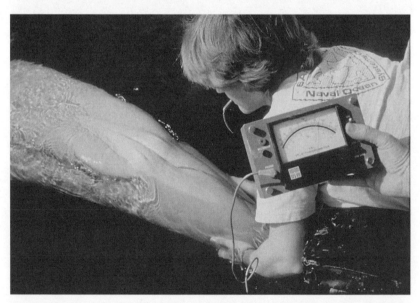

Fig. 42. As part of efforts to better understand the ability of dolphins to thermoregulate in cold water, a scientist takes a rectal temperature of a dolphin. Official U.S. Navy photograph.

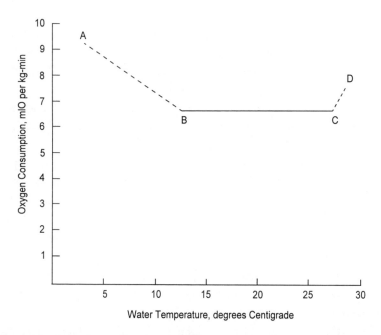

Fig. 43. The thermal neutral zone represents a range of ambient temperatures where a species can maintain its body temperature without elevating its resting metabolic rate. The upper critical temperature (C) and lower critical temperature (B) are the points at which energetic costs to maintain body temperature become noticeable. Sentiel A. Rommel.

ENERGETICS—SUMMARY THOUGHTS

Peppered throughout our discussion of dolphin adaptations are words such as *energy, energetic efficiency,* and *energetic cost.* To a large extent, marine mammal adaptations reflect ways in which the animals can balance energy expenditures with intake of food (not unlike a cost-benefit model used by an economist). The problem, as we have seen, is more acute for marine mammals than for terrestrial ones due to the ability of cold water to "steal" heat (that is, energy) from the body.

Costs for a dolphin or other marine mammal include those associated with foraging, with heat loss, and with maintenance of body functions. At least some of the energy taken in is used to support individual growth and reproduction.

Costa and Williams review the topic of marine mammal energetics.[111] They note that the study of energetics provides considerable insight about the relationship between an individual animal and its environment. Marine mammals have developed a suite of traits, discussed in this chapter, that permit them to survive and propagate. Large and fusiform bodies, modified integument, special circulatory system traits, specialized swimming behaviors, elevated metabolic rates, and unusual diving adaptations all help marine mammals "balance the equation" in terms of intake and outflow of energy.

Since so much of what marine mammals do involves conserving or optimizing use of energy, the field of marine mammal energetics offers considerable insight into the biology of species. And while the discussion in this chapter has involved energetics of individual animals, Costa and Williams extended their discussion to include population level energy use, foraging ecology, and conservation (see also chapter 6). The broader approach has implications for fishery conflicts with humans and for understanding population changes as they may relate to environmental changes (for example, El Niño Southern Oscillation, global warming).

While still in something of a fledgling stage of development relative to certain other approaches to the study of marine mammals, the field of bioenergetics offers some exciting challenges to creative scientists seeking to understand better how marine mammals make a living.

Sensory Biology

"Sensory systems evolved to allow animals to receive and process information from their surroundings."[112] Since a dolphin's surroundings are so different from our own in terms of factors such as light availability, speed of sound transmission, and pressure, one might reasonably expect significant differences in dolphin sensory systems. In this section, we consider organs that receive and detect stimuli; in chapter 7 we deal with the site of information processing—the brain.

One important bias which we, as humans, have involves our reliance on vision as our primary source of information regarding our environment. We sometimes tend to assume that other animals perceive the world as we do. In the case of the bottlenose dolphin, nothing could be further from the truth. In fact, it has been suggested that marine mammals are de facto crepuscular species (that is, species that are active around dawn and dusk).[113] Given the limitations imposed by attenuation of light and the relative ease with which sound travels in seawater (approximately 4.5 times faster than in air), it is no wonder that the importance of vision is reduced and that acoustics plays such an important role in communication in marine organisms in general and in marine mammals specifically.

It is also worth noting that animals do not give equal attention to all stimuli to which they are exposed. Rather, species are exquisitely attuned to certain stimuli (for example, those associated with predators and prey or social cues) and virtually impervious to others. The sensory systems act as the selective filters that permit a species to avoid being barraged by stimuli.

As noted above, bottlenose dolphins are likely to perceive their world primarily through auditory or acoustic stimuli. Marine mammal scientists have suggested that the extreme development (hypertrophy) of acoustic regions of the dolphin brain (see also chapter 7) is a reflection of the extent to which rapid processing of sounds, especially high-frequency echolocation clicks, is important to the species.[114]

Sound energy in the environment is converted by biomechanical transducers of the middle and inner ear into nerve impulses that travel via the eighth cranial nerve (the acoustic or vestibulocochlear nerve) to the brain. Mammalian ears are intricate structures that have more than 75,000 mechanical and electrochemical components packed into a minute space of just one cubic centimeter. Not surprisingly, given the theme of this chapter, the number and *structure* of those components determine functional hearing (see chapter 7 for discussion of cranial nerves and regions of the brain).

Even though dolphins lack an external ear, they possess the same fundamental parts to their middle and inner ears as do terrestrial mammals. In terrestrial mammals the typical middle ear is an air-filled canal with small bones (malleus, incus, and stapes) located between tautly stretched membranes. The middle ear serves as a transducer of energy from air to the liquid contained in the inner ear. The inner ear (specifically the cochlea, a fluid-filled spiral structure) is the site where mechanical energy is converted into nerve impulses. The specific regions where this occurs in the cochlea are called the organ of Corti (with receptor cells) and the basilar membrane (a resonator).[115] As noted, human and other mammalian ears possess cochleae, although the frequencies of sound detected vary greatly among species and individuals.

Some significant changes have developed in specific regions of the dolphin ear. For example, most odontocetes lack any bony connection between

Table 2. Sounds Produced by Dolphins

Sound Type	Frequency Range	Function
Clicks	0.2–150 kHz	Echolocation
Whistles	0.2–24 kHz	Individual recognition Group cohesion
Low frequency, narrowband	0.3–0.9 kHz	Unknown
Rasps, grates, mews, barks, yelps	0.2–16 kHz	Communication?

the ear bones and the rest of the skull. Instead, the ears are acoustically isolated by being suspended from the skull by ligaments. In addition, there are no air-filled canals in dolphin ears, since such structures would be susceptible to pressure changes during deep dives. Instead, fat bodies (notably the intramandibular fat bodies noted earlier) are used to channel sound. The ossicles of the dolphin middle ear are stiffened with bony struts and inflexible joints; such stiffening is thought to be essential for dolphins to be able to echolocate using ultrasonic frequencies.

Dolphins, of course, produce a variety of sounds, not just those associated with echolocation. Table 2 lists the sounds, together with their frequencies and speculated functions. Students should note how incomplete our knowledge is about the functions of many dolphin sounds—good topics for future research.[116] For reference, the upper bound of human hearing is only 20 kHz, compared to the 150 kHz limit for the bottlenose dolphin; in fact, even the peak acoustic sensitivity of dolphins, up to 100 kHz, is much higher than the human hearing threshold.[117]

The two types of dolphin sounds that have been studied most thoroughly are echolocation clicks and signature whistles. Signature whistles were first assessed, and the term *signature whistle* coined, by the late, eminent husband-wife team of Melba and David Caldwell,[118] who demonstrated that individual captive dolphins produce distinctive whistles,[119] although it is apparently not unusual for individuals to mimic the whistles of other dolphins with which they associate.[120] Signature whistles are used, at least in part, to help maintain group cohesion.[121]

Recent work has demonstrated that free-ranging dolphins also possess signature whistles.[122] Calves as young as one month of age (or as old as two years of age) develop signature whistles, which presumably contribute to maintenance of contact with the mother. Once established, the signature whistle remains virtually unchanged for the rest of the dolphin's life. Thus, signature whistles help dolphins maintain relationships with other animals for very long periods of time. Interestingly, signature whistles of male calves tend to resemble those of their mothers more than whistles of female calves do.[123] The reasons for this are not well understood; once thought to possibly function to reduce inbreeding,[124] scientists now feel more strongly that the sex difference is driven primarily by a need for female distinctiveness, since female dolphins associate, at least in Sarasota Bay, with close female relatives, including siblings, mothers, and offspring.[125]

Results of playback experiments indicate that free-ranging dolphins respond more strongly to recorded signature whistles of kin and other familiar dolphins than they do to whistles of less familiar animals. This provides

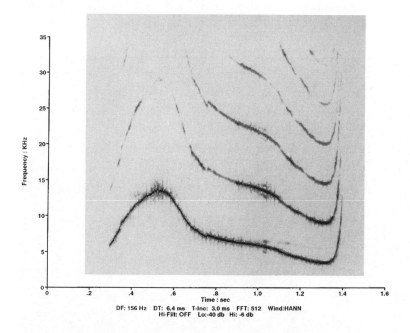

Fig. 44. Dolphins produce a variety of sounds, the functions of which are generally not well understood. This picture shows a spectrogram of whistles produced by a dolphin. Each spectrogram plots sound frequency in kilohertz versus time in seconds. L. Sayigh.

further support that signature whistles function to identify individual dolphins.[126]

Echolocation can be defined as the ability to produce high-frequency sounds and to detect and analyze echoes of those sounds that bounce off objects.[127] Echolocation serves as a useful tool by which the animal can probe its surroundings to detect factors such as bottom topography, food availability and type, and presence of predators.[128] The high resolution of dolphin echolocation is difficult for humans to comprehend; imagine being able to use sound to detect an object approximately the size of a Ping-Pong ball a football field away![129] Also amazing is the suggestion that bottlenose dolphins may even vary the frequency of the clicks they produce to avoid "competition" from background noises.[130] It has even been suggested that dolphins and other odontocetes can produce such an intense sound field, using echolocation clicks, that they can stun their prey before actually making physical contact.[131] Sounding to human ears more like a buzz than a series of distinct individual clicks, echolocation provides a dolphin homing in on prey or simply investigating a novel object with a sophisticated means of probing the environment and perhaps even catching a meal, night and

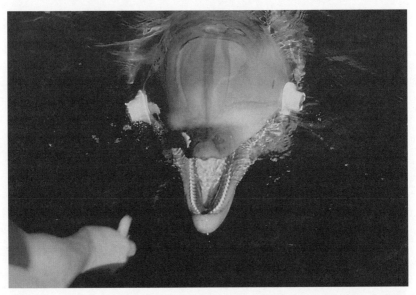

Fig. 45. In an effort to study the ability of dolphins to navigate or orient using echolocation, soft rubber eyecups are used to prevent the animals from using vision. Official U.S. Navy photograph.

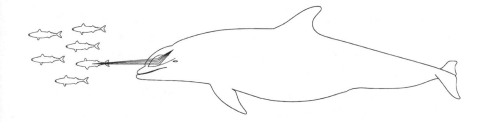

Fig. 46. Scientists have hypothesized that dolphins can produce such intense, focused beams of sound that they can actually use sound to stun prey. Sentiel A. Rommel.

day. Contrary to popular belief, however, echolocation is used only as needed—it is not a constantly operating scanning system.

Effective echolocation requires special anatomical "equipment" both to produce appropriate sounds and to receive and process them. The use of melon and intramandibular fat as acoustic lenses has been mentioned above. Part of the ability of these structures to focus sound is due to the presence of special fats, sometimes referred to as acoustic lipids.[132] The melon allows production of a narrow cone or beam of sound that can be more or less focused, depending on the needs of the animal emitting the sound. For example, echolocation clicks might be relatively focused in order to gain precise information about a nearby object. On the other hand, a dolphin might produce a somewhat more diffuse sound field when scanning a wide area for the presence of predators or prey.

Humans and most terrestrial mammals cannot hear directionally under-water, a function of a small interaural (between the ears) distance and the fast rate with which sound travels underwater. For dolphins, the presence of an acoustic lens (that is, the intramandibular fat body) that abuts each ear facilitates directional hearing by causing sound (especially ultrasonic echolocation clicks) that is lateral to the dolphin to be channeled to one ear before the other; it does this by acting as a "preferential low impedance path to the middle ear."[133] The thin lower jaw bone (sometimes called the pan bone) overlying the fat body acts as a "window" between the environment and the ear region.[134]

Thus, echolocation, directional hearing, and acoustic communication in dolphins are permitted by a cadre of features not associated with typical mammals: the presence of a special sound-production site (the area of the nasal plug and sacs), a special lens to focus outgoing sound (the melon), a low impedance pathway for incoming sound (the intramandibular fat body), ears that have become isolated from the rest of the skull, a cochlea possessing specialized features (stiffening, sensory cells sensitive to particular frequencies), and greatly expanded acoustic regions of the brain. In few other anatomical systems that we have discussed in this chapter have so many fundamental changes occurred.

Acoustics may dominate the sensory input of a bottlenose dolphin, but other senses are also used. Because light is attenuated (absorbed) as depth increases, eyes of marine mammals must be adapted to low-light levels. For example, the number of rods and cones (collectively called photoreceptor cells) in the retina of the eye varies among species. The visual sensitivity of marine mammal eyes relates to both the number and type of photoreceptor cells and to the presence of a tapetum lucidum, a reflective layer located behind the retina. The tapetum reflects incoming light back through the retina, thereby increasing the likelihood that a photoreceptor may be stimulated (note that "eyeshine" in a cat or other crepuscular/nocturnal animal is caused by reflection of light from the tapetum lucidum).

Bottlenose dolphins have 400,000 photoreceptors per mm^2 of retinal surface,[135] compared to 120,000 or so per mm^2 in humans.[136] In addition, as in humans, bottlenose dolphins possess duplex retinas—that is, with both rods (better for vision in low-light environments) and cones (best for acuity in circumstances with good light). Such an arrangement permits dolphins to use vision at different times of day and at different depths. The presence of cones, incidentally, does not necessarily mean that dolphins possess color vision;[137] instead, cones may function simply to provide good visual acuity when light levels are high. Visual acuity of cetaceans appears to be similar to that of a cat. Unlike many other species that possess good visual acuity, the dolphin lacks an area of very densely packed cones called a fovea centralis in the retina.[138]

In the typical terrestrial mammal's eye, focusing of light onto the retina occurs due to both the lens and the cornea. In fact, in humans, around two-thirds of the total focusing power of the eye involves bending of light at the air-cornea interface. Because the refractive index of water is similar to that inside the eye, an eye adapted to terrestrial conditions (as eyes of cetacean ancestors undoubtedly were) loses its ability to focus underwater with the cornea. To compensate, dolphins have developed stronger lenses, which are spherical in shape, much like a fish lens. This allows dolphins and other cetaceans to focus light precisely on the retina when looking at objects underwater,[139] but causes myopia (nearsightedness) when viewing objects in air. How dolphins are able to adjust to the latter condition is not well understood. However, the precision with which dolphins in marine parks and aquaria can locate and touch objects suspended above their pools provides proof that they do make the adjustment quite well, and often make appropriate adjustments while still underwater.

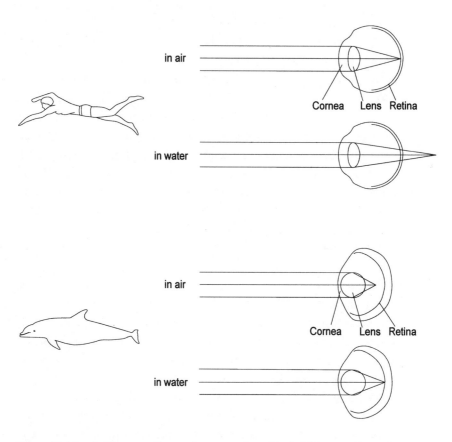

Fig. 47. The "typical" mammalian eye becomes adapted in dolphins to withstand pressure, saltwater immersion, and the fact that the cornea, which focuses light in air, no longer does so underwater. As a consequence, a dolphin is able to focus light on its retina underwater but not in air, where the animal becomes nearsighted (myopic) but can quickly learn to compensate. Humans have the opposite problem—we focus on the retina in air but become farsighted (hyperopic) under water. Sentiel A. Rommel.

The field of vision of dolphins is also different from that of humans. The positioning of the eyes on each side of the dolphins' head provides the animals with some degree of binocular vision forward. However, the positioning provides optimal viewing laterally, below the plane of the body, and even caudally. Muscular manipulation of the eye results in outward "pooching" that permits enhanced vision in front of and behind the animal as well. This extensive field of view complements the forward-oriented echolocation system and provides the dolphin with greater ability to sense approaching predators, maintain position relative to other members of the group, or view subtle visual signals from companions.

Dolphins use other senses that have not been studied as well as vision and acoustics have; these include magnetic reception, tactile sensation, and detection of chemicals (termed chemoreception). Chemoreception typically occurs via taste (gustation) and smell (olfaction). The slow speed with which chemicals diffuse through water (10,000 times slower than in air), and the slow speed of water currents (on average, fifteen times slower than air currents) limit how effective the chemical transfer of information under water can be. Olfaction involves detection of chemicals using sensory areas associated with the nose and nostrils. Since dolphin "nostrils" (that is, the blowhole) remain closed much of the time, it comes as no surprise to find that dolphins lack olfactory bulbs in the brain.[140] On the other hand, it appears that dolphins have the ability to discriminate different tastes,[141] and taste buds are present on the tongue.[142]

Cetaceans' abilities to detect magnetic sensations, primarily to assist in navigation, have received considerable attention because some scientists have related locations of strandings to geomagnetic fields along certain coastlines such as the United Kingdom.[143] However, in other parts of the world, such as New Zealand, there appears to be no correlation between stranding locations and geomagnetic fields.[144]

Magnetite has been found in the membranes covering the brain and spinal cord of the bottlenose dolphin and other cetaceans,[145] but this may relate to structural support of the membrane rather than to orientation and navigation. The question of the extent to which magnetic sensation plays a role in dolphins' and other cetaceans' ability to orient remains unclear.

Finally, studies have demonstrated dolphin abilities to detect tactile stimuli. The most comprehensive study used electroencephalograms to map locations on the dolphin body where sensitivity was greatest.[146] In decreasing order of sensitivity, these included the angle of the jaw, the area around the eyes and melon, the tip of the rostrum and the blowhole, and the rest of the body. Clearly the head region in general is most important for detection of tactile cues. The possibility exists, but has not been conclusively demonstrated, that swimming dolphins may be able to detect pressure differences associated with local turbulence and use their superficial muscles to actively dampen that turbulence, thereby reducing drag.

Behavioral evidence also exists to support the idea that dolphins use tactile cues a great deal. Socializing dolphins tend to rub against one another frequently as they travel or interact. This behavior, perhaps, is analogous to social grooming that occurs in some terrestrial mammals, including primates.[147]

In summary, scientists have learned about some sensory adaptations and their functions in bottlenose dolphins. But there is still much to learn. Noted sensory biologists Douglas Wartzok and Darlene Ketten[148] have observed that the tools we use to investigate marine mammal sensory biology are still limited and that we still do not really understand what stimuli dolphins and other cetaceans encounter as they conduct their daily lives. In addition, some research tools that are accepted and applied to other species may not be used, for legal or ethical reasons, on marine mammals. As technology produces new, noninvasive scientific "tools" that can be used to assess dolphin and other marine mammal sensory capabilities, exciting insights will certainly result.

Conclusions

We began this chapter by observing that form and function go together, and that, even in the face of inadequate experimental evidence, knowledge of the former may permit assumptions to be made regarding the latter. What may be surprising is that there are still major deficiencies in our knowledge of structure, leaving scientists a considerable number of interesting questions to address. In the decade between 1978 and 1987, nearly fifteen hundred carcasses of bottlenose dolphins were reported (and most were also recovered for study) in the southeastern United States alone;[149] what a gold mine of specimen materials for the opportunistic anatomist.

We also raised the question early in the chapter: Is dolphin anatomy fundamentally similar to our own, or basically different? The question actually leads to more than a philosophical exercise. If dolphins are like humans and other terrestrial mammals, what does this tell us about evolution and connectedness among living organisms? If dolphins are so very different, we might ask how and why fundamental biological attributes have come to vary so.

As we and our colleagues work with dolphins and talk about structures and functions, we remain excited and enthralled by what dolphins can do. The forces that shaped their bodies created something exquisite. The study of dolphin functional morphology and physiology represents an exciting field, and creative minds regularly discover new tools or ask questions in novel ways that expand what we know.

Life History Strategies

The study of a species' biology involves, to a large extent, a consideration of adaptations. When people are asked to consider adaptations that animals possess which allow them to survive and propagate, what comes to mind typically involves anatomical structures. As we saw in chapter 4, it is often quite easy to examine the structure of a particular morphological trait in a dolphin (for example, the powerful flukes, the intramandibular fat bodies, the streamlined body) and perceive why the trait is useful for the species. But adaptations are not limited to gross morphological attributes; for example, as we have seen, the presence of the respiratory pigment, myoglobin, in skeletal muscle is a biochemical, rather than an anatomical adaptation, that facilitates diving in dolphins and other marine mammals. Yet another view of dolphin adaptations is offered here.

In this chapter we deal with life histories, defined as "the significant features of the life cycle through which an organism passes, with particular reference to strategies influencing survival and reproduction."[1] Relevant features or stages of the life cycle could include birth, weaning, independence from parental care, sexual maturity, physical maturity, social maturity, pregnancy, parturition, lactation, and senescence—in other words, almost anything an organism is and does. Such a broad and vague definition is so all-encompassing that it is not very useful. A more specific and practical definition of life history might be those traits (that is, adaptations) for which

Fig. 48. A mother dolphin and her calf swim in a typical formation. Flip Nicklin and Minden Pictures.

variation directly influences fecundity (the rate at which individuals produce offspring), survival of individuals, and population growth.[2] Among the more commonly assessed life history traits are reproductive rate, age at sexual maturity, and life span. It is important at this point to realize that (1) expression of life history traits by individuals varies due to both environmental factors and population status and growth; and (2) life history attributes make up a vital suite of a species' adaptations. An excellent review of evolution of life history strategies appears in Ricklefs.[3]

It seems obvious that, within a particular habitat or environment, not all residents behave the same way or play the same role. In coastal waters of Florida, for example, individual pink shrimp (*Penaeus duorarum*) possess rather short life spans; produce hundreds of thousands, if not millions, of eggs per adult female; do not care for their offspring at all; and attain relatively small size.[4] In contrast, bottlenose dolphins in the same habitat may live more than fifty years, produce a single offspring every few years, demonstrate intense and prolonged care of their few offspring, and slowly reach large body size. The shrimp and the dolphin have clearly evolved entirely different strategies for success in the same habitat. In fact, shrimp and dolphins lie at different ends of a gradient of such strategies, with the shrimp being called r-strategists and dolphins being considered K-strategists.[5]

The r-strategists (sometimes called r-selectors) of the world have evolved traits (termed life history attributes) that maximize "r," which in ecological equations stands for intrinsic rate of increase. The K-strategists (or K-selectors) have done the opposite, in that their life history attributes maximize the probability that population size will remain relatively stable and approximate "K," which denotes the carrying capacity of the environment. Strictly in terms of reproduction, r-strategists produce a lot of offspring, the vast majority of which do not survive. A goal of this process, sometimes referred to as "flooding the market," is to produce so many offspring that not all can be consumed by predators. After all, if only a few female pink shrimp reach adulthood, they have the potential to produce enormous numbers of offspring that can repopulate an area. The K-strategists, conversely, produce few offspring, which are typically well attended and well trained by their

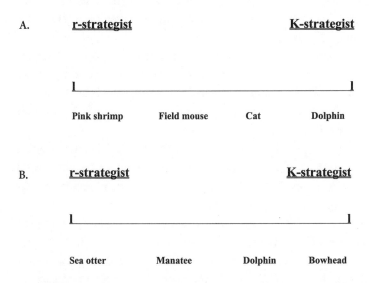

Fig. 49. The concept of r- vs. K-selection involves a gradient along which different species lie. The r-strategists of the world are relatively small, produce large numbers of offspring, and have short life spans. The K-strategists, on the other hand, are larger, produce fewer offspring, and live longer lives. No matter what the other species to which a dolphin is compared, the dolphin always exists at the K-strategist end of the gradient. John E. Reynolds III.

parents or other members of a group and which, therefore, have a good survival rate.

So far, the concept of r- vs. K-selection may seem quite simple and straightforward. But there are some confounding factors. First, one must bear in mind that the concept involves a gradient along which species lie. In other words, most species are not absolutely r-selected or K-selected, but possess attributes that place them somewhere in the middle. Again, based strictly on reproductive output (or fecundity), where would one place a mouse such as the common deer mouse, *Peromyscus maniculatus*? Clearly a mouse produces many more young (a few a year) than a dolphin, but equally clearly, mice produce nowhere near as many offspring as pink shrimp do. Based just on fecundity, one might make a case for mice being either relatively r-selected or relatively K-selected, depending on one's frame of reference.

The other confounding factor is that life history strategies involve far more than simply reproductive output. Rather, a suite of attributes is used to assign a particular species to a particular location along the r- and K-strategist gradient. A list of attributes associated with the different poles of that gradient appears in table 3.

To illustrate how consideration of several attributes may contribute more insight into species' life history strategies than consideration of only one or two attributes, consider yet another resident of coastal Florida waters: the manatee. Exactly how do dolphins and manatees compare in terms of their life history attributes?

One feature common to K-selectors is large body size. Manatees reach a body weight of about 3,600 pounds (1,500 kilograms),[6] a weight several times that of the largest bottlenose dolphins. This single observation suggests that manatees might be more K-selected than dolphins.

Another feature of K-selectors involves species life span. Dolphins in Sarasota Bay may live into their forties (males) and fifties (females);[7] this has been documented by sectioning dolphin teeth and counting growth layer groups therein.[8] Until recently, no reliable method existed to assess age of manatees, since they replace their teeth throughout their lives. However, using growth layer groups in ear bones, scientists have demonstrated that manatees may live to be as old as fifty-nine years, although relatively few manatees live past the age of twenty.[9] It seems fair to say that manatees and

Table 3. Attributes of r-Strategists and K-Strategists

ATTRIBUTE	MANIFESTATION	
	r-strategists	K-strategists
Fecundity	High	Low
Age at sexual maturity	Young	Old
Rate of development of offspring	Fast	Slow
Breeding episodes/life span	One (semelparity)	Numerous (iteroparity)
Body size	Small	Large
Life span	Short, often <1 year	Long
Population size	Variable, often well above or below carrying capacity	Stable, at or near carrying capacity
Mortality	Often catastrophic, density independent, nondirected	Noncatastrophic, density dependent, directed at certain demographic groups
Survivorship	Very poor for newborns, improves later; so-called Type III survivorship curve	Better at any age than for r-strategists; Good–excellent survival after newborn period; Types I and II survivorship curves
Colonizing ability	Great	Limited
Energy utilization	Opt for production	Opt for efficiency
Climate	Often uncertain, variable	Predictable
Social behavior	Weak, few short-term bonds	Strong, prolonged bonds
Parental Care	Little	A lot, extended over time

Sources: E. R. Pianka, "On r and K Selection," 592–97; R. E. Ricklefs, *Ecology*, 577–79, 173–86; and R. Brewer, *The Science of Ecology*, 173–86.

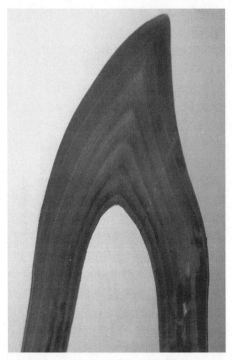

Fig. 50. Much like rings in a tree, the presence of growth layer groups in the teeth of dolphins permit scientists to determine age of individual animals. In this photograph, a tooth has been sectioned and stained to show the layers. Megan K. Stolen, Hubbs-Sea World Research Institute.

dolphins have comparable life spans, suggesting, based on this feature, that the two species are comparably K-selected.

But wait! Other factors must be considered, and when they are, dolphins emerge as somewhat more K-selected than manatees. For example, the onset of sexual maturity influences species or individual reproductive potential a great deal. Thus, assessment of sexual maturity status becomes very important for biologists and conservationists interested in the life history of a particular species. How can attainment of sexual maturity be determined?

For males, several features are routinely used. Mass of the testes is assessed, since testicular size increases dramatically in many species when sexual maturity is reached. Also, the microscopic anatomy of the testes and epididymides[10] is examined to assess the condition of the cells in and around the seminiferous tubules[11] or to reveal mature spermatozoa in either the seminiferous tubules or the lumen (the open part of a duct) of the epididymis. Scientists may create a "smear" of epididymal fluid on a microscope slide and examine the slide for the presence of sperm. Sometimes scientists also assess levels of reproductive hormones (for example, testosterone) in blood, since mature individuals produce more of these hormones. Finally, ultrasound may be used to gauge testicular dimensions. Interestingly enough, the first three methods depend on availability for examination of recently deceased animals (it is rather impractical, for example, to do testicular biopsies on species that lack scrotal testes!), and the fourth method can use blood from either living or recently deceased individuals. This observation reinforces how vital efficient stranding networks are to understanding and conserving marine mammals.[12]

Determining sexual maturity of females also relies to at least some extent on specimens obtained through stranding networks. A female that is ovulating is sexually mature. Hence, it is common to examine the ovaries for scars resulting from ovulation. Recent ovulations are marked by prominent yellowish bodies called corpora lutea (singular is corpus luteum), whereas ovulations that occurred in the more distant past may be, but are not always, indicated by white scars called corpora albicantia (singular, corpus albicans), which actually represent regressed, inactive corpora lutea. Scientists may also examine the uterus for scars indicating the implantation of a fetus during pregnancy, another surefire indicator of sexual maturity. Uteri and ovaries are available for study only from deceased animals. However, as with males, living animals can also provide clues. Levels of hormones (for example, estrogen, progesterone) in the blood can reflect where in an estrous cycle a particular female is. Ultrasound can detect the presence of a fetus. And, of course, the presence of a nutritionally dependent, suckling calf indicates that a female is sexually mature.

Assessment of reproductive status becomes more meaningful when the age of the animals is determined. That is why the scientific community becomes excited when the presence and periodicity of growth layer groups (or other reliable means of aging individuals) are developed as described above.

Florida manatees reach sexual maturity as young as two years of age for males[13] and three years for females,[14] whereas male and female bottlenose dolphins in Sarasota Bay, Florida, do not reach sexual maturity until ten to thirteen years old and five to twelve years old, respectively.[15] Most female dolphins in this group reach sexual maturity at about eight to ten years of age. In addition, female Florida manatees may produce a calf every 2.5 to 3

Fig. 51. Ultrasound provides a valuable, noninvasive means to help scientists and veterinarians assess the health of dolphins both in captivity and in the wild. Here scientists examine abdominal organs using ultrasound. Official U.S. Navy photograph.

years,[16] a period that approximates the minimum intercalf interval for dolphins. During the time between calves, female dolphins appear to invest more into the offspring energetically (through very prolonged lactation) and socially than manatees do. In addition, juvenile dolphins develop close and long-lasting relationships with other individual dolphins besides their mothers;[17] this long-term relationship is less clear in manatees.

These traits, as noted, indicate that although both species clearly belong at the K-selector end of the r- vs. K-selector gradient, dolphins are actually somewhat more K-selected than manatees. Assuming an intercalf interval of three years and a life span of twenty-five years, a female Florida manatee reaching sexual maturity at age three could produce seven calves. A female dolphin from the Sarasota Bay population, sexually mature at nine years of age, may continue to reproduce until she is in her late forties. Assuming an average intercalf interval of five years, the female dolphin may produce seven or eight calves in her lifetime. Thus, in this hypothetical situation, lifelong reproductive output for both animals would be approximately equal, although the reproductive life span and degree of parental care of the dolphin would be far greater.

Before providing additional information regarding life history attributes of bottlenose dolphins, it is appropriate to explain why a focus on such attributes is useful. As we will elaborate in chapter 10, an understanding of life histories is important to effective conservation of a species. For example, it is relatively difficult to overharvest a strongly r-selected species, but very easy to overharvest a K-selector. After all, as noted earlier in this chapter, even a few female pink shrimp can provide many millions of eggs. The most common way in which populations of r-selectors are decimated by human activities involves destruction of habitat vital to their survival. Thus, the more K-selected a species is, the more conservative any direct or incidental take must be, because such species are *biologically incapable* of dramatic recoveries. Yet traditional methods by which take levels have been determined (for example, maximum sustainable yield, to be discussed in chapter 10) were developed for highly fecund r-selectors! This tragic mismatch of harvest of K-strategists using approaches designed for r-strategists has had terrible consequences for some commercially harvested species.[18]

For most species, we lack optimal life history data. Therefore, we must make assumptions based on data we *do* have. However, the case of Florida manatees (extremely large animals with surprisingly early onset of sexual maturity) shows that untested assumptions must be treated with some caution.

Another reason to monitor life history attributes is that they are actually somewhat variable within a particular population or species, depending on social and environmental conditions. For example, it is well documented that age at sexual maturity decreases in many exploited populations, including fin whales (*Balaenoptera physalus*).[19] This presumably occurs, at least in part, because the remaining animals have more food available to them, and better nutrition permits females to reach breeding size earlier. Thus, neither carrying capacity of environments nor life history traits of species are constant; monitoring the latter may provide important clues about the status of the former.

It should be clear that an understanding of life history strategies employed by a species is vital to biologists interested in species adaptations and to conservationists interested in effective management of human activities. Lack of life history data causes managers to fall back on assumptions that may or may not be accurate or appropriate.

So let's return to the bottlenose dolphin and examine aspects of its life history, recalling from chapter 3 that there may well be more than one type of bottlenose in the world. At the very least, we know that different groups of dolphins reach different adult sizes, occupy and exploit different habitats, and may, therefore, be expected to demonstrate somewhat different life history strategies. We shall use the criteria listed in table 3 as a road map for general attributes to discuss; specific life history traits for bottlenose dolphins and selected other odontocetes appear in table 4. It is important to note that there are still many gaps in our understanding of life history traits for bottlenose dolphins, generally, and for most dolphin groups occupying specific locations. This is another important area where aspiring marine mammalogists can make a real impact, and the acquisition of meaningful data does not necessarily even require access to living animals, since age, sexual maturity, length, and weight can all be assessed using stranded individuals.

Age at onset of sexual maturity is, as we have seen, influenced by a number of environmental factors.[20] As mentioned in the well-studied Sarasota Bay dolphin population, females reach sexual maturity as young as five years of age or as old as twelve, although most females are eight to ten years old before they have their first calf.[21] Body length of females at sexual maturity is about 220 to 235 centimeters, and growth slows dramatically after females start to breed. Male dolphins in Sarasota Bay reach sexual maturity at ten to thirteen years of age, at which time they measure about 245 to 260 centimeters long. The males also begin to show elevated testosterone levels as early as eight years of age.[22] Male dolphins rapidly increase their mass when they reach puberty, and they continue to grow until they reach about twenty years old. Thus, in males, sexual and physical maturity are separated by several years, whereas the two events are temporally closer in females. As occurs in other species in which sexual dimorphism is the rule, differences in adult male and female sizes probably relate to the latter diverting much of their

Table 4. Life History Parameters of the Bottlenose Dolphin and Selected other Odontocetes

Species	Adult Length (cm) Male/Female	Age at Sexual Maturity (Years) Male/Female	Max. Age (Years) Male/Female	No. Calves, Lifetime	Average Age at Weaning (Months)	Intercalf Interval (Years)	Gestation (Months)	Social Bonds
Tursiops truncatus	261/251	8–12/5–10	41+/50+	6–8	18–20	3–6	12	Long-term, fluid
Phocoena phocoena	160/180	4/4–6	12/24	>12	8	1	11	Short, loose
Globicephala macrorhynchus	545/381	16/9	45+/62+	4	42	7	12	Long-term, tight

Sources: R. S. Wells, D. J. Boness, and G. B. Rathbun, "Behavior"; W. F. Perrin, R. L. Brownell, and D. P. DeMaster, *Reproduction in Whales, Dolphins, and Porpoises*, 495. Note: Some ages used by Perrin, Brownell, and DeMaster and in this table differ slightly from those provided by individual recent papers cited in the text.

energy to fetal development and lactation, while the males continue to fuel only their own bodies. Interestingly, males may not be competitive in terms of actually breeding until they are into their twenties (that is, until they reach yet another life history plateau—social maturity).[23]

Another relatively well-studied group of dolphins exists off the coast of South Africa. There females reach sexual maturity at 9 to 11 years of age. Puberty may begin as early as 9 years of age for males, but average onset of sexual maturity is 14.5 years old. As is the case with Sarasota Bay dolphins, male dolphins off South Africa continue to grow well past puberty, so they grow somewhat longer and much heavier than females.[24]

Sexual maturity is reached much earlier in dolphins off Japan, where 50 percent of the females were sexually mature by age 7, and at least one animal appeared to be sexually mature at only 3.5 years old.[25] Despite their youth at sexual maturity, the female Japanese dolphins were quite large: 50 percent of the females were sexually mature at about 267 centimeters long, or nearly one-half meter longer than Sarasota Bay females when they reached sexual maturity.[26] Recall that relatively larger body size and earlier onset of sexual maturity provide rather contradictory indications of where along the r- vs. K-selector gradient a species or population belongs.

Finally, along the Atlantic coast of the south-central United States, both male and female dolphins reach physical maturity at 13 years of age, with females reaching sexual maturity as early as 7 years old. A lack of mature males in this particular sample prevented the authors from defining age at sexual maturity for males. However, it appeared that both sexes approached physical maturity at a length of about 250 centimeters (that is, there appears to be less sexual dimorphism than in some other dolphin populations).[27]

Clearly some variation exists in terms of age and size of individuals at sexual maturity, a factor that affects reproductive potential a great deal. For example, all other things being equal, a female dolphin from Japan that reaches sexual maturity at 3.5 years of age would produce two more calves than an animal from Sarasota or South Africa that was sexually mature at 11 years of age. If a female dolphin typically produces only six to eight calves per lifetime, an increase of two calves represents a sizable percentage increase in reproductive capacity over the life of the animal.

As is the case for data on sexual maturity, there are few data available from different dolphin populations on developmental rates for offspring, longevity, and patterns of mortality and survivorship. And as before, we

Fig. 52. Dolphins copulating. Randall S. Wells, Chicago Zoological Society.

Fig. 53. The body of a female dolphin flexes during contractions as her baby enters the world. Randall S. Wells, Chicago Zoological Society.

turn to the Sarasota Bay population as "the norm," fully recognizing that it may not be!

The K-selected species show slow growth and development of young, and dolphins clearly fit the K-selector mold in this regard. Newborn dolphins vary in length from about 84 to 140 centimeters long,[28] depending on geographic location. Average length is about 103 centimeters for dolphins off southern Africa, approximately 115 centimeters for calves in Sarasota Bay, about 117 centimeters for animals along the Atlantic coast of the United States, and 128 centimeters for Japanese dolphins.[29] Calves from the Sarasota Bay population grow most during the 1.5 to 2 years in which they typically suckle, although weaning may occur when offspring are much more than 2 years old. In at least one instance in Sarasota Bay, a 7-year-old apparently still suckled from its lactating mother, and among Shark Bay dolphins, weaning occurs when calves are between 2.7 and 9 years old.[30] Such late ages for weaning provide testimony to the enormous extent of maternal energetic "investment" in offspring.[31] Perhaps the most telling indication of maternal investment is reflected simply by the extended time calves remain with their mothers. For Sarasota dolphins, calves remain closely associated with the mother for an average of more than five years, with occasional individuals staying with their mothers up to eleven years;[32] for dolphins in Shark Bay, Australia, and Moray Firth, Scotland, the ties last an average of four years.[33] Thus even after the nutritional dependency of a calf ceases, it continues to need its mother for other reasons, including protection from preda-

Fig. 54. A mother dolphin and her calf. Randall S. Wells, Chicago Zoological Society.

Fig. 55. A mother dolphin and her calf. SeaWorld.

tors and social development and integration into the group. Long-term social bonds (other than with the mother) begin to develop prior to separation
but develop further and mature afterward. The social tie between a mother
and her calf is striking. On numerous occasions mother dolphins (both in
the wild and in captivity) have been observed carrying the body of a deceased calf for days.[34]

Ultimately, calves tend to go their own way around the time when the
next calf is born. At separation from their mothers, Sarasota Bay dolphins
average approximately 225 centimeters long. Interestingly, a female dolphin
in Sarasota Bay, orphaned at 1 year of age, has survived for at least 8 years on
its own and even gave birth to its first calf at 8 years of age.

Fig. 56. A mother dolphin and her calf. Jason B. Allen, Eckerd College Dolphin Project.

Although Sarasota Bay female dolphins grow somewhat faster initially than males and reach asymptotic length (that is, the body length at which growth nearly ceases and full body length is approximated) earlier than the males, the males exhibit a growth spurt around puberty and, as noted earlier, ultimately reach their asymptotic length later and achieve a larger size than the females.[35] For either sex, physical maturity, like sexual maturity, takes a long time to reach: about 12 years for females and 20 for males in Sarasota Bay; thus, a long period of physical development is clearly evident.

Bottlenose dolphins can live for several decades (more than four for males and more than five for females). There does not appear to be any reproductive senescence for the females, with individuals 48 years old continuing to give birth and rear calves successfully in Sarasota Bay. During the long life span, mortality (and the converse, survivorship) vary. Recall the various life history milestones noted at the outset of this chapter—animals are more vulnerable during certain phases of their lives (for example, initial independence from maternal care; being born) than during others. In addition, males and females may be exposed to different risks, resulting in different mortality rates according to gender. In fact, one study noted that there is a 2:1 sex ratio favoring females, due to high juvenile male dolphin mortality in Sarasota Bay.[36]

Various studies have attempted to calculate what are termed *vital rates* for dolphin populations. Crude birth rates (that is, the estimated number of newborn animals divided by the estimated total population for a particular area) range from 0.012 to 0.156.[37] For Sarasota Bay dolphins,[38] crude birth rate was 0.055, and recruitment rate of calves to age 1 was 0.048, indicating excellent survival of newborns (another attribute of K-selected species).

Juvenile males and very young (so-called young of the year) dolphins of both sexes suffer higher mortality than do dolphins in general.[39] Such trends, incidentally, characterize other mammalian species as well. In Sarasota Bay, annual mortality from all causes and for all ages and both sexes was approximately 0.010 to 0.038;[40] however, annual mortality of only young of the year was 0.189, about an order of magnitude higher than mortality for the general dolphin population in Sarasota Bay.[41] For comparison, the overall annual mortality ranged from 0.069 to 0.092 for dolphins in the Indian River, along the east coast of Florida.[42] South African scientists estimated an annual mortality rate of 0.022 due only to shark predation on dolphins off the Natal Coast.[43]

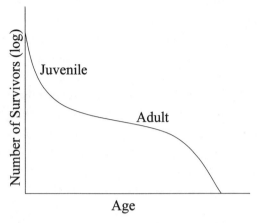

Fig. 57. Different types of survivorship curves characterize r-strategists and K-strategists (see table 3). Bottlenose dolphins exhibit a curve indicating that following a period of infant/juvenile mortality, dolphins may survive for a long time. Adapted from R. Brewer, *The Science of Ecology.* Samantha D. Eide.

Even though the annual mortality rates for dolphin calves are higher than the rates for all dolphins in a population, even the calf mortality is low relative to what would be found in r-selected species. A survivorship curve for dolphins would indicate that, following a period of moderate mortality in the first year of life, survival remained fairly high for a number of years until old age was reached and mortality increased dramatically. Brewer discusses theoretical survivorship curves and provides a hybrid curve that approximates what is found in dolphins.[44] A more empirical assessment of dolphin survival is provided by a histogram of the age distribution of the Sarasota Bay dolphin population.[45]

Relatively low mortality of young dolphins is, at least in part, a consequence of care provided by both mothers and other members of the population. As will be discussed in greater detail in chapter 6, dolphins in Sarasota Bay and at least some other geographic locations frequently form nursery groups in which a number of females can collectively watch out for the young; such groups often occupy protected shallow waters where predators are largely absent or can presumably be easily detected and avoided. As noted, growing up as part of a relatively stable group facilitates development of social skills and of individual long-term social bonds that allow young dolphins to be integrated into a local population.

Predation is one natural cause of death in dolphins. Attacks by sharks are not always successful, as evidenced by scars and wounds on the bodies of dolphins studied worldwide.[46] However, slightly more than 1 percent of the sharks caught off Natal (89 sharks out of 6,000) had remains of cetaceans in their stomachs,[47] providing some indication of the success of sharks as predators on *Tursiops* and other species. Various studies suggest the following: (1) a preference by sharks to attack young animals or mothers with calves; and (2) that certain species of sharks, such as tiger (*Galeocerdo cuvieri*), great white (*Carcharodon carcharias*), bull (*Carcharinus leucas*), and dusky (*Carcharinus obscurus*) sharks, are the primary species involved in predation on dolphins. Dolphin deaths may also result from attacks by killer whales.[48]

Dolphins may die due to nonpredatory interactions with other occupants of the marine and coastal environments. For example, there are numerous instances where dolphins have died from the effects of embedded stingray spines.[49]

Dolphins die for other reasons as well. Some common diseases of bottlenose dolphins include bacterial pneumonia, pox and other viruses, erysipelas, hepatitis, gastric ulcerations, and pancreatitis.[50] In addition, parasites of a variety of types may use dolphins as hosts and perhaps compromise their survival.[51] Human-related causes of death have already been mentioned elsewhere and will be dealt with in some detail in chapter 8.

Referring back to table 3, one can appreciate that *Tursiops truncatus* would rank as a K-selected species by virtually any measure. But how do bottlenose dolphins compare with other odontocetes? A detailed comparison is clearly beyond the scope of this book, but table 4 indicates that the species is actually somewhat intermediate in its life history attributes relative to the larger, more social pilot whale[52] and the smaller, less social harbor porpoise.[53] Such an intermediate position in terms of life history adaptations parallels the intermediate position bottlenose dolphins demonstrate morphologically and ecologically relative to other odontocetes (refer to chapter 4).

Better recognition of dolphin life history strategies will take a long time; after all, it is extremely difficult to understand what happens during all phases of life for species that live for many decades. It takes dedication and commitment for scientists to unravel the complexities of life for the very social, long-lived, K-selected species. Ultimately, however, such information

Fig. 58. Scientists carefully capture and release bottlenose dolphins for studies of health, life history, and communication. Knowledge gained by examining the animals closely helps conserve them. Flip Nicklin and Minden Pictures.

is necessary to optimally conserve species, and in the case of the bottlenose dolphin, for which so little is known worldwide, assumptions based on data from the long-term Sarasota Bay study simply may not be appropriate or correct when applied to all other populations; in fact, the more we learn, the more it appears that Sarasota Bay dolphins are pretty representative of the normal range of anatomical, physiological, and behavioral attributes for the species.

In chapter 4 we considered dolphin adaptations that amaze people because dolphins can do certain things so much better than we can (for example, diving, thermoregulating in cold water, detecting direction of sound underwater, and fast, efficient swimming). People admire and applaud dolphin superiority in these regards.

In this chapter and the two that follow, we consider other adaptations, many of which endear the species to people because dolphins remind us so much of ourselves. Dolphins possess attributes such as long life spans, intricate social dynamics, prolonged parental care, delayed onset of sexual maturity, and cognitive abilities that our species tends to admire in itself.

In terms of life histories, humans and bottlenose dolphins are quite similar in most regards; by virtually any measure, both would be considered to be extremely K-selected. In fact, there is probably only a single substantial difference between the life histories of the two species: dolphin populations, as might be expected of a true K-strategist, remain at levels around the carrying capacity of their local environments, whereas human populations have expanded to the point where local carrying capacity is often greatly exceeded. This single difference is not insignificant—human population size, growth, and resource consumption are looming threats for the survival of *all* species on Earth.[54]

The Daily Lives of Dolphins

Introduction

A number of authors have noted that behavioral attributes exhibited by a particular species are part of an adaptive suite, along with morphological or anatomical traits, life history characteristics, physiological capabilities, and biochemical possibilities.[1] In other words, these features all represent adaptations that allow each species to function in particular ways in its environment. The genetic makeup of a species helps to define how particular traits are expressed, but the environment also influences their expression.

Thus, the behavior of particular species is influenced by both internal and external constraints. Internal constraints are those imposed, for example, by the structure (morphology) and function (physiology) of the species. A couple of very simplistic examples illustrate the point: For example, bottlenose dolphins lack hind limbs, so they can never move about on land; on the other hand, the species possesses anatomical and physiological adaptations that permit it to dive fairly well, thereby allowing it to exploit food resources that are unavailable to most mammals. The large body size of dolphins means that they are not subject to predation by many other species, a factor that would affect social behavior and group defense. We began our consideration of dolphin anatomy and physiology (chapter 4) by suggesting that it is often interesting and fun to consider how a particular structure could function in a species. It is equally useful to imagine how such adaptations relate to a species' behavior and ecology.

Among a species' adaptations, behaviors can be plastic in response to particular environmental conditions (that is, external constraints). This is not true of many anatomical adaptations (for example, structure of the retina, number of limbs) that are permanent features, unaffected by environmental conditions, of an individual and which can only vary across generations. But behaviors can be changed during the lifetime of an individual, or even during a single day, in response to changing conditions and needs of the animal.

If morphology and physiology are relatively static, the social and physical environment that an animal encounters may, conversely, be quite dynamic. This is certainly the case for species like the bottlenose dolphin, which need to find and capture mobile prey of a variety of types, fend off predators, survive various environmental stresses, find and compete successfully for mates, and rear offspring that will be equally competitive. Just as humans exhibit a variety of social and other behaviors that depend on their surroundings, so do dolphins.

The study of behavioral ecology attempts to explain observed behaviors by understanding why they are adaptive under particular environmental conditions. Two main approaches to the field have been employed: optimality theory and the comparative approach. Using optimality theory, one attempts to explain why a particular behavior may be predicted based on the relative costs and benefits of the behavior. For example, scientists have noted that bottlenose dolphins occupying different habitats possess dramatically different group sizes, with larger groups being associated with animals in deep, offshore waters. Why might that be the case? Why would small groups be optimal in one setting and large groups be best in another?

First it is useful to note that living in groups automatically carries with it certain costs. Animals in groups can spread disease more easily than do solitary animals; animals in groups are more apparent to predators than single animals are; groups must share food resources, whereas a solitary animal can consume all the food it finds; and groups are more easily detected by predators. So group living per se isn't necessarily a good thing due to certain obvious costs.

But there can be benefits as well, although, as mentioned, there are not automatically going to be benefits to group living. Having several individuals present may allow easier detection of predators and even better defense against predators. If the group contains both males and females, it is easy for group members to find mates. Additionally, it may be easier for many animals to find and acquire certain types of food than for solitary individuals to do so.

Let's return to optimality theory and different dolphin group sizes. One could hypothesize that the benefits of being in a large group in deep water far outweigh the costs, but that the benefits are relatively less for the shallow-water animals. Reasons for the difference could include relative risk of predation and the distribution and abundance of prey.

Let's consider predation effects first. In shallow water, large sharks (the main predators on bottlenose dolphins) are less abundant than they are in deep water. In addition, it would be difficult for a shark in very shallow water to attack dolphins from below, thereby reducing somewhat the area that would need to be surveyed for sharks. Conversely, in deep water, sharks could easily attack from below, thereby causing dolphins in such areas to have to be more vigilant than would be the case in shallow water. Thus, from

Fig. 59. Three generations of related female dolphins swim together in Sarasota Bay. Kim W. Urian, Dolphin Biology Research Institute.

the standpoint of vulnerability to predation, deep-water dolphins may have both more and larger predators to avoid and more directions from which attacks could come. Large groups could contribute to detection and defense and reduce the probability that any particular individual will be singled out, given the cover and confusion provided by schoolmates.

From the standpoint of prey abundance and patchiness, one can also deduce why large groups might be better offshore. In shallow waters, prey are more evenly distributed than is the case in deep water, where prey tend to be found in patches. Having evenly distributed but not densely packed prey in shallow water means that (1) food is not all that hard to find (that is, large groups are not necessary to locate prey); and (2) small groups could share prey that is found, but some members of a large group might go without food. Thus, in coastal, shallow areas, small group size of dolphins is favored—the costs of very large groups outweigh the benefits there. Not so in the offshore areas, where food resources are distributed patchily but are dense. In such settings, having many animals, potentially spread over a large area, may permit easier detection of a patch, and once a patch is found, there is enough to feed a large group. Here, the benefits outweigh the costs of large group size.

The comparative perspective is also very useful in understanding animal behavior patterns. For obvious reasons, terrestrial animals tend to be easier and cheaper to study than marine species. However, knowing something about internal and external constraints that affect species in general allows scientists studying marine mammals, like dolphins, to make certain inferences based on what has been documented in terrestrial species. Understanding something about maternal care in primates (for which prolonged maternal care and socialization are typical) has facilitated our understanding of maternal care and social behavior of dolphins. Similarly, studies of other aspects of terrestrial mammalian behavior have enhanced understanding of marine mammal behavior. One of the most insightful comparative papers we have encountered recently demonstrates incredible similarities in social structures and life histories of elephants and sperm whales.[2]

This chapter is about dolphin behavioral ecology. Among marine mammals (or even among mammals in general), bottlenose dolphins exhibit a rich variety of behaviors related to their intricate social patterns and their ability to exploit a variety of habitats. For most readers, we expect that fascination with behavior constitutes a major reason for interest in the species.

Studying Behavior

To develop a comprehensive view of the behavior of a species, it is important that individual animals be clearly identified, that these individuals be "tracked" over time, and that attributes of those individuals be known (for example, age, sex, reproductive status). Given the longevity of many marine mammal species, an interest in comprehensively understanding species behavior must be accompanied by a long-term commitment. In the case of the Sarasota dolphin project initiated by Blair Irvine, Randy Wells, and Michael Scott, the commitment is approaching three decades in duration—virtually the professional life span of a scientist.

How can individual animals be distinguished by scientists? Some clue may be derived by understanding how we distinguish among ourselves. As visually oriented animals, people tend to distinguish individuals by their appearance. So, as might be expected, scientists use scars, color patterns, body shape and size, and other natural features to identify particular animals. With bottlenose dolphins, the dorsal fin, so obvious as an animal surfaces to breathe, provides a lot of distinguishing marks, such as nicks and notches, as well as differences in shape and size.[3] In fact, the use and value of "photo identification" to study cetacean populations was pioneered by scientists working with bottlenose dolphins in Sarasota Bay, Florida, in the early 1970s.

More broadly, it should be noted that the logistic obstacles associated with studying dolphin behavior (for example, the requirement for long-term commitments; the difficulty in contacting, staying with, and carefully observing animals that spend much of their time out of sight) have caused the field of marine mammal behavior to be relatively new. In fact, many of the truly pioneering studies did not occur until the latter part of the twentieth century.[4] Although we feel strongly that anyone entering the field of cetacean behavior would benefit enormously by understanding the methods used by some of the early leaders in the study of bottlenose dolphin behavior and ecology,[5] we also recognize that the application of modern technology has contributed to the growth and great popularity of the field in recent years.

For example, some individual animals may be difficult to recognize based just on natural marks. In addition to using photo identification, therefore, scientists may treat the fin in ways that permit easier identification (for ex-

Fig. 60. Distinctively marked dorsal fins allow scientists to recognize individual dolphins. Eckerd College Dolphin Project.

ample, freeze brands or rototags)[6] or ease of following the individual (radio and satellite tags).[7]

To gather information regarding age, sex, reproductive status, and genetic relationships of dolphins, the animals can be captured and briefly handled. Sectioning of a tooth allows age to be determined.[8] Sex can be determined by examining the ventral side of the animal; in males the genital and anal openings are positioned farther apart than in females. Reproductive status can be assessed by examining hormones in the blood,[9] by examining the size of gonads or determining the presence of a fetus using ultrasound,[10] or by presence of a calf. Finally, relationships among individuals, including paternities, have been assessed by using genetic or molecular techniques to examine blood samples.[11]

Armed with patience, a lot of time, and techniques such as those mentioned above, scientists may have the keys to further unlock the mystery of why bottlenose dolphins behave the way they do.

As is the case with humans, dolphins engage in certain activities or behaviors on a daily basis. For example, in the course of a single day a human may eat two to three times, sleep, and interact under a variety of circum-

Fig. 61. Gulliver's dorsal fin carries tags to assist scientists in following him upon release. This particular fin has a satellite-linked tag and a plastic rototag with a small VHF transmitter on it. Randall S. Wells, Mote Marine Laboratory.

stances with other humans. The timing and precise nature of the activities depends on both internal (health, reproductive state) and external (climate, social setting) constraints. Dolphins also have typical daily activities, which can be affected by a suite of biological or climatic variables. Of course, the influence of social factors on dolphin behavior cannot be underestimated; in studies of both captive and wild dolphins, certain behaviors may be dictated by where the animals are or what other dolphins are present. Common daily activities, which scientists often note in their studies, include socializing, feeding, traveling, and milling.[12] These behaviors will be described in detail later in this chapter.

Similar to what occurs when humans come together to enjoy each other's company or to work for a common goal, social interactions among dolphins can be extremely complex and diverse, whether they are overt or subtle in nature. Understanding these interactions can be even more difficult than understanding human social interactions, since scientists cannot actually communicate with dolphins to find out what they are thinking and because observations of dolphin behavior may be limited by distance and by those actions that are visible when the animal appears at the surface of the water. The husband-wife team, David and Melba Caldwell, spent decades studying the bottlenose dolphin in both the wild and captivity. They, more perhaps than virtually anyone else, set the stage for other studies of the species by describing aspects of dolphin communication and behavior such as home ranging, dominance relationships, care giving, and interactions with humans.[13]

Whereas solitary dolphins are not infrequently observed in the wild, dolphins are often seen in groups, ranging in size anywhere from two to hundreds of dolphins. However, one should bear in mind our human perceptual bias. What we visually consider to be widely separated, solitary dolphins may, in fact, be part of a well-organized social group whose members are in constant touch with one another using sounds they produce.

People have applied various terms to groups of dolphins—terms such as pod, herd, school. To at least some extent, the cohesiveness of the group determines the most preferable term. In this book, we consider a pod to be a group of animals that remains together for a long time and whose membership is virtually unchanged during that time;[14] thus, this term is inappropriate for describing the typically fluid groups of bottlenose dolphins. Groups (and subgroups) of dolphins represent congregations—that is, relatively temporary collections of individuals in the same general area and often engaged in similar activities.

After nearly three decades of studying dolphins in Sarasota Bay, scientists have identified some characteristics of group dynamics in a community of resident bottlenose dolphins.[15] For the most part, groups are defined by age and sex but are often fluid. Groups that are commonly recognized include female bands/nursery groups, subadult groups, or male pairs. Female bands include adult females and their calves; at times, more than two generations (that is, a grandmother, a mother, and a newborn daughter) may occupy the same female band and may explain why it is advantageous for females to develop different signature whistles. Older offspring of both sexes have been observed associating with their mother following the birth of a new sibling.

Nursery groups tend to be composed of females that share home ranges—ranges that are maintained from generation to generation. The composition of a particular nursery group at any given time depends on the reproductive condition of the females more than on their degree of relatedness; females with calves of similar ages tend to swim together, as do pregnant females. The nursery groups typically include females of several matrilines that have associated over several generations. In cases where related females are synchronized reproductively, the probability that they will be found together in the same nursery group is higher. For example, Ms. Mayhem, an older female resident of Sarasota Bay, raised her daughter, Pumpkin, in nursery groups with other females in similar phases of their reproductive cycles. Upon the birth of Ms. Mayhem's next calf, a male, Pumpkin left the nursery group, though she returned from time to time and apparently engaged in babysitting for her younger brother. Upon the birth of her own calf, Pumpkin has been observed in the company of her mother and her subsequent calves, as well as with other females present in the nursery groups that included Ms. Mayhem and Pumpkin as a calf.

After young dolphins (juveniles) separate from their mothers, they join together to form subadult groups, which are among the most physically active in Sarasota waters, with much socializing, chasing, and leaping. These subadult groups comprise both males and females, starting as young as three years of age. Males tend to associate with subadult groups longer (ten to fifteen years) than females (eight to twelve years). The latter reach sexual maturity, become impregnated, and join female bands at a younger age than the age at which males reach physical and social maturity.

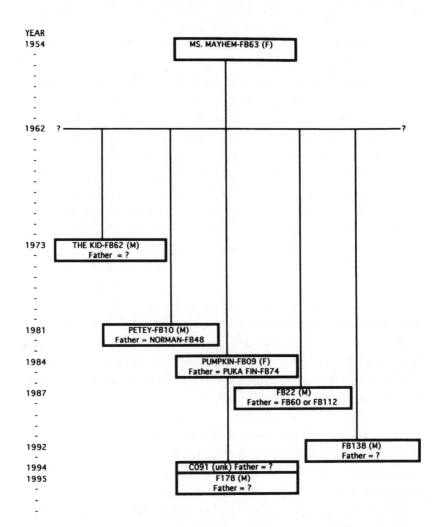

Fig. 62. Ms. Mayhem, a female dolphin living in Sarasota Bay, produced five calves from 1973 through 1992. At least three different males sired the calves. Randall S. Wells, Chicago Zoological Society.

Around the onset of sexual maturity, male dolphins in many locations tend to form coalitions of two or three animals that can last for at least several years[16] or even for a couple decades, until one member of the pair dies.[17] In some cases, males whose companions have died may form new pair bonds.

Examples of this process exist from long-term studies in Sarasota Bay. The Kid, one of Ms. Mayhem's sons, grew up in a juvenile group that typi-

Fig. 63. Ms. Mayhem's third known calf, Pumpkin, was struck by a boat, the propeller of which sliced her dorsal fin. Sue Hofmann, Chicago Zoological Society.

cally included five other males of similar age. Upon reaching sexual maturity, three stable male pairs were formed, including The Kid and Nat, dolphins FB18 and FB44, and dolphins FB36 and FB38. When Nat died of pancreatitis several years later, The Kid was left without a partner. Though he spent brief periods of time (up to several months) with other partnerless males of disparate ages and backgrounds, none of these pairings was stable. Upon the disappearance of FB18, however, The Kid and FB44 immediately formed a stable pair that lasted for a number of years, until the disappearance of The Kid. It seems that the factors of primary importance in developing long-term male pair bonds are similar age and growing up as members of a cohort.[18]

Of course the group dynamics in Sarasota reflect an inshore, residential community for the most part. Scientists assume that large offshore groups of dolphins contain both sexes and animals of all ages.

What mechanisms exist to facilitate maintenance of groups of dolphins, as well as hierarchical relationships therein? To begin with, it is important to realize that the development of different relationships with a number of individuals requires that those individuals be distinguished from one another easily. As noted in chapter 4, the Caldwells were the first to suggest that individual dolphins could be distinguished using "signature whistles."[19] After individuals are distinguished from one another, relationships may be reconfirmed using various signals.[20] Signals used by various species may be conveyed via one or more of the senses, including vision, acoustics, smell (olfaction), taste (gustation), or touch.[21] To be most effective in transmitting information, signals tend to be relatively few in number and to be unambiguous. For example, two humans might encounter one another walking down a street; visual cues allow individual recognition. Once the two people identify each other, they may signal—a smile, a wave, and a hello (a combination of visual and acoustic signals) connote and reinforce a friendly relationship, whereas a scowl, a clenched fist, and a shouted profanity reinforce just the opposite.

Research into dolphin communication is still in its infancy. Although we recognize that acoustic cues are very important to dolphins to reinforce either friendly, or affiliative, or antagonistic/hierarchical relationships, the functions of many of the sounds they make (for example, rasps, grates, mews, barks, yelps; see table 2, chapter 4) are still unknown.

We also know that dolphins reinforce social bonds within groups using other sensory cues as well. For example, scientists have suggested that the tremendous amount of touching and rubbing that occurs among dolphins may serve the same function (that is, establishing and maintaining strong intragroup relationships) as social grooming in primates.[22] Not all tactile cues are kind and affiliative, however; an examination of the skin of many dolphins, especially males, reveals so-called rake marks, evidence that dolphins bite one another.

As a special extension of the use of tactile cues, dolphins of a number of species besides the bottlenose (for example, spinner dolphins) engage in copulatory behavior a lot, even when there is no possibility of impregnating a female.[23] Perhaps this nurtures bonds among individuals; a proponent of this belief, the late Ken Norris was fond of saying that dolphins use sex the way humans use a handshake! It has been observed that very young male dolphins may copulate with their mothers, again reinforcing the likely utility of sexual behavior to promote social bonds.[24]

Other signals and cues that dolphins may use include visual or chemical ones. Although the role of body postures in dominance hierarchies of bottlenose dolphins is not entirely clear, in another small delphinid, the spinner dolphin, adult males assume a posture, accentuated by a hump in the anal region, that mimics an aggressive posture used by sharks.[25] Similarly, dolphins sometimes mouth one another, perhaps using taste buds on the tongue to help learn something about the identity or the status of other dolphins.

As mentioned earlier in this chapter, optimal group size reflects the physical environment, predation pressures, prey type and availability, and other factors. In any size group, bottlenose dolphin social interactions, as well as those of other small cetaceans, may involve a whole suite of specific behaviors (to be discussed in detail later in this chapter), including traveling, group defense, cooperative feeding, caregiving, mating, and playing. Altogether, these behaviors and the roles played by different individuals contribute to the overall social order.[26]

Reproduction

As noted above, dolphins engage in copulatory behavior a great deal. Although much of such behavior is not involved in procreation, some of it clearly is. In most parts of the species' range, male alliances and coalitions traverse their home ranges seeking estrous females with which to mate. Once the males separate a female from the other members of her group (that is, form a "consortship" with her),[27] they may compete for the chance to actually copulate with her.[28] At least in Shark Bay, herding of females may last up to several weeks.[29] During that time, aggressive and even violent encounters

Fig. 64. Three dolphins swimming parallel to each other. Flip Nicklin and Minden Pictures.

with other male coalitions may occur, although high levels of aggression are not necessarily the case among males.[30]

In at least one location (Moray Firth, Scotland), male dolphins apparently do not form wandering coalitions; rather, individual males resident in particular locations may await females that enter those areas.[31] This arrangement may have some attributes of a lek, a breeding system in which males display themselves (acoustically, visually, etc.) to females in hopes of attracting them to mate.[32]

Copulatory and precopulatory behaviors may be complex,[33] but they typically involve considerable rubbing of the animals' bodies, flukes, and pectoral flippers. The males in a coalition frequently flank the female as she swims, perhaps to restrict her movements, or perhaps for energetic reasons (for example, to avoid excess drag). Another hypothesis for why flanking occurs is "mate guarding." In Sarasota Bay, for example, the close proximity of flanking males often may not represent active herding of the female, but instead may be simply a means of ensuring that the flanking males have access to the female when she becomes receptive, while preventing such access by other males.[34]

In Shark Bay, Australia, male dolphins produce a popping sound, apparently as a threat, while they accompany females;[35] interestingly, the sound has not been recorded for male dolphin consorts in other locations. Actual copulation often occurs with the animals positioned belly to belly and facing in the same direction, although nonparallel positions have also been recorded. Intromission is very brief—just a few seconds—and involves vigorous pelvic thrusting.[36]

Dolphins exhibit what is termed a promiscuous mating system, which means that both males and females may mate with many partners.[37] Such a system is facilitated by the fact that males and females may have overlapping home ranges, which permits individuals to encounter members of the opposite sex frequently. During peaks in the breeding season, the testes may enlarge and become capable of producing enormous quantities of sperm, up to about 5×10^{13} per ejaculate.[38] Very large testes and copious semen characterize species in which sperm competition may be involved; for example, in cases where promiscuity exists and where more than one male might mate with a particular female during a short time period, a male that produces a lot of semen may, during copulation, be able to outcompete by displacement of sperm a male that produces less.

Scientists have conducted paternity testing of dolphin calves in Sarasota Bay and discovered that, although some males may sire more than one calf from a particular female, it is more common for subsequent calves to have different fathers. Interestingly, not all males in an area appear to have an equal chance of impregnating a female; for example, males that have reached sexual but not full physical maturity do not compete well for access to females. Thus, fathers are typically fully grown and more than twenty years old.[39] The large size of males may confer either or both of a couple advantages: (1) it may allow the males to control access to females better (that is, they can physically prevent smaller males from gaining access); or (2) it may be an attribute that influences female choice of her mates.[40] In fact, differences in intensity and aggressiveness of male guarding of females by Shark Bay dolphins and Sarasota Bay dolphins may relate to the presence of sexual dimorphism (much larger size of the males) in the latter population;[41] in other words, more fighting may be necessary to establish superiority in instances where differences in body size are not available to use as clear signals to challengers.

Rearing of Young, Altruism, and Epimeletic Behavior

In K-selected animals, such as dolphins and humans, which produce few offspring and possess long and strong social bonds, it is not surprising to find that mothers make a considerable investment, nutritionally and otherwise, into each offspring they produce. In humans and some species, fathers may contribute to child rearing, but in the promiscuous species such as dolphins, males are not obviously involved. Rather, females, often as a part of a nursery group containing calves of similar ages, spend several years helping their precious, few calves adjust to the social and physical environment in which they will live.

One of the most obvious ways in which a mammal provides care for young is through milk, provision of which takes some toll on the mother. For example, lactating female dolphins in captivity require over twice as many calories per kilogram of body weight (88–153 kcal/kg) as do nonpregnant/nonlactating females or males (34–67 kcal/kg). Even pregnant females do not require as much nutrition (36–89 kcal/kg) as do the lactating females.[42]

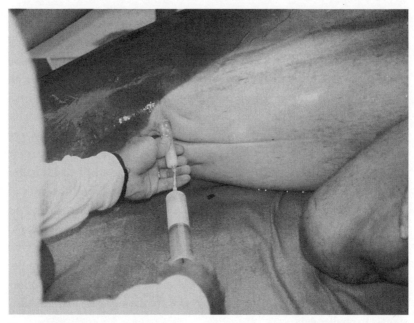

Fig. 65. Milk from free-ranging dolphins may be collected for analysis of environmental contaminants and composition as part of efforts to better understand dolphin health. Kim W. Urian, Chicago Zoological Society.

With the mother gliding through the water, nursing may be initiated when a calf nudges its mother's mammary glands, which may elicit the let down of milk.[43] Although calves can create suction, it has also been suggested that the mother can contract her abdominal muscles such that milk is squirted into her offspring's mouth.[44] Bouts of suckling may be very brief (a few seconds long) but become longer as the calf matures.[45] Females may lactate and presumably suckle their own or other calves for up to seven years. Imagine the energy investment that a female makes over several years in a single calf!

The circumstance in which other dolphins besides the mother provide care for offspring is termed allomaternal care. In dolphins, this phenomenon has been recognized for some time and it leads to more successful rearing of young than is the case for females that opt to rear their young outside such groups.[46] Rather amazingly, as noted earlier, in at least one instance the introduction of a young orphaned dolphin into an enclosure precipitated lactation to occur in nonlactating, nonpregnant females.[47]

Allomaternal care may be important in other energetic ways. For example, "baby-sitting"[48] may provide a lactating mother with time to rest or even to forage.[49] Such behaviors certainly are not unique to bottlenose dolphins, but rather characterize a number of social breeding mammals.[50]

An interesting new perspective[51] regarding the function of allomaternal care is that it does *not*, in fact, benefit mother dolphins by allowing them to have more time to forage. Mother dolphins in Shark Bay, for example, spent less time foraging when their calves were with inexperienced escorts than when the calves were alone; even when the escorts were experienced, the mother dolphins did not forage more than they did when their calves were alone. It was suggested that, since most escorts of calves were inexperienced young females, allomaternal care occurred primarily as a mechanism to help such animals learn how to be parents.

Mother dolphins invest in their young in other ways besides providing food. Mothers may protect their offspring from predators. In addition, mother dolphins in nursery groups in Sarasota Bay may facilitate social development among their calves by creating "playpens," or areas where the young animals interact while the adults form a protective ring around them.[52] The female bands with nursery groups, in fact, appear to select protected shallow-water habitats where food is plentiful and predators are scarce.[53] Females in Sarasota Bay that choose to raise their offspring in large, stable nursery groups are much more successful than are mothers that choose not to be part of such groups.[54]

The strength of the bond between mother and calf can be manifested in a way that tugs at human heart strings. If their calves die, we and others have seen mother dolphins carry the bodies around on their rostra, or simply remain with the carcass. As noted in chapter 5, however, dolphins carry a whole range of items on their rostra, including dead sharks! So even though people may be moved by the sight of a mother dolphin carrying her dead calf, we must be careful how we interpret such behavior.

Just as humans sometimes lend helping hands to other humans, whether they are related or not, dolphins may provide assistance to other dolphins. Many behavioral scientists are careful to distinguish between nurturant behaviors (directed toward young) and succorant behaviors (directed toward animals in distress).[55] Caregiving behavior, termed epimeletic behavior, can be seen when a calf or indeed any dolphin in a group is injured and another dolphin aids the injured animal by "standing by," interposing itself between the injured animal and perceived threats, or even physically supporting it at the surface to facilitate breathing.[56] In addition, dolphins have been suggested (but certainly not proven!) to exhibit reciprocal altruism, which could be manifested by mutual assistance in combat, in feeding, and in various protective measures that members may take either individually or as a group.[57]

Playing

Playing is often included as a type of social behavior; however, some definitions do not suggest playing to be an obligatory social activity. One such definition of playing states that it may include a dolphin's preoccupation with an object, such as a piece of kelp, a sponge, or refuse like plastic bottles or bags, which means only one dolphin need be preoccupied to have play occur.[58] Scientists, however, are not sure why a dolphin would be interested in a piece of kelp or refuse. Seemingly, the activity holds no biological benefit for the dolphin(s) other than to be a source of enjoyment.[59]

A broader definition of play distinguishes between structuralist and functionalist approaches. The former considers play as "any activity that is exaggerated or discrepant, divertive, oriented, marked by novel motor patterns or combinations of such patterns, and that appears to the observer to have no immediate function."[60] The functional definition suggests that play "involves probing, manipulation, experimentation, learning, and the control of one's own body as well as the behavior of others, and that also, essentially, serves the function of developing and perfecting future adaptive responses to the physical and social environment."[61]

Thus, functionalists have linked play behavior with social activity, including sexual behavior. Scientists studying captive dolphins in South Africa, for example, identified play groups in their studies.[62] While rarely defined as such in wild dolphins, play groups in captive dolphins generally consisted of two to four subadult animals within close physical contact, leaping over adult animals on the periphery of the activity, chasing each other, and with much splashing about. In the wild playful activity similar to that in captivity was identifiable by the same attributes, but was often categorized as social rather than play behavior.[63] In adult captive animals play behavior was not readily distinguishable from sexual behavior.[64]

The functionalist definition of play makes a lot of sense when one considers the amount of "practice" young, and even older, animals need in societies that are as complex as that of the bottlenose dolphin. Thus, even adult animals may play, but the frequency of the activity is less than is the case for younger animals. Only by trying out different approaches can a dolphin learn how to survive in its diverse physical world and become integrated into its social world.

Home Ranging and Migrations

David Caldwell[65] was the first scientist to attempt to assess the home range (an area that an animal knows thoroughly and patrols regularly)[66] of a bottlenose dolphin; he calculated that a distinctively marked (and therefore easily recognized) dolphin occupied a tiny area, only 0.4 km²! Although Caldwell's limited number of observations led to the calculation of an unrealistically small home range, later scientists have found it useful to consider dolphin home ranging behavior. In Sarasota Bay, the one hundred or so resident dolphins (and their immediate predecessors), have a year-round home range of about 125 km². This, of course, does not mean that all one hundred animals are in the same place at the same time; rather, the different social groups or individuals tend to have different but overlapping core areas within the bay.[67] The size of the home range is governed, to at least some extent, by the age and sex of the animals, with adult males ranging most widely.[68] North of Sarasota Bay, in southern Tampa Bay, home ranges for individual dolphins may be as large as 73.5 km².[69]

Different regions within the Sarasota Bay home range are used preferentially by dolphins at different times of year.[70] This should not be surprising in light of seasonal changes in the biotic (for example, prey availability) and abiotic (for example, water temperatures) environments. Similarly, home ranges can shift from one year to the next as conditions change; this phenomenon was perhaps best illustrated when dolphins in southern California shifted their range north over 500 kilometers during an El Niño event.[71]

A number of studies worldwide (for example, United States, Scotland, Argentina, Australia) have shown that dolphins are at least seasonal, if not year-round, residents of particular coastal areas.[72] However, it can be quite difficult in some cases to understand what constitutes a home range for a group of dolphins. Part of the problem is that not all dolphin communities are as stationary or stable as that in Sarasota Bay. The seasonal residency patterns suggested to exist in some locations (for example, along the Carolina coasts)[73] means that an effective home range or multiple home ranges linked by travel corridors or ranges may span tens to hundreds of kilometers of coastline.[74] In such cases, collaborative interactions among different research groups can often illuminate what dolphins do in the wild.

Agonistic Behaviors—Dominance and Competition

Although the public image of dolphins is often that of peaceful, social animals, not all relationships among dolphins fit that mold. Both wild and captive bottlenose dolphins have demonstrated dominance relationships and competition. Among the agonistic behaviors exhibited by dolphins are biting and tooth raking, ramming, and striking with the flukes or peduncle, and mothers may discipline their calves by lifting them out of the water on their flukes or rostra, or even holding them underwater.[75] In captivity, fights may even lead to death.[76] Possibly the most dramatic examples of aggressive or agonistic behaviors occur when males compete for access to females to breed.[77]

In the early to mid-1990s, infanticide occurred in dolphins in the Moray Firth, Scotland.[78] Given the small size of the dolphin population there (about 130 individuals) and the small number of calves produced annually (six to seven) such behavior could have dramatic effects on the long-term viability of the population. More recently (1996–97), off the coast of Virginia, several calves have been recovered and found to have died from trauma.[79] The carcass of an adult male was also recovered; he, too, died from trauma. Due to the nature of the injuries, scientists suggested that adult *Tursiops* were the culprits.[80] Infanticide by male dolphins may increase reproductive fitness of individuals doing the killing if (1) the offspring being killed were sired by other males, and (2) the bereft mother becomes sexually receptive very soon following the loss of her calf.[81] We note that infanticide does occur in many other species of mammals; the lack of reports of the phenomenon in bottlenose dolphins may relate to the lack of detailed necropsies of newborn or very young dolphins.[82]

Dominance relationships, or even simple aggression, have also played a part in feeding sessions. For example, during the disposal of fish off a trawler, male dolphins in Moreton Bay became almost territorial.[83] While certain males tolerated the presence of females in their vicinity during such a feeding session, they would drive off the other males. A male bottlenose dolphin may exert this dominance through certain actions such as tail slapping.[84]

Captivity provides an opportunity to acquire a clearer picture of dominance relationships in dolphins. Studies indicate that dominance relationships are not limited to males in a social setting; females have also demonstrated dominance. Usually in captivity when a mature male is present, he will be the dominant animal in the group,[85] sometimes ensuring this dominance by severely injuring other group members. The presence of dominance hierarchies among free-ranging dolphins is not as easy to document as it is among captives, where it has been carefully quantified.[86]

Social Interactions with Other Species

Of course dolphins do not only interact with each other. Just as people interact with other animals in their environment (such as dogs, cats, horses, or birds), dolphins interact with people (see chapters 2 and 8) and other animals within their marine ecosystem as well.

MARINE MAMMALS

Bottlenose dolphins, for example, may interact with other cetaceans or even with coastal manatees. In the eastern tropical Pacific, bottlenose dolphins have been observed with at least thirteen other cetacean species.[87] Dolphins' interactions with other marine mammals may be benign or aggressive.[88] In many cases, scientists are uncertain why members of different species form groups.

In both South Africa and Australia, bottlenose dolphins have exhibited aggression toward or dominance over humpback dolphins, *Sousa chinensis*.[89] In the Bahamas, male bottlenose dolphins fight with male Atlantic spotted dolphins, *Stenella frontalis*.[90] Conversely, captive tucuxi (*Sotalia fluviatilis*) may band together and attack bottlenose dolphins in the same enclosure.[91]

Scientists have documented the deaths of a number of harbor porpoises due to attacks by bottlenose dolphins.[92] Due to the small size of the porpoises, it is possible that the attacks may relate to infanticidal behavior.[93]

In captivity bottlenose dolphins mate with other cetacean species and produce offspring. Among the species with which *Tursiops truncatus* has successfully mated are false killer whales (*Pseudorca crassidens*), Risso's dolphins, short-finned pilot whales (*Globicephala macrorhynchus*) and rough-tooth dolphins (*Steno bredanensis*).[94] It has also been speculated that bottlenose dolphins and Risso's dolphins may interbreed in the wild.[95] Hybridization in free-ranging whales (particularly mysticetes) is not that unusual an event.[96]

SHARKS AND RAYS

Sharks are the primary predators of the bottlenose dolphin. However, the prevalence, or success, of shark attacks varies in different areas of the world. Healed scars representing failed attacks by sharks on dolphins occur in only about 10 percent of the dolphins found off South Africa;[97] contrast this figure to the nearly 37 percent of bottlenose dolphins scarred by sharks in Moreton Bay, Queensland, Australia,[98] and the 31 percent figure for Sarasota Bay dolphins.[99] Aside from scarred but living dolphins, the success of sharks as predators can be gauged by records of dolphin remains in the stomachs of sharks,[100] such as tiger, dusky, and bull sharks. These sharks are not only found in offshore waters but also have been caught in inshore waters such as passes between bays and open waters. In Sarasota, dolphins' seasonal movements have even been correlated with the seasonal abundance of some sharks, and as noted above, nursery groups with calves are found in shallow protected waters, where chances of predation on the vulnerable calves are reduced.

How might dolphins respond to large predatory sharks? In at least some cases,[101] the dolphins simply swim away to try to avoid the predators.[102] On the other hand, there are occasions where dolphins might ram or bite attacking sharks.[103] In one case several captive dolphins developed a coordinated attack and killed a sandbar shark (*Carcharinus plumbeus*).[104]

Interestingly, attacks on dolphins by sharks have also been suggested to be accidents in cases where both sharks and dolphins feed on the same school of fish.[105]

In Sarasota Bay it appears that groups of dolphins (or pairs of males) may suffer lower mortality than do single animals; for example, males that exist in pairs have more shark scars than do solitary males, but the pair-bonded males live longer on average. We suggest that pairs of males may be detected and attacked by sharks more often than are single males, but that an injured member of a pair is assisted and provided more opportunity to recover from an attack. As noted at the outset of this chapter, living in groups carries with it certain disadvantages (costs, such as disease transmission), but that certain advantages (benefits, such as group detection of and defense against predators) may make being a group member, overall, quite beneficial.

As noted earlier, dolphins also interact with stingrays, sometimes with fatal results. Because dolphins and stingrays share the same shallow aquatic habitat they are bound to come into contact. Physical contact by the dolphin can result in dolphin injury and mortality. Stingray barbs have been found in a number of animals along the central west coast of Florida since 1987.[106] At least four dolphins between 1987 and 1992 died because of these barbs.

Feeding

Feeding involves the pursuit and capture of prey. Bottlenose dolphins employ many strategies for feeding, depending on habitat, group dynamics, prey type, and other variables.[107] Essentially the food resources available in an environment can dictate how the dolphin goes about acquiring food.

The bottlenose dolphin's behavioral flexibility, also referred to as plasticity, is most apparent in the diversity of its feeding techniques. Dolphins take advantage of any readily available food source, including various fish, shellfish, and squid,[108] and they adapt their feeding methods according to food type and local conditions, similar to humans. Succeeding generations of bottlenose dolphins apparently continue to use the same innovative strategies and feed on the same types of food. This is reflected, for example, by several generations of dolphins "strand feeding" on mullet that are driven onto the mudbanks of the Carolinas[109] or by dolphins following working shrimp boats to acquire discards.[110]

For many dolphins, however, listening may be especially essential since many of the prey items of the bottlenose dolphin are highly soniferous, or sound producing.[111] The sounds produced by prey species have spectral energies and source levels that fall within the hearing range of bottlenose dolphins. As in humans, dolphins constantly hear noises, but there is, no doubt, a certain degree of censoring or ignoring of extraneous sounds to permit focusing on those noises that are biologically important—sounds from predators or prey, for example (see chapter 4). Scientists suggest that as dolphins swim along channels bordered by sea grass beds, they may exhibit what is referred to as passive listening in which they simply try to quietly

Fig. 66. A dolphin successfully captures a fish. Randall S. Wells, Chicago Zoological Society.

listen for soniferous fish, rather than actively exploring for prey using echolocation. Such dolphins are said to be channel stalking. Following detection of prey, they may either rush in for capture or alert other dolphins of the prey's presence. Under some circumstances, passive listening may be an energetically cheaper strategy than actively spending time searching and hunting for food.

In effect, as dolphins prowl along the edges of channels, they may hear the proverbial "dinner bell." Primary prey species that produce sounds include spotted sea trout (*Cynoscion nebulosus*), pinfish (*Lagodon rhomboides*), silver perch (*Bairdiella chrysoura*), striped mullet (*Mugil cephalus*), Atlantic croaker (*Micropogonias undulatus*), and oyster toadfish (*Ospanus tau*).[112] Such species are often represented in dolphin stomach contents at a level that is disproportionate to their abundance in a particular habitat.

The ecosystem and prey type have much to do with how a dolphin may go about feeding. Since dolphins inhabit such diverse habitats and have such catholic diets, feeding methods vary considerably. Dolphins in shallow waters may employ different strategies than do those dolphins found in deeper offshore waters. To understand why a dolphin feeds the way it does, one must ask what the dolphin is consuming, what the group dynamics are at the time of the feeding session, and, maybe most importantly, what the physical characteristics of the environment are.

The abundance, distribution, and ease of access to food supplies can influence numerous social factors, such as group size, group composition, sex ratios, frequency of aggression, and the frequency of exploration and social play. Duration and frequency of feeding may also depend on prey availability, energetic requirements, and reproductive status. Sex and size of dolphins also play a role in when and where dolphins feed.[113]

Bottlenose dolphins may utilize several different foraging strategies.[114] Often these strategies require a high degree of cooperation and synchrony of action. A number of dolphins may simply chase or rush after the prey, which may result in the latter being driven into the waiting mouths of the other dolphins.[115]

Fishing dolphins may take advantage of barriers to fish movements to herd their prey. For example, dolphins may form a semicircle to patrol the edge of a mullet school that has been herded against an oyster bar or mangrove stand; individual dolphins cease patrolling to grab a fish. Similarly, dolphins may use the surface of the water as a barrier to schooling fish.[116] In such cases, the dolphins herd the fish into a tight knot at the water's surface and then strike from below. Often in such instances feeding birds dive into the packed fish.

In a specialized case of prey herding, dolphins may also chase prey into areas where the dolphins have more maneuverability than the prey. This is the case in South Carolina, where dolphins drive prey up onto mudbanks and then strand themselves to feed on the helpless fish;[117] this is termed

Fig. 67. Fishwhacking involves dolphins slapping a fish with their flukes. As a result, the fish is knocked out of the water; when it reenters, the waiting dolphin consumes it. Here, an unlucky mullet goes flying. Randall S. Wells, Chicago Zoological Society.

strand feeding. Interestingly, all the dolphins that strand themselves do so on their right sides—for reasons unknown to scientists.[118]

Yet another method used by dolphins is called fishwhacking, occasionally seen in Sarasota Bay and Boca Ciega Bay, Florida. Dolphins use their tails to strike the fish, often sending it out of the water; this in turn stuns or kills the fish. Some observers speculate that hitting the fish softens or beheads the fish, whereas others speculate it is merely a form of playing with food.[119] As early as 1938, dolphins were photographed off northeastern Florida catching mullet in midair, which may have been the initial strategy or form of fish-whacking.[120]

In a somewhat similar vein, scientists surveying the Indian River, Florida, from an airship observed a dolphin whacking a mass of algae. As a result, fish were dislodged and captured.[121]

Another unusual feeding technique called kerplunking has been exhibited by dolphins in both Australia and Florida.[122] A kerplunking dolphin lifts its flukes and peduncle out of the water and then drives them hard through the water's surface, creating the sound for which the behavior is named. In addition to the loud splash, a trail of bubbles is created; hypothetically, fish located in sea grasses are driven out of their hiding places but then constrained in their movements by the barrier imposed by the bubbles. This technique apparently mimics to some extent the bubble curtains made to consolidate prey by humpback whales.

One poorly understood technique for food acquisition involves dolphins in Shark Bay, Australia, placing sponges on the tips of their rostra while apparently foraging in the sediments on the bottom.[123] Although the way in which the sponges are used is uncertain, this behavior provides additional evidence that dolphins are among the very few tool-using animals.

Perhaps the most unusual feeding method employed by dolphins is so-called crater feeding, in which dolphins attempt to excavate prey located several centimeters into the sediment.[124] As a result of their efforts, the dolphins may work their bodies into the bottom all the way to their pectoral flippers.

As noted earlier, dolphins can also be opportunistic feeders by following fishing boats, especially shrimping boats, and eating the fishermen's discarded bycatch. As early as 1938, scientists observed dolphins following working shrimp boats and even damaging the trawls as they attempted to get to the catch.[125] Three types of feeding in specific association with shrimp

Fig. 68. A most unusual feeding method called crater feeding is demonstrated by a dolphin in the Bahamas. Wild Dolphin Project.

trawlers have been delineated: (1) feeding behind actively trawling shrimp boats, (2) feeding on trash fish, which are the discards from a shrimp boat after a trawl, and (3) feeding around nonworking anchored shrimp boats.[126] Seemingly, this proves to be an energetically inexpensive strategy to gather food. Other ways in which dolphins may interact with humans to acquire food are discussed in chapter 8.

A theoretical feeding strategy, which also incorporates the bottlenose dolphin's extraordinary echolocation system, is called prey-stunning (see fig. 46).[127] By using focused beams of intense sound, dolphins might be able to stun or kill their prey once detected in nearby waters. If this system exists, it would save the dolphin time and energy by not having to chase the fish. However, this technique has yet to be demonstrated.

Altogether, bottlenose dolphins have demonstrated an uncanny ability to take advantage of what nature offers them to eat. Through a variety of individual and group techniques, dolphins around the world, in shallow coastal waters or deep offshore areas, make the world "their oyster."

Diurnal, Seasonal, and Other Behavior Patterns

In between and during social interactions and feeding bouts, dolphins usually engage in traveling, milling, or resting activity. In the wild, traveling generally refers to dolphins involved in persistent, directional movement.[128] In shallow inshore waters, traveling dolphins generally use channels for this directional movement. As noted above in the discussion of feeding behaviors, at such times dolphins may be passively listening for food.

Milling, a somewhat ambiguous category, involves dolphins moving within a given area but with frequent changes in heading. Many studies have associated milling with other behaviors such as feeding, socializing, or playing.[129]

The term *idling*, while often used synonymously with milling, refers to less physical activity such as resting.[130] At such times the dolphin barely moves. Resting may involve an animal facing into a strong current and maintaining position there.[131]

Now that one is familiar with the behaviors of dolphins, the next questions to ask are when and where do dolphins engage in such activities? Humans have a typical daily routine. During the day, humans interact, work, play, and eat. During the night, humans mostly sleep or rest. Dolphins may have similar day and night habits. This is referred to as diurnal activity patterns.

Are dolphin behaviors affected by the time of day or night? Several studies have shown that indeed dolphins do exhibit diurnal activity patterns. For instance, dolphins were slightly more active at night on the Pacific coast. For dolphins near Port O'Connor, Texas, traveling and mating increased gradually in frequency throughout the day, while feeding declined throughout the day.[132] Sexual activity occurred throughout the day but peaked during midday hours for South African dolphins in captivity.[133]

A satellite-tagged bottlenose dolphin in Florida rested in the early morning hours, around 2 to 4 A.M.,[134] perhaps because fishing effort is less productive than at other times of day. This supports the theory that during that time period, dolphin activity is comparable to daylight levels of activity in Florida waters and corresponds to resting.[135]

Scientists may know optimal times of day that dolphins engage in certain behaviors such as feeding, but how much time does a dolphin actually spend feeding? Some humans go to fast food restaurants and eat whole meals in less than thirty minutes, while others spend hours at the dining room table consuming seven-course meals. Some humans commute sixty to ninety minutes to work every morning, while others take a quick five-minute drive down the street to get to work. Do some dolphins eat more food less often or less food more often? Do some dolphins travel longer and farther to utilize more habitat than others?

Activity budgets have been described for bottlenose dolphin communities such as ones in Indian River Lagoon and Sarasota Bay, Florida, and off San Diego, California. Travel dominates the amount of time spent each day, hovering at 45 to 50 percent or more. Socializing and feeding each usually occupy around 12 to 20 percent of each day. However, these activity budgets appear to be dependent upon seasonal, ecological, and spatial considerations.[136]

Specifically, in the Indian River Lagoon, an estuary on the east coast of Florida, dolphins spent 57 percent of their time traveling, 16 percent milling, 14 percent feeding, and 13 percent socializing.[137] The dolphins around Sanibel Island, located on the west coast of Florida and a generally similar type of habitat as that of the Indian River Lagoon, spent 46 percent of their time traveling, 38 percent feeding, and 17 percent of the time socializing.[138] In Sarasota Bay, traveling occurred 67 percent of the time, followed by milling at 14 percent, feeding at 13 percent, socializing at 4 percent, and resting at 2 percent.[139] On the Pacific coast, dolphins occupying San Diego waters traveled 63 percent of the time, fed 19 percent, socialized 12 percent, played 3 percent, and rested 3 percent of the time.[140] San Diego dolphins tend to be migratory, but it appears that some of the population is fairly residential.[141] Differences in the percentages of time spent in different activities could reflect differences in behavioral definitions by various researchers, habitat differences, or the seasons when observations were made.

Based on comparisons of activity budgets, it appears that optimal activity budgets are primarily determined by morphological and physiological constraints of the bottlenose dolphin, which are fairly similar among populations. Yet variations in percentages within a given study area also reflect ecological parameters such as season. Traveling occupied a significantly greater proportion of all observed behaviors in January–April and June than during other months, and feeding occupied about twice as much time in August–

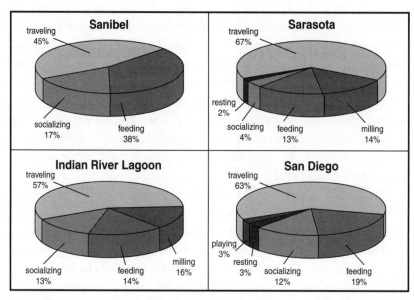

Fig. 69. Different studies of bottlenose dolphins provide glimpses into the typical daily routines of the animals. Such differences likely reflect regional differences in behavior, but are probably also due to differences in observer definitions of behaviors and observer experience. The data used to compile the pie diagrams are from studies by Hanson and Defran (San Diego), Waples (Sarasota), Shane (Sanibel), and Hart (Indian River). Samantha D. Eide.

December and May as in other months. These feeding peaks were associated with distributional changes of fish and invertebrates in the fall and spring.

Off the west coast of Florida, habitat use of bottlenose dolphins was significantly dependent on season, largely due to a seasonal change in the locations where the dolphins fed.[142] The dolphins fed more frequently in sea grass flats during the summer and in deepwater passes and coastal Gulf waters in the winter.[143]

Changes in activity patterns between seasons could be attributed to the need for the dolphins to vary the thickness of their blubber layer throughout the year. Scientists have determined that blubber layers were thicker in the winter than the summer in the Sarasota bottlenose dolphin population.[144] An increase in caloric intake has also been noted for dolphins in the Florida Keys during the fall, which coincided with an increase in blubber thickness. Increases in feeding during the fall and winter months have been noted for dolphins in Texas, but not necessarily around Sanibel Island, in southwestern Florida.[145]

Seasonally, an association between traveling, feeding, and mating exists for dolphins in Matagorda Bay, Texas.[146] Traveling and mating occurred more frequently in spring and summer than in fall and winter, but feeding occurred about 25 percent of the time in fall and winter and only 5–10 percent of the time in spring and summer. Copulatory behavior was seen throughout the year in both captive and wild dolphins, but spring and early summer saw the most frequent copulatory activity in both cases. Socializing and mating peaked in April and May, corresponding with a peak in calving in the spring.

As mentioned in the introduction, the physical environment can affect social dynamics dramatically. The social structure of different bottlenose dolphin populations can be quite diverse as a result of the wide variety of environments that they occupy.[147] High social diversity within a closely related group of mammals has been primarily attributed to differences in food resources, predation pressures, and the physical characteristics of the environment.[148]

Tidal state significantly influenced the frequency of both resting and bow riding in the dolphins of southern Texas.[149] Resting occurred almost exclusively at ebb tide; at the same time this could have been a form of feeding, with the dolphins facing into the current and capturing fish carried out with the tide. Bow riding was generally restricted to ebb and flood tide, suggesting an energetic causation.

Inshore populations of bottlenose dolphins off the northeastern coast of North America exhibited a trend for increased seasonal migratory behavior at higher latitudes.[150] The Moray Firth contains the world's highest latitude population of bottlenose dolphins yet studied, so one might predict them to be migratory and for their occurrence in the inner Moray Firth to be highly seasonal. Despite seasonal fluctuations in the number of individuals present, dolphins were observed in the area at all times of the year.[151] The highest number of individuals occurred in the summer and autumn.

In the Moray Firth, salmon have been identified as a prey species of the dolphin. The fish migrate through the Firth during spring and summer to spawn in the rivers, and this would partially explain why there is an increase in dolphin abundance starting in the summer.[152]

Similar seasonal influxes have been reported from several studies in tropical or subtropical regions. Such changes have been attributed to spatial variations in local conditions, resulting in certain areas being more suitable for predator avoidance, the rearing of offspring, mating, or foraging.[153]

Conclusion

When people encounter dolphins in the wild, a common question is "What are the animals doing?" Even for scientists who have spent years studying dolphins, the answer may not be apparent as the mammals disappear below the surface. But patience, dedication, and ingenuity are paying off as we are afforded better and better glimpses into the world of bottlenose dolphins. What we *do* know is that they live complex lives; develop strong, individually distinctive, and lasting bonds with other members of their social groups; and are able to adjust their behaviors depending on the environmental circumstances they encounter. They live in a world where they receive support from their group members, but where they face the grim realities of harsh competition for resources and sudden death from predators.

Their society is categorized as a fission-fusion society—one in which there are "fluid long-term, repeated rather than constant associations."[154] Such a social system, of course, is not entirely unfamiliar to primates such as humans and chimpanzees,[155] in which much of the day is spent interacting with and reinforcing relationships of various types with a variety of individuals.

What are dolphins doing when we see them glide by a boat? Myriad subtle and overt behaviors that allow them to exploit habitats all over the world, to develop and maintain bonds with others of their kind, and simply to survive.

Intelligence and Cognition

Few topics associated with bottlenose dolphins have stirred the imagination of the general public more than claims that the species possesses near-human "intelligence." The publication in 1967 of John Lilly's book *The Mind of the Dolphin: A Nonhuman Intelligence* triggered much of the interest, which has waned little among the general public.[1] In this chapter we explore the evidence in support of dolphin intelligence and whether or how that intelligence may be manifested or assessed.

An attribute that sets humans apart from most species is our large and complex brain. Humans have an average body weight of 36–95 kilograms and brains that weigh 1.10–1.54 kilograms;[2] thus, the brain can represent between 1.2 and 4.2 percent of the total body weight. Similar types of data exist for bottlenose dolphins.[3] For coastal animals from the western north Atlantic, for example, body weight ranged between 120 and 225 kilograms, with a mean of 165 kilograms, and brain weight averaged 1.53 kilograms. So the brain represented roughly 0.9 percent of the total body weight, a smaller percentage than is the case for humans. The point on which many people fasten their attention is that dolphin brains can be absolutely larger than our own. However, because it is expected that large animals have absolutely large brains, the more meaningful comparison among species is relative, not absolute brain size. For the record, sperm whale brains are the largest in the animal kingdom, weighing a whopping 7.8 kilograms or more, approxi-

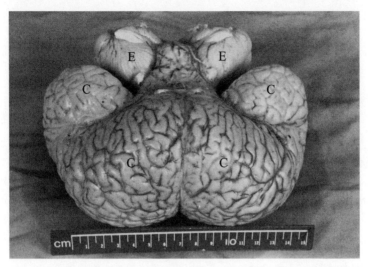

Fig. 70. Anterior view (ventral side up) of the brain of a bottlenose dolphin. C represents cerebrum, E represents cerebellum. From Ridgway, "The Central Nervous System of the Bottlenose Dolphin," with permission of S. H. Ridgway.

mately the weight of a nine-month-old human infant;[4] less impressive is the percentage of the body weight this brain represents—a paltry 0.2 percent.[5]

Of course, the brain has a number of components, not all of which relate to intellectual capacity. The human brain is dominated by the forebrain (or prosencephalon), especially the cerebral hemispheres (the telencephalon).[6] The other, and much smaller, part of the forebrain is the diencephalon, which includes the hypothalamus (involved in autonomic and neuroendocrine functions) and the thalamus (where a number of important nuclei—that is, clusters of nerve cell bodies—involved in processing of sensory information exist). The midbrain (mesencephalon) is relatively small, but it is important especially as a region for processing visual stimuli. The hindbrain (rhombencephalon) comprises three regions: the cerebellum, the pons, and the medulla oblongata. The cerebellum is large and distinctive, and it is especially important to active animals since it coordinates muscular activities. The pons is a small region notable for the large and important sensory and motor cranial nerves associated with it.[7] Finally, the medulla oblongata includes nerve centers that deal with important body functions such as circulation or respiration. The medulla oblongata, pons, midbrain, and diencephalon collectively make up what is called the brainstem.

Of all the regions of the brain, the telencephalon is the one we associate with intelligence. The two cerebral hemispheres, connected medially (along the midline) by a thick corpus callosum, are superficially distinctive due to the large number of sulci (grooves) and gyri (ridges). The outer layer of the telencephalon (termed the cerebral cortex) is made up of gray matter—nerve cells or neurons. Since the number of nerve cells presumably relates in some fashion to a species' potential for complex brain functions, volume of gray matter in the cerebral cortex is an important criterion to assess. White matter, located inside (medial to) the gray matter of the telencephalon, consists of processes (that is, axons and dendrites) that extend to and from neurons, as well as a sheath of lipid called myelin. The myelin, like most fats, appears white—hence the name white matter.

Very thorough descriptions of the dolphin central nervous system (brain and spinal cord) appear in a number of references.[8] These sources point out some important differences between dolphin and human brains.

For example, a relatively large portion of the dolphin brain (15 percent of the total brain mass, compared with 11 percent for the human brain) is represented by the cerebellum;[9] a large- bodied, muscular animal such as a dolphin *should* have a large cerebellum. Since the cerebellum takes up a surprisingly large fraction of the total brain volume, it might come as no surprise to find that the cerebral hemispheres of the dolphin, while impressive compared to those of most mammals, are relatively small, compared to those in a human. The volume of dolphin cerebral cortex is, in fact, only 80 percent of that of the human.[10] The point is that, although dolphins possess large brains, the percentage of brain that is associated with "intelligence" is less than that in humans, and the percentage of total body weight that is brain is also less than in humans.

There are other structural and therefore functional differences in human and dolphin brains. Odontocete cerebral hemispheres have more surface folding than human brains do. This increases surface area and therefore, number of nerve cells.[11] The degree of folding of the cerebral hemispheres (termed cortical folding) is sometimes assessed as a Gyration Index (GI) in which the higher the value, the greater the degree of cortical folding; in humans, the GI may approach 3, whereas in odontocetes, the GI can exceed 4.[12]

On the other hand, the thickness of the cerebral cortex (another factor that would influence number of nerve cells present) is about half in dolphins and other odontocetes what it is in humans.[13] In fact, one cell layer

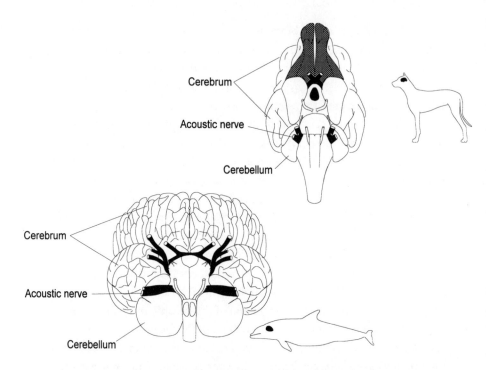

Fig. 71. The diameter of a particular cranial nerve reflects its functional importance. It is no surprise, therefore, that acoustically oriented animals such as the bottlenose dolphin possess greatly enlarged acoustic nerves (cranial nerve VIII). Sentiel A. Rommel.

present in humans is totally absent in dolphins.[14] Recall that even though the dolphin cerebral cortex is more convoluted than that in the human, the volume of the dolphin cortex is only 80 percent of that of the human cortex.

A couple of other differences between dolphin and human brains warrant brief discussion. The corpus callosum is a dense region of nerve fibers that connect the two cerebral hemispheres. The corpus callosum of the pantropical spotted dolphin brain has a cross-sectional surface area that is significantly smaller than that in the human brain, and scientists estimate that the cross-sectional area of the bottlenose dolphin corpus callosum is only about 25 percent the size of the cross-sectional area of the human corpus callosum.[15] The functional significance of this observation is that there are either fewer fibers (which reduces amount of communication between cerebral hemispheres) and/or smaller fibers (which reduces speed of communication between hemispheres) in the dolphin corpus callosum.

The degree of connectedness between cerebral hemispheres may be related to dolphin sleep patterns, in which one half of the brain stays awake and alert while the other half rests. When dolphins do sleep, there is some evidence that, like some other mammals, they exhibit REM (rapid eye movement) sleep.[16]

Another feature of the dolphin brain that makes functional sense involves the diameter of some of the cranial nerves, because larger nerves can either have more fibers for more information transfer or larger fibers for faster transfer.[17] In other words, there is presumed to be a direct relationship between diameter of cranial nerves and their functional importance to a species. As might be expected, olfactory nerves (which in mammals convey information about airborne scents), which clearly exist in dolphin fetuses, degenerate and are absent in adult dolphins,[18] although olfactory lobes of the brain remain prominent.[19] Gustation (taste) may, like olfaction, seem like a relatively unimportant sense in dolphins (since they swallow their prey whole, without chewing), but well-developed facial (cranial nerve VII) and glossopharyngeal (cranial nerve IX) nerves, together with distinctive areas of the brain associated with processing of information regarding taste, indicate that the sense is important to dolphins; as noted earlier, dolphins possess taste buds on their tongues.[20] The facial nerve is exceptionally large, due at least in part to its involvement in the important task of coordinating muscle movements associated with sound production in the nasal sac region of the head.[21] Under certain circumstances, vision is an important sense in dolphins (see chapter 4), and the optic nerves (cranial nerve II) are prominent, although the extent to which optic fibers cross over to the contralateral side (opposite side from the eye from which an optic nerve originated) of the brain is uncertain.[22] The second largest cranial nerve in dolphins is the trigeminal (cranial nerve V), which is involved in tactile stimulation of the head. Finally, the acoustic or vestibulocochlear nerve (cranial nerve VIII—the largest cranial nerve in dolphins) and acoustic regions of the brain are much larger than those in typical terrestrial mammals.[23] Cranial nerve VIII in odontocetes contains the largest nerve fibers measured in *any* vertebrate, permitting conduction of information at a rate possibly five times that found in terrestrial mammals.[24]

Thus, anatomists do infer function from size of particular regions of the nervous system. So what can be inferred from the presence of a large brain, and how can one assess whether a brain is larger than one might expect for an animal of a particular size? How might brain size relate to that elusive term *intelligence*?

To begin with, people don't really understand how to assess intelligence in people,[25] so it is a bit presumptuous to assume we can come to grips with intelligence in other species. There are, in fact, "hundreds of tests for intelligence within our own species."[26] Clearly we don't know how to test for this trait, and instead specialists now discuss multiple human intelligences.[27] Scientists have noted that there is no relationship between brain size and intelligence in humans, but "this observation cannot be extended to differences between species."[28]

It is difficult to make the leap from presence of a large brain to being intelligent.[29] Accepting Funk and Wagnalls's definition of intelligence as the faculty of "perceiving and comprehending, understanding," scientists have stated that "intelligence is a hypothetical concept: it does not occupy space or have *physical* or chemical correlates."[30] Thus, brain size and intelligence are to some degree de-linked. Care must be taken not to carry the de-linkage too far, however. There has to be some critical mass of circuitry (brain cells and processes) present for a species to have the potential to be intelligent, however we may define the term.[31] So we return to the question, do certain species have more circuitry than we would expect, based on their size?

A measure of relative brain size that has been applied to a variety of species is the encephalization quotient (EQ).[32] The EQ for a particular species is the ratio of the observed mass of the brain to the mass of the brain one would expect based on body size. The latter is calculated based on allometric relationships established by measuring the relative size of different body parts over a wide range of taxa.

An EQ of 1.0 means that the brain is exactly the size one would expect for an animal of a particular size; an EQ higher than 1.0 means that a species is relatively brainy (but recall that having a large brain does not necessarily mean that the telencephalon, specifically, is large). Bottlenose dolphins have a very high EQ, about 2.8 or higher.[33] Thus, dolphin brains are not simply absolutely large; they are relatively very large as well. Humans, by the way, have extremely high EQ values, estimated by some to be in the neighborhood of 7.5, making our species the brainiest in existence.[34] Scientist and essayist Stephen Jay Gould humorously notes that such measurements may simply "reinforce an ego we would do well to deflate."[35] Nonetheless, it is worth noting that EQ levels in several species of odontocetes, including

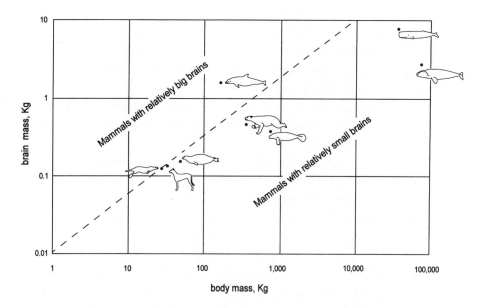

Fig. 72. How brainy are dolphins? One way by which to address this question is to examine relative brain size (the ratio of brain size to body size) for a variety of mammals. In this graph, the dotted line represents the ratio for mammals in general. Those species that appear above the line (like the dolphin) have larger than average brains; those below the line (like the manatee) have smaller than expected brains. Sentiel A. Rommel.

Tursiops, are significantly higher than is the case for any primate except our own species.[36]

The EQ value for a species relates to "a number of general measures of cognitive processing ability in different mammals," as well as to "a number of life history patterns in mammals."[37] For example, EQ may be correlated with life span, home range size, and social systems that characterize a particular species.[38] Oddly enough, the relationships found between EQ and other factors in primates and some other mammals do not appear to apply as well to cetaceans, including the bottlenose dolphin.[39]

The reasons for the larger than normal brain of the bottlenose dolphin (and indeed of small odontocetes in general) are not clearly understood. Among the more plausible suggestions are that: (1) the complexity of processing high-frequency echolocation information requires the development of large centers in the cerebral hemispheres; and/or (2) the degree of sociality exhibited by many species, in which individual animals recognize and have particular long- and short-term relationships with a number of other individuals, has placed a premium on the evolutionary development of a large, complex brain.[40] Some authors develop a strong case that "hypertrophy of the auditory system may be the primary reason for the dolphin's large brain."[41] This opinion is supported by observations that the auditory regions of the dolphin brain are 7 to 250 times larger than the equivalent regions of the human brain and by noting very fast auditory brain stem responses to sounds.[42]

Some confounding observations exist, however. Sperm whales are good echolocators and are very social, yet their EQ values are low (that is, only about 0.3).[43] Even some small, less social odontocetes such as Indus river dolphins (*Platanista minor*) echolocate well but do not possess the exceptionally large brains that bottlenose dolphins do.[44]

Noted cetacean acoustician and ethologist Peter Tyack argues persuasively that large brains evolved in dolphins to permit complex social functions.[45] As is the case with certain primates, bottlenose dolphins and certain other large-brained odontocetes have developed societies in which there exists a balance between cooperation and competition among particular individuals (see chapter 5). The social politics of chimpanzees (*Pan troglodytes*) and dolphins show some remarkable similarities, especially in terms of the importance of "individual-specific social relations" extending far beyond the mother-offspring relationship to include individuals of all ages and both sexes.[46] The development of such complex societies may have favored the evolution of large brain size.[47]

So the reason for dolphins having a large brain continues to be somewhat elusive; but there must be a reason, since maintenance of brain tissue is metabolically expensive.[48] The adult human brain, for example, may only represent 2 percent of the body weight, but it can account for nearly 20 percent of the basal metabolic rate.[49] Since animals tend not to develop energetically draining attributes that do not provide some benefit, large-brained animals must certainly derive something from that structure. It has been observed that "brains are metabolically expensive and don't get bigger (phylogenetically) unless in some fashion they are more than paying for their upkeep."[50]

The primary message of the discussion to this point is that, despite all the interest that exists regarding human and dolphin intelligence, and in what the presence of a large brain really means, scientists do not have a clear idea of whether dolphins (or any other species for that matter!) are or are not intelligent. But the search for answers continues, especially in terms of research on species cognition and communication. After all, "in the final analysis, intellectual *performance*, rather than structural criteria, defines the quality of a brain."[51]

Lilly attempted to find correlations between large brains, intelligence, and "language-like" communication.[52] Even though, as described above, intelligence and brain size are difficult to relate, people have suggested that use of language may be an appropriate barometer of relative levels of animal intelligence. This supposition has led to research on both communication and cognition, two closely related topics.[53] Cognition involves how animals process information internally, as well as how information is processed between the animal and its environment; communication relates to information transfer among individuals.[54] In this book most aspects of communication were covered in chapters 4 and 6; here we consider dolphin cognition.

As noted, one approach by which scientists have attempted to assess cognitive abilities of various nonhuman species, including other primates, is through language studies.[55] Although it has been difficult to interpret the results of studies in which attempts were made to teach our close primate relatives, especially chimpanzees, to communicate with us, the same approach has been used by individuals wishing to assess cognition in dolphins; in the latter case, the results were clearer.

Lilly believed that dolphins could learn to converse with humans.[56] He went so far as to have a volunteer inhabit a shallow pool containing a dolphin for 2.5 months in order to establish a rapport.[57] The results of Lilly's work did little to convince the scientific community of dolphins' language ability, but his books, in which he made wild claims that dolphins and other odontocetes could talk, captivated the imagination of the public. Tyack maintains that although Lilly's "books stimulated popular interest, their unsubstantiated claims scared several generations of behavioral scientists away from a potentially fascinating group of mammals for comparative study."[58]

The assessment of dolphin cognition lay rather dormant until Louis Herman, a psychologist at the University of Hawaii, began a series of studies to assess dolphins' ability to comprehend, rather than to speak, language. This approach has been more fruitful and has produced results that the scientific community recognizes.[59]

Fundamentally, Herman and his associates employ the sorts of animal training techniques used in oceanaria (that is, operant conditioning) to train dolphins to associate objects and actions involving those objects with particular gestures or sounds.[60] For example, a captive dolphin may perform a desired behavior in response to a particular hand signal. Trainers can reinforce the occurrence of such behaviors, and even shape the behaviors, by providing food or other rewards (for example, rubbing) when the dolphin does the appropriate behaviors on cue. In modern animal training procedures, an incorrect response is not punished; rather, the trainer responds by doing nothing, either positive or negative (that is, a neutral response).

With great patience, dolphins, and other animals for that matter, can be taught a vocabulary that permits them to do both simple and complex behaviors without error. Instructing a dog or dolphin to perform without error the relatively simple act of "fetch the ball" suggests that the animal understands (1) what fetch means, and (2) the difference between a ball and other fetchable objects in the area.

Once an animal has established a broad vocabulary relating signals, behaviors, and objects, scientists can test cognitive ability as manifested by its ability to use language in terms of syntax (the way in which words are put together in phrases and sentences), semantics (meanings of different words or signs), and reference (the extent to which the animal relates signs or symbols to the actual object they represent).[61] In this arena, dolphins trained by Herman and his colleagues performed better than do chimpanzees and other primates, although the training methods used with primates may have sometimes prevented assessment of syntactic ability to be done.[62]

Before considering exactly what scientists in the field have observed, it may be helpful to illustrate why syntactic ability may be important to assess when attempting to understand cognitive ability. Let's assume that a variety of objects float in the pool of a dolphin whose vocabulary includes those objects. If a trainer were to give a command of "ball-hoop," with no frame of reference as to what to do with the objects, the dolphin would have a dilemma: Should the ball be carried to the hoop? The hoop taken to the ball? The ball placed inside the hoop? The hoop put over the ball? The hoop and the ball moved in tandem?

However, if the dolphin had been trained to understand a general "rule" that the first object to which it is referred is the direct object of a phrase, and the second object is an indirect object of the same phrase, then "ball-hoop" becomes clearer—the dolphin must do something with the ball, in relationship to the hoop, rather than the other way around. Instruction in verbs allows the dolphin to complete the task well; for example, the command, "ball-fetch-hoop," would elicit a response in which the ball is taken to the hoop.

The above example could simply reflect intensive training of a particular animal, rather than comprehension of syntactic rules. In fact, some scientists have made precisely that argument based on research with captive California sea lions.[63] Herman and his group feel differently—that their work with dolphins suggests linguistic ability.

Well-designed experiments have shown that dolphins apparently do not simply learn to respond to verbal or gestural commands; rather, they appear to learn the grammatical rules involving indirect and direct objects, prepositions and verbs.[64] Thus, commands regarding new objects in the pool elicited the same sorts of responses as did commands regarding balls and hoops. The dolphins appeared to master syntax, a process that involves some higher-level processing of information by the brain.

As noted, the idea that dolphins possess certain linguistic abilities is supported by strong empirical evidence. On the other hand, some scientists interpret the data differently and believe that there is no reason to believe that dolphins "possess a sonic language which they use to communicate with one another about past and future events" or that their "sonic emissions reflect a language analogous to human spoken language which enables them to think in 'words' as well as in 'images.'"[65] "Many linguists would agree . . . that grammatical categories only make sense as part of a richer syntactic structure, developed with much less formal training."[66] The debate about language continues to generate, in Tyack's words, "more heat than light."[67]

But syntactic ability is not the only criterion that has been assessed to understand dolphin cognitive ability. We noted earlier that reference plays an important role in animal cognition. One way to test whether an animal can use a verbal or gestural signal to symbolize an object is to ask the animal to locate and perform some action with that particular object when it is actually absent.[68] Under such circumstances, dolphins appear to search for the object. Eventually, dolphins so trained press a special paddle to indicate absence of the requested object.[69] Interestingly, sea lions would simply not perform the requested action if the object were missing. Evidently, dolphins have some ability to envision an absent object, based on a signal and past experience.

Fig. 73. A tight group of dolphins swimming in shallows. Flip Nicklin and Minden Pictures.

Dolphins demonstrate other capabilities that suggest unusual information processing and response. Herman, for example, says that dolphins are the only animals that exhibit both vocal and motor imitation.[70] There is a clear need for the latter in species such as dolphins, in which young animals must learn complex social and predatory behaviors to survive.[71] In addition, scientists performed a series of experiments and suggested that dolphins can share information through a single set of echoes produced by one of the group.[72] For example, if a particular dolphin focused echolocation clicks on a school of fish, nearby dolphins could also listen to the echoes. The passive listeners might know the following: (1) a school of fish is nearby; and (2) the echolocating dolphin is aware of and attending to the fish. Such a system, if it exists, could facilitate synchronous behavior of hunting dolphins.

To this point, we have established that dolphins possess at least some attributes associated with cognition. A synthesis of the topic in mammals in general lists seven social and cognitive attributes (object manipulation, concept learning, concept memory, repertoire diversity, use of referentia, vocal mimicry, and dependency on social tradition), and indicates that bottlenose dolphins have been shown to possess six of the seven (all but concept learning) to at least a moderate extent.[73]

But the demonstration of cognitive abilities under well-controlled experimental conditions does not necessarily demonstrate their use in the wild. And, if present, do such abilities truly make dolphins "intelligent?" After all, attributes associated with intelligence in dolphins are not necessarily so associated with other species. For example, honeybees possess an amazing ability to communicate locations of flowers to other bees via the "waggle dance," but honeybees are not commonly considered to be intelligent animals.[74] Social insects (bees and ants) also exhibit amazing coordination of behavior by different social groups; yet intellect seems lacking. Mynah birds and parrots are excellent vocal mimics like dolphins, but the birds, too, are not really considered intelligent.

What dolphins and some social primates share is a suite of attributes: long lives; prolonged parental care; delayed onset of sexual and physical maturation; development of social bonds of different types with different group members; excellent communication, leading to cooperation and even perhaps to altruism; large brains, with large telencephalons; high encephalization quotients; and signs of diverse cognitive abilities. The suite is what endears dolphins to people and makes some people want to believe that dolphins share what we value most in ourselves, something reflected in the name we conferred upon our own species: *sapiens*.

In some circles, the debate over dolphin intelligence may never end. Even the pessimistic statement that "trying to arrive at an airtight definition of intelligence is as thankless a job as trying to define Life or Man" will probably not deter those for whom it is important to attempt to show the position occupied by dolphins along a continuum of animal intellect.[75] But is the question of relative intelligence really a vital one to answer?

Peter Tyack has stated, "I personally do not believe it is meaningful to attempt to fit different species along a linear scale of intelligence."[76] We agree. Such an exercise is likely to do little more than reinforce our species' overinflated ego. What seems more productive and enjoyable is to indulge in contemplation of the remarkable suite of dolphin adaptations that endear the species to people: cooperative behavior; coordinated movements; close, long-term ties among individuals; adaptability to different environmental conditions; communication; echolocation; and large and specialized brains. This suite is truly no less wonderful and presents no less cause for admiration than the presence of intelligence.

Human Interactions with Dolphins

As noted in chapter 2, people have interacted with dolphins for centuries. It seems safe to suggest that, as more and more people have inhabited the earth and used coastal and offshore waters for a growing range of activities, the nature and consequences to dolphins of human interactions have changed over time. Interactions 2,500 years ago involving a few Mediterranean fishermen who employed hook-and-line fishing from sailboats probably were inconsequential for dolphins. On the other hand, groups of local gillnetters today can have quite an effect on abundance of local species, including both the target species (for example, fish and squid) and nontarget species such as bottlenose dolphins.[1]

In this chapter, we examine the range of consequences of interactions between dolphins and humans. In some cases (for example, incidental take in nets) the consequences are clearly negative for the dolphins, but in other cases there may be a positive outcome. For many activities, there are both pros and cons in terms of effects on dolphins. It is important to note that bottlenose dolphins occupying coastal and inshore waters are vulnerable to impacts from a variety of human activities. It will become apparent that scientists often do not understand well the effects of single activities on individual or populations of dolphins; cumulative or synergistic effects are even less well understood, but may impair dolphin survival in many parts of the world.

Positive Relationships

COOPERATIVE FISHING

One of the few instances in which dolphins appear to benefit from interactions with people involves artisanal fisheries in a number of countries around the world.[2] Cooperative fishing has apparently occurred at least since the time of Pliny the Elder (A.D. 23–79).[3]

In the town of Laguna, Brazil, for example, cooperative fishing has been reported since 1847, and at least three generations of dolphins are involved at present.[4] When schools of mullet are expected to be close to shore and available for easy harvest (that is, from November to April), the Laguna fishermen, equipped with circular throw nets, and the dolphins position themselves in shallow water, facing seaward. In the murky water, the humans have trouble seeing the mullet, so they rely on the behavior of the dolphins as a cue to when to throw the nets. The dolphins detect and then herd the fish toward their human partners. The vigor with which the dolphins chase mullet provides information to the awaiting fishermen as to the size of the fish school; thus, several fishermen may toss their nets during a single herding incident. As the nets hit the water, the schooling fish that are not caught apparently become confused and are easy targets for the dolphins. This sort of working relationship is appropriately called a symbiosis.[5]

Local fishermen recognize the individual dolphins with which they work. Interestingly, not all dolphins in an area may choose to cooperate with fishermen. Those that do not participate are called *ruim*—that is, "bad dolphins"—by the Laguna fishermen.[6]

Controversial Relationships

PUBLIC DISPLAY OF DOLPHINS

We opened this book by noting that the maintenance of marine mammals, including dolphins, in captivity has been and continues to be extremely controversial. The bottlenose dolphin is the cetacean most commonly held in captivity. Although dolphins have been held in oceanaria and aquaria for more than 125 years, the debate about the propriety of public display and other uses of captive dolphins remains heated. "Depending on how . . . questions . . . are answered, an oceanarium might be regarded as an amusement park, an educational center, a research laboratory, a genetic bank, or a prison."[7] Before addressing controversial aspects of captive maintenance of dolphins, we provide a little history of the issue.[8]

Oddly enough, given the prevalence of bottlenose dolphins in oceanaria today, the first cetacean species to be kept in captivity was probably the harbor porpoise, which was held in private collections in France as early as the fifteenth century.[9] The first dolphin to be held in captivity was a stranded animal maintained briefly at Boston's Aquarial Gardens in 1861;[10] the first dolphin kept in captivity in Europe was maintained at the Brighton Aquarium in England in 1883.[11] In 1914, the New York Aquarium acquired several dolphins from a net fishery in North Carolina, becoming the first facility in the United States to actively seek to maintain the species in captivity. But it was not until the opening in 1938 of Marine Studios (more recently called Marineland of Florida) in St. Augustine, Florida, that the public display industry began in earnest.[12] Currently, nearly sixty facilities in seventeen countries hold nearly 650 captive dolphins.[13]

To satisfy the demand for dolphins for public display and research, approximately 1,500 animals were removed from the wild between 1938 and 1980.[14] Following the passage of the Marine Mammal Protection Act of 1972, permits were issued by the National Marine Fisheries Service authorizing the collection of more than 530 dolphins from waters of the southeastern United States.[15] However, the development of very successful captive breeding programs has virtually eliminated the need to take additional specimens from the wild.[16] In fact, by 1995, the percentage of captive dolphins born in captivity in the United States and Canada reached 43 percent.[17]

Since 1989, there have been no bottlenose dolphins captured from continental United States waters for public display or research, although a few individuals of other dolphin species have been live-captured.[18] Live capture of bottlenose dolphins may have been focused in coastal waters of the southeastern United States, but it has also occurred off Hawaii, South Africa, Japan, Mexico, the Bahamas, the Philippines, and some Mediterranean countries.[19] Some small-scale live capture for the species still apparently occurs around the world.[20]

Once dolphins are placed in captive facilities in the United States, standards for their maintenance are enforced by the Animal and Plant Health Inspection Service (Department of Agriculture), as stipulated under the 1994 amendments to the Marine Mammal Protection Act. Inspections by the service are typically conducted when a facility opens, but may be redone if complaints arise. Prior to 1994, the National Marine Fisheries Service (Department of Commerce) and the Animal and Plant Health Inspection Service (APHIS) shared oversight duties. The existing standards, it should be recognized, stipulate *reasonable* (in some people's minds) conditions that must be met or exceeded, not necessarily the *optimal* standards. Some facilities have the affluence and the will to build enclosures that far exceed the minimum APHIS standards, whereas other organizations simply meet what is required of them. Thus, quality of facilities and their success in maintaining marine mammals are not consistent.[21]

The impact of the Marine Mammal Protection Act on the care and maintenance of captive marine mammals actually extends globally. The 1994 amendments to the act require, for example, that foreign facilities wishing to import marine mammals from the United States must show evidence that their maintenance standards match those imposed on United States facilities. In reality, standards for keeping marine mammals in captivity vary a great deal around the world.[22]

With this background information, what is the nature of the controversy surrounding captive maintenance of dolphins? There are actually a number of arguments in favor of keeping animals in captivity.[23]

Among the most often heard justifications for maintaining captive bottlenose dolphins and other cetaceans is that they serve at facilities that display them as ambassadors for wild animals. In other words, captive mainte-

Fig. 74. Students receive instruction in a classroom at Sea World. Such zoological parks provide an opportunity to educate and instill a conservation ethic in an enormous number of children each year. SeaWorld, Florida.

nance of a few individuals has the potential to pay great dividends in terms of enhanced public and legislative interest, and subsequently in protection of large numbers of dolphins and their habitat in the wild. More than 122 million people in the United States visited zoos and aquaria in 1997;[24] this represents a huge audience whose opinions and actions could be shaped. According to recent amendments of the Marine Mammal Protection Act, public display of marine mammals must be accompanied by education and public awareness efforts with a strong conservation message. Some people feel that this translates into greater interest among the general public in conservation of species and habitats. In fact, a recent poll indicated that most of nearly two thousand respondents considered oceanaria to perform valuable education functions that enhanced conservation efforts.[25] However, a couple of factors must be borne in mind: (1) the quality of education programs at individual facilities varies considerably; and (2) there have not been rigorous assessments of the effectiveness of education programs or of how they might be improved. Nonetheless, there is evidence in this poll and elsewhere

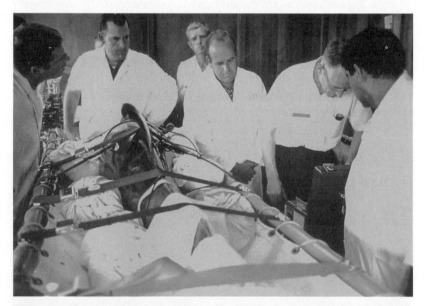

Fig. 75. Prominent scientists, including Dr. Kenneth Norris (center) and Dr. Sam Ridgway (left) remove a foreign object from the forestomach of a dolphin. People such as Norris and Ridgway, David and Melba Caldwell, and Steve Leatherwood (among others) set the stage for much of the scientific research occurring today. From S. H. Ridgway, *Mammals of the Sea*, with permission of S. H. Ridgway.

Fig. 76. A stranded dolphin at Mote Marine Laboratory receives an injection for treatment of an infection. To minimize stress and to facilitate handling, the dolphin has been trained to remain stationary at poolside for medical procedures. Randall S. Wells, Mote Marine Laboratory.

Fig. 77. Effective rehabilitation of dolphins requires extensive, specialized facilities and well-trained staff. At Mote Marine Laboratory's Dolphin and Whale Hospital, a dolphin named Gulliver is lifted from the critical care pool on his way to a large rehabilitation lagoon in preparation for his ultimate release. Jay Gorzelany, Mote Marine Laboratory.

Fig. 78. Births of dolphins in captivity are no longer unusual. Official U.S. Navy photograph taken by Michelle Reddy.

that public display of marine mammals affects public attitudes and may contribute to conservation of the species being displayed.

Another stated benefit of keeping dolphins in captivity is that the captive environment provides a setting in which many aspects of dolphin biology can be studied very well. This justification is especially important for species such as dolphins, for which many aspects of their biology are logistically difficult to study in the wild. Captive studies have involved assessments of "intelligence" and cognitive ability, physiology, and reproductive endocrinology, which are all difficult topics to address in free-ranging dolphins.[26]

Certainly the captive environment has provided opportunities to study the health of dolphins and to create an understanding of what constitutes a healthy individual. Some of the more common diseases of bottlenose dolphins include bacterial pneumonia, pox viruses, erysipelas, hepatitis, gastric ulcerations, enteritis, pancreatitis, and hepatic degenerative disease.[27] As noted elsewhere in this book, scientists and veterinarians have recently devoted more attention to examining the species for evidence of morbillivirus and have noted its occurrence in various locations. Not surprisingly, dolphins and other marine mammals seem generally to suffer from the same range and types of diseases as their terrestrial counterparts, including humans. The techniques and "standards" created by captive studies of blood chemistry and other aspects of dolphin medicine have even been applied to field studies in which wild dolphins are handled briefly by scientists who assess such things as blood chemistry and blubber thickness to develop a "health assessment score" for individuals.[28]

However, people raise the question of whether the results of such research merit keeping animals in captivity. For example, do studies of captive dolphins really provide information that allows scientists to clearly understand what dolphins do in the wild? Some scientists have extrapolated and applied data from captive animal communication and cognition research to what may happen in the wild; their conclusions, while reasonable, nonetheless remain conjectural.[29] Whitlow Au, a noted biosonar researcher, states: "Our perception of how dolphins utilize their sonar in the wild is based on extrapolation of knowledge obtained in 'laboratory' experiments—we do not have the foggiest idea of how dolphins utilize their sonar in a natural environment."[30] On the other hand, one might well argue that information gained from captive animals is clearly better than having no information at all on aspects of dolphin biology!

In a similar vein, people have questioned whether the captive environment induces atypical behavior patterns and other aspects of dolphin biology; in other words, do data from captive studies have any relevance to wild dolphins at all? Results of some studies indicate that bottlenose dolphins tend to exhibit generally similar behaviors in the wild and in captivity.[31] Furthermore, round-the-clock studies of captives in clear water may provide insights that would be extremely difficult to obtain in the wild. As noted by one study: "Zoo-based research revealed patterns of behavior that conformed to current knowledge about bottlenose dolphin social structure. Moreover, research in a zoo setting facilitated development of a quantitative technique that can be used to assess cetacean dominance relationships in field research."[32]

On the other hand, noted cetacean biologist Ken Norris has observed that certain natural behaviors (for example, migrations and daily home ranging patterns) of dolphins are distorted or blunted in a captive environment, no matter how large or how refined the facility is.[33] However, Norris also has stated that captive dolphins "have told us all we know about the dolphin mind, . . . how their senses work, how they echolocate, how they dive, and much of what we know about how their societies work."[34] Norris even discusses development of studies of wild and captive dolphins that would complement one another, perhaps using the idea of a "dolphin sabattical," in which wild animals would be brought into captivity briefly and then released back to their home waters.[35] This creative approach has, in fact, already been tried once, with the animals being successfully reintroduced to their original waters and social groups.[36]

One of the ways in which data from captive animals are useful to understanding and conserving wild animals involves rescue and rehabilitation of stranded individuals. Within the United States and elsewhere in the world, well-organized networks of scientists and oceanaria exist to respond to stranded marine mammals.[37] Without data from captive animals regarding blood chemistry and other medical attributes of healthy dolphins, it would be extremely difficult to effectively treat compromised animals that come up on the beach.[38] Because scientists and veterinarians do know so much about dolphin health, in several cases injured or sick dolphins have been treated and released. For example, a bottlenose dolphin was rescued by Mote Marine Laboratory staff in 1993, treated for 107 days, and released back into his home waters. This animal, named Freeway because he stranded within sight of an interstate highway, suffered from severe shark bites, massive quantities of fluid in the pleural cavity interfering with lung function, and a host of other health problems. Applying new and well-tested techniques learned from years of caring for captive dolphins, we returned Freeway to health. Based on five years of photographic identification records of Freeway prior to stranding, we were able to return him to familiar waters, where we observed him over the next six months. Although uncertainty exists regarding the extent to which such releases affect wild populations of dolphins, the process of rescuing, rehabilitating, and ultimately releasing animals to the wild certainly does a lot to cause people to care about dolphins and their conservation. Thus, the net effect on wild populations could be substantial. However, there are risks of releases as well, including affecting social order, introducing animals with "maladaptive traits" (for example, seeking food from humans), and introducing diseases to wild populations.[39]

The idea of reintroduction raises another issue. It has been argued that maintenance of animals in captivity provides assurance that, if a species becomes extinct in part or all of its range in the wild, there will still be some individuals left that could be reintroduced to natural areas with proper habitat for that species. In a similar vein, captive animals provide some genetic diversity for wild populations that have been reduced to the point where genetic bottlenecks occur. Although the development of captive breeding programs, with a possible long-term goal of restocking decimated wild populations, for species other than marine mammals have met with some success,[40] the idea has not been considered seriously until recently for a cetacean species, the highly endangered baiji (*Lipotes vexillifer*) from the Yangtze River in China.[41] For the bottlenose dolphin, it seems *extremely* premature to consider restocking programs. If people manage natural habitats and human activities properly, restocking will never become an issue for the bottlenose.

We intimated in chapter 1 that animals maintained in captivity may exist under better water quality and certain other conditions than some of their wild counterparts do. Earlier, we cited the case of dolphins residing in the Moray Firth, where nearly 100 percent of the animals possess skin lesions or anatomical deformities, perhaps as a result of poor habitat quality.[42] In cases where ecosystems are heavily polluted or otherwise degraded, this argument may have some merit. However, an extension of the argument to suggest that we view captive environments as good surrogates for nature and, therefore, place less emphasis on maintaining diverse natural environments, is extremely dangerous.[43] Ultimately, it is vital for the well-being of all wild living resources (and for people, too) to preserve natural environments in as healthy a condition as possible.

As is the case with any controversy, cogent arguments exist to support opposite points of view. Thus, there is opposition to captivity for a number of reasons.

One argument is that removal of animals from the wild could stress or even jeopardize the survival of wild populations or stocks. As noted above, this point no longer applies to bottlenose dolphins in United States waters, for which capture operations ceased in 1989. Historically (prior to 1972), however, live capture operations may have affected local dolphin populations due to unregulated takes. Take quotas were established following passage of the Marine Mammal Protection Act of 1972 by the National Marine Fisheries Service. The quotas capped live captures at a level no more than 2 percent of the minimum estimated number of dolphins in a particular "management area" (that is, from what was considered to be a particular stock—see chapter 9). The so-called 2 percent rule was based on estimates of dolphin productivity.[44] This system theoretically permitted more than one hundred dolphins a year to be taken from various locations in the southeastern United States, but the highest number ever actually captured in a year was fifty-six, in 1988, and as few as sixteen animals were captured in a single year after the quota system was initiated in 1972.[45]

The issue of live captures affecting wild dolphin populations seems laid to rest at present, at least in the United States. Similarly, the argument that survival of dolphins in captivity is reduced (relative to that of free-ranging animals) has been challenged by rigorous scientific analyses.[46] Although mortality is relatively high during acclimation periods of up to sixty days, long-term survival of dolphins in captivity has improved over time, apparently as a result of improved husbandry practices.[47] Survival of wild dolphins is, in fact, generally quite comparable to that of captives.[48] One interesting finding was that, despite APHIS regulations for care and maintenance of dolphins, survivorship varies significantly among facilities.[49]

An argument against captivity that is difficult to counter is the ethical one, which has been applied to the issue of captivity in general, but which seems to generate the most heat when applied to large-brained, social mammals such as the nonhuman primates and dolphins. The argument is that such animals have rights similar to those of humans and that captivity violates those rights. A corollary to the argument is that the development of whale-watch industries and the proliferation of high-quality videos provide other avenues by which people can learn about and see dolphins and other marine mammals firsthand, thereby, at least in theory, reducing or eliminating the need to keep the animals in captivity at all. As we shall discuss later in this chapter, dolphin watching ventures are not necessarily conducted in ways that prevent impact to wild animals, and, in fact, they may cause obvious harassment of dolphins.

The reason that the animal-rights argument against captivity continues to be hard to resolve is that it is fundamentally a philosophical one, not a scientific one that can be addressed with data. At the 1983 Global Conference on the Non-Consumptive Utilization of Cetacean Resources (also known as the "Whales Alive" conference), captivity was "the most volatile and divisive subject" discussed.[50]

The issue of captive maintenance of dolphins thus may never be completely resolved. On the one hand, captive maintenance is perfectly legal; maintenance standards exist and are enforced; the animals may survive (according to certain measures) as well as their free-ranging counterparts; and scientific evidence suggests minimal detriment to wild or captive animals and possible enhancement to the wild populations as a result of greater public interest. On the other hand, certain people feel that it is simply unethical to keep dolphins in captivity under any circumstance or for any reason. It is the sort of issue for which each person simply has to make up his or her own mind.

SWIM-WITH-THE-DOLPHIN PROGRAMS

As a very specialized aspect of the captivity issue, swim-with-the-dolphin programs merit separate consideration. The issue is especially contentious because it involves people actually paying substantial amounts of money (in some cases more than $150 each for several swimmers) to spend ½ hour to an hour in the water with one or more dolphins.

Originally, only four facilities in the United States (three in the Florida Keys and one in Hawaii) were provisionally authorized to conduct the swim program. By late 1998, fourteen others were authorized as well, with most permitting wading but not actual swimming with the dolphins.[51] Although the programs have some fundamental similarities, there have been great differences in terms of the extent to which the dolphins have been controlled by professional trainers. Such differences have created situations in which

Fig. 79. Children participating in a swim-with-the-dolphin program at Dolphin Quest, Hawaii. Flip Nicklin and Minden Pictures.

Fig. 80. A trainer at a swim-with-the-dolphin program interacts with a dolphin at Dolphin Quest, Hawaii. Flip Nicklin and Minden Pictures.

either the dolphins or the humans were at risk.[52] In fact, one study "found no behavioral evidence that Controlled Swims with adequate refuge were deleterious for human swimmers or dolphins."[53] This stands in stark contrast with the situation where control is minimal; in such instances, humans have been injured and dolphins have exhibited behaviors that have caused them to be permanently removed from the programs. Behavior, especially of social animals, often reflects physiological state, and some dolphin behaviors associated with swim programs may indicate that involved animals feel some stress.[54]

As noted earlier in this book, humans have, for centuries, swum with free-ranging dolphins, creating an image that dolphins are friendly animals that enjoy human companionship. What is less advertised is that, on occasion, dolphins and other wild cetaceans have injured people and even killed one individual in Brazil in 1994.[55] These incidents "should serve as a reminder to humans that cetaceans, even when behaving non-aggressively, can pose a serious threat."[56] As it turns out, adult and maturing male dolphins were "most likely to engage in high-risk activity resulting in swimmer injury" in the swim-with-the-dolphin programs, although female dolphins also could put human swimmers at risk.[57]

So what are the potential benefits of swim programs? Advocates mention that people who engage in these programs often comment about the extent to which the experience "changed their lives." In particular, several reports suggest that swimming with dolphins provides excellent therapy for children with severe disabilities.[58] These reports claim that a program called Dolphin Human Therapy is both clinically and cost effective when compared to conventional programs that treat disabled children. Even though water therapy *without* dolphins can provide certain health benefits (for example, stress relief, pain relief, reduction in anxiety and depression), the reports suggest that dolphin-assisted therapy can, over both the short and long term, increase attention, motivation, and language and other skill development. Such findings led to the recommendation of dolphin-assisted therapy "as a complement to, not a replacement for, conventional therapies."[59] Another study noted that mentally retarded children working with dolphins learned two to ten times more quickly and exhibited longer retention of information than did children who were exposed to similar material but did not have dolphins present.[60]

The work with mentally retarded and otherwise disabled children has suggested that controlled swimming with dolphins may provide beneficial therapy. However, critics have stated that the data and analyses are flawed, leading to equally flawed conclusions.[61] Thus, the evidence regarding the benefits of swimming with dolphins is controversial. However, in instances where people swimming with dolphins are affected positively by the encounter, those people and their families are, as suggested earlier in this chapter, likely to become advocates of programs that protect and conserve free-ranging dolphins.

Thus, the swim-with-the-dolphin issue bears many of the same questions and concerns as does the issue of dolphin captivity in general. But the alleged and demonstrated potential for harm to dolphins and humans on the one hand, and the alleged benefits to humans on the other, make the issue somewhat special. Nor has it been solved at the level of federal regulations.

Prior to 1994, regulation of swim-with-the-dolphin programs rested with the National Marine Fisheries Service, but with passage that year of amendments to the Marine Mammal Protection Act, jurisdiction passed to the APHIS. With prompting from the Marine Mammal Commission, APHIS has drafted new rules to regulate the programs. Those rules were disseminated for comment and scheduled to be adopted in 1998, but by late 1999 final guidelines and rules had not been adopted.

DOLPHIN WATCHING AND DOLPHIN FEEDING VENTURES

In recent years, there has been a dramatic increase in activities that promote direct interactions between wild marine mammals and people. Whale watching is probably the best known of such commercial ventures. There are actually a couple categories of entrepreneurial activities that could or do affect wild marine mammals: (1) activities that bring people close to marine mammals to observe, photograph, or even swim with or otherwise make physical contact with the animals; and (2) activities where people feed the animals, in some cases to entice them to approach vessels. Both types of activities involve bottlenose dolphins. In the United States, these activities exist primarily in the southeastern part of the country.[62]

Although commercial operators have argued that dolphin watching and dolphin feeding ventures are benign,[63] feeding of wild marine mammals, including dolphins, is expressly forbidden as a type of "take" under the Marine Mammal Protection Act.[64] One important reason (of several) for this designation is that feeding of wild marine mammals can cause them to

Fig. 81. Dolphins attract the attention of the general public at Monkey Mia, Australia. Flip Nicklin and Minden Pictures.

Fig. 82. Dolphins being fed by the general public at Monkey Mia, Australia. There has been speculation that this activity has affected survival of young dolphins there. Flip Nicklin and Minden Pictures.

change their normal behavior patterns in detrimental ways. For example, large powerful marine mammals that become accustomed to being close to people who feed them may become irritated with and attack people who do not. At Tangalooma, Australia, dolphins became "pushy" with people during feeding sessions, and such behavior "may be a precursor to more aggressive actions on the part of the dolphin."[65] In Florida, we have witnessed a number of incidents in which a begging dolphin has bitten people, with serious injuries resulting. In addition, wild animals that become dependant on humans for food may, in fact, have their survival jeopardized when the source of food is terminated and they have to feed themselves. This has been speculated as a possible cause of very poor recent survival of juvenile bottlenose dolphins around Monkey Mia, Australia.[66]

Other reasons why dolphin feeding may create problems for dolphins include the following: Dolphins that learn to approach boats for food may be more susceptible to becoming entangled in fishing gear, hit by propellers, shot, poisoned, or fed foreign objects. In addition, migratory patterns could be affected in ways that expose dolphins to inhospitable environmental conditions. Further, animals exposed to humans and pets on boats could be more susceptible to disease transmission.[67] Finally, the animals may also be distracted from natural activities, such as being vigilant regarding predators.[68]

Dolphin watching has the potential to be a relatively benign (that is, nonconsumptive) activity, and some operators are careful to minimize their disturbance of dolphins.[69] However, dolphin watching is sometimes conducted in ways that are extremely disruptive to dolphins. In our own work in Boca Ciega Bay, Florida, for example, certain commercial dolphin watch operators "home in" on dolphins being observed (with appropriate federal authorization) as part of a scientific research program. Although the scientists attempt to conduct activities in ways that minimize disruption of the animals in order to observe "normal" behaviors, some dolphin watch boats may deliberately race through the group in order to induce bow riding or other dramatic behavior for the benefit of the paying customers. At the least, the speeding boat disrupts normal behaviors and scatters the group, and at times it comes perilously close to females with young calves. This sort of activity clearly constitutes harassment and is considered illegal.[70]

In 1997 the National Marine Fisheries Service responded to the growing problem by having agency representatives meet with local federal representatives, members of the general public, and dolphin tour operators in the southeastern United States to explain what constitutes proper interactions between marine mammals and humans. That same year, the service contracted with the Florida Marine Patrol (a state enforcement agency with numerous officers patrolling the coastal waters of Florida) to increase enforcement. In 1998, the service planned to add six new enforcement officers in the southeastern United States to concentrate on preventing feeding or other activities that harass dolphins.[71]

On the larger scale, activities such as dolphin watching and dolphin feeding constitute ecotourism, a growing development worldwide. Often viewed simplistically as a solution that provides for the economic needs of local people while allowing natural resources to be maintained, ecotourism, or nature tourism, like all forms of economic development, can have undesirable and unforeseen impacts if it is not planned and subsequently monitored very carefully.[72] For example, in southern Japan we have observed as many as eight dolphin watching vessels converge on a single school of bottlenose dolphins *upon every single surfacing* over periods of more than an hour.

On occasion, people have questioned whether scientific research conducted on marine mammals may have adverse impacts on the animals. For example, if scientists were to conduct studies that affected dolphins by causing them to leave preferred habitat, the survival of the animals could be impaired as they seek to feed themselves in areas where prey are either less available or less nutritious.

To prevent undue or unforeseen adverse effects of research on marine mammals, scientists in the United States must obtain permits from the appropriate federal agencies.[73] Permit applications are reviewed by scientists and other personnel at these agencies, as well as by the members of the Marine Mammal Commission and its Committee of Scientific Advisors on Marine Mammals. The permit applications are also made available for public comment. Unless the reviewers are satisfied that the research activities will not have undue adverse impacts, a permit is not granted.[74]

It should be noted that some research does have some impact on the animals being studied. For example, if an animal is captured and handled by scientists, the procedures may have the potential to cause some discomfort or pain (for example, if a tooth is extracted under local anesthesia in order to age the animal, or a stomach lavage is used to collect gut contents for analysis of food habits). In approving the permit, the scientific and other reviewers must feel that (1) the scientists doing the work are highly qualified and are conducting an important, well-designed, "bona fide" study; (2) the cost of potentially creating some discomfort in some individuals is more than balanced by the benefit of obtaining particular scientific information; (3) the scientific data are being collected in the most humane manner possible; and (4) both the long-term and short-term adverse effects of the study are as small as possible. It is very important to realize, as discussed in chapter 10, that effective, rational conservation programs require good knowledge of the species being conserved and its habitat.

Interestingly enough, the restrictions on scientific research activities far exceed those placed on the general public. For example, a scientist conducting photo-identification research on a local group of bottlenose dolphins needs to acquire permission (via a research permit or a letter of authorization) to approach the animals and potentially to harass them.[75] On the other hand, members of the public may, with absolutely no legal authority or insight into animal behavior, approach dolphins closely and, without meaning to do so, harass them. In fact, because the lay public generally knows less about dolphin behavior than do scientists holding a permit or letter of authorization, the chance for harassment by the public is increased. In reality, anyone without a permit who harasses marine mammals violates the Marine Mammal Protection Act, but it is impossible to enforce the act well.

In summary, research activities involving dolphins must be approved by scientists and managers. The work is done in ways that minimize detrimental effects. And the data generated by such studies contribute to our ability to understand what dolphin populations do and need, and therefore, to conserve those populations.

MILITARY USES OF DOLPHINS

In 1959 the U.S. Navy initiated its Marine Mammal Program with a single dolphin named Notty; the initial goal of the program was to learn more about dolphin hydrodynamics to assist in the design of naval vessels.[76] Since that time, the navy has maintained bottlenose dolphins to study the animals and learn more about such abilities as diving, orientation, sound production and reception, and thermoregulation. Such studies contributed to work that enhanced human underwater capabilities. This research also contributed a great deal to scientific understanding of dolphin neuroanatomy, physiology, health, sensory biology, and behavior.[77] The dolphins also

Fig. 83. Dolphins have been used to assist navy divers in a number of ways. From S. H. Ridgway, *The Dolphin Doctor*, with permission of S. H. Ridgway.

helped navy divers by bringing them tools and helping to locate submerged objects in the open ocean.[78] Questions of an ethical nature have been raised about the extent to which dolphins held by the military might be involved in warfare (for example, carrying messages, placing or searching for underwater mines, guarding underwater areas).

The navy has over time diminished the size of its marine mammal program and its captive colony of dolphins; recently, this trend has been reversed. Although the Office of Naval Research continues to fund research on dolphin hydrodynamics, health (for example, immunology), and acoustics, much of the work is done not by naval personnel but by independent scientists.

Negative Relationships

DIRECTED TAKES

Although people often associate commercial whaling with the large baleen whales or sperm whales, a number of smaller cetaceans have historically been harvested for meat, blubber, or other products. Some species still are killed and used today.

Bottlenose dolphins are no exception to the rule. In the United States, a thriving fishery for the species began in 1797 and peaked in the late nineteenth century at Cape Hatteras, North Carolina, with annual catches sometimes in excess of two thousand animals. The history of this particular fishery after 1893 is not clear, but it seems to have ceased operations in 1929.[79] Smaller fisheries that took, or probably took, bottlenose dolphins existed in the late nineteenth century at Cape May, New Jersey, and at Long Island. Among the products of the take was meat for human consumption. The federal government even published recipes for bottlenose dolphins and other cetaceans in 1918.[80]

The largest fishery for dolphins existed in the Black Sea, where the carcasses were used for oil, meat, leather, and fish meal.[81] Three species (common dolphin; harbor porpoise; and bottlenose dolphin) were taken in this fishery, which crashed in the mid-1960s. Take data do not differentiate well among the various species, so it is difficult to know the overall magnitude of the harvest. However, dolphin numbers were so depleted that in 1966 the governments of Bulgaria and the Union of Soviet Socialist Republics prohibited killing of dolphins in the Black Sea. Turkey continues to take animals, although the size of the harvest is not known.[82] However, the populations of small cetaceans affected by the Black Sea fishery are considered to be at risk.[83]

Directed take of bottlenose dolphins continues in various parts of the world besides Turkey, including in Peru, Sri Lanka, and Japan.[84] Such takes occur either for human consumption or to reduce perceived competition for fish resources.[85]

In the United States, commercial hunting and killing of marine mammals, including dolphins, has been illegal since passage of the Marine Mammal Protection Act in 1972. However, as noted elsewhere in this chapter, the take of dolphins for public display continued for almost two decades after passage of the act, and incidental take of dolphins by commercial and recreational fishing gear continues to this day.

INCIDENTAL TAKES

In 1972 the Marine Mammal Protection Act was passed due to public concern about three issues: commercial whaling, hunting of baby harp seals, and incidental take of dolphins of various types by the purse seine fishery for yellowfin tuna in the eastern tropical Pacific Ocean.[86] The latter issue actually involved what is termed bycatch (take of a nontarget species) more than it did incidental take (inadvertent catching of nontarget species) since the purse seiners deliberately set their nets around dolphins, below which the tuna swim.

Over the years, more and more issues have been detected and have become cause for concern among marine mammal scientists and managers. In 1994, the vast majority of the amendments to the act concerned one issue: assessment and mitigation of incidental take of marine mammals by fisheries.[87]

Effects of incidental take have been considered most commonly at the population level; in other words, what effect can such take have on a particular stock or population? For example, a Taiwanese gill net fishery operating off Australia may take more than two thousand bottlenose dolphins a year;[88] if such a level of take continues, it is difficult to imagine that the local or regional population of dolphins could avoid adverse impact. A number of other fisheries worldwide take the species in smaller numbers.

In the United States, as stipulated in the 1994 Amendments to the Marine Mammal Protection Act, commercial fisheries were classified as Category I (those that frequently kill or seriously injure marine mammals), Category II (those that occasionally kill or injure marine mammals) and Category III (fisheries that rarely harm marine mammals).[89] Reporting requirements and other regulations are strictest for the most harmful fisheries (Categories I and II) and virtually nonexistent for Category III fisheries. This creates an interesting catch-22 in which a fishery might be listed originally as a Category III fishery but, because monitoring and reporting requirements are minimal, it would be difficult to amass data sufficient ever to cause that fishery to be reclassified as a Category I or II fishery. For example, in the southeastern United States, the primary fisheries that historically appeared (based on results of a questionnaire) to take bottlenose dolphins were the shrimp trawl and menhaden seine fisheries.[90] In the 1998 listings of fisheries by category by the National Marine Fisheries Service, neither of these fisheries was classified as either a Category I or II fishery.[91] The primary Category I and II fisheries that are reported to take bottlenose dolphins in the waters of the United States are the pelagic drift gillnet fishery in the Atlantic Ocean, Caribbean Sea, and Gulf of Mexico (Category I), a multispecies sink gillnet fishery in the northeastern United States (Category I), a longline fishery for large pelagic fishes in the Atlantic, Caribbean, and Gulf of Mexico (Category I), a drift gillnet fishery for shark and swordfish off California and

Fig. 84. It is not unusual for dolphins to become entangled in fishing nets and drown. Statewide inshore bans on netting, as have been implemented in Florida, have reduced dolphin mortality due to entanglement in commercial fishing gear, but recreational fishing line injures or kills increasing numbers of animals. Randall S. Wells, Chicago Zoological Society.

Oregon (Category I), a mid-Atlantic coastal gillnet fishery (Category II), a southeastern Atlantic shark gillnet fishery (Category II), a North Carolina haul seine fishery (Category II), and an anchovy, mackerel and tuna purse seine fishery off California (Category II). Note two things about the list of involved fisheries: (1) the frequency with which gillnets are involved in incidental take of bottlenose dolphins; and (2) many other species of marine mammals are also taken in these fisheries.

Taking a broader view, bottlenose dolphins were among the stocks and species listed as potentially injured or killed in three out of the four Category I fisheries and three out of six Category II fisheries in the Atlantic, Gulf of Mexico, and Caribbean waters of the United States. Among Pacific fisheries in the United States, bottlenose dolphins were listed as potentially impacted by one out of two Category I fisheries and one out of eighteen Category II fisheries.[92]

There are, of course, effects of incidental take that can be assessed at the level of the individual animal rather than the population. For example, recreational fishing gear has been implicated in the deaths or injuries of dolphins in Florida.[93]

An interesting observation made by scientists in Australia involved a calf that became entangled in discarded monofilament fishing line.[94] Prior to the entanglement, the calf and its mother mainly rested and traveled slowly. Following the entanglement, vocalizations occurred immediately. Then the pair traveled quickly, with synchronous leaping and frequent changes of direction. They were joined briefly by other dolphins which also engaged in synchronous leaping. Calves may be more susceptible to entanglement than adults, due to their "inexperience, playfulness, curiosity, and small size."[95] This sort of behavior suggests that entanglement induced some sort of "sympathetic" behavior by members of the group. Also, if the entanglement had involved a net, rather than a single fishing line, the vigorous post-entanglement behavior could have resulted in entanglement of other individuals.

Is it possible to prevent dolphins and other cetaceans from becoming entangled in nets and drowning? Although scientists do not know why cetaceans do not detect netting and avoid it, the idea has been proposed that, if the nets were somehow made more apparent to marine mammals but not to target species of fish, the former could avoid becoming entangled without detriment to the catch for market.[96] In the northeastern United States, active acoustic alarms, called pingers, have been successfully used to dramatically reduce incidental take of harbor porpoises in groundfish gillnets.[97] Scientists believe that the use of passive sonar reflectors, called cats eyes, may increase the likelihood of bottlenose dolphins detecting and avoiding becoming entangled in nets in the Moray Firth.[98] Although it is uncertain whether such devices solve the problem of incidental take of dolphins, tests provide hope that the magnitude of the problem can be reduced for some fisheries.

The general public may tend to lump all types of commercial fishing together in terms of impacts to nontarget species. For example, the 1995 ban on commercial netting by the state of Florida was extended to all types of commercial netting (but not to recreational fishing) in inshore waters of the state.[99] However, it is clear that certain types of fishing (for example, gill netting and trawling) are especially wasteful and/or damaging to the environment, whereas other types of fishing are much less so.

Another type of incidental take of dolphins involves nets placed around swimming beaches to prevent sharks from attacking swimmers. Such nets have been used extensively in Australia and South Africa, where they have entangled and killed dolphins.[100] To date, attempts to prevent entanglement of dolphins by using active or passive devices in these particular nets have been unsuccessful.[101] Off South Africa, the incidental take of dolphins is sufficiently high to cause concern about the sustainability of the take.[102]

A final way in which people take dolphins and other marine mammals incidentally to human activities involves boating. As noted below, dolphins may occasionally be struck by fast-moving motorboats. Such mortality is not usually, but perhaps should be, considered under the Marine Mammal Protection Act as "incidental take." For the Florida manatee, another marine mammal that is vulnerable to watercraft collisions, such incidents represent a major source of mortality and injury that grows annually.[103]

HABITAT DEGRADATION

Although it is clear that human activities have degraded habitat used by bottlenose dolphins, the extent to which the dolphin populations have been impacted has not been assessed well. However, a number of authors have speculated that local dolphin abundance has been reduced in areas (for example, Galveston Bay, Biscayne Bay, San Diego Bay) where human activities have adversely affected habitat quality.[104]

Fig. 85. Bottlenose dolphins live in close proximity to human activities, some of which pose threats to the animals. Here, dolphins are swimming with an oil drilling platform in the background. Flip Nicklin and Minden Pictures.

Point and nonpoint sources of pollution may have significant impacts to dolphins. For example, human sewage apparently contributed to the deaths of several dolphins at Monkey Mia, Australia.[105] Dolphins may have extremely high levels of chlorinated hydrocarbons and other toxicants in their tissues,[106] and toxicant accumulation has been suggested as a likely cause of immunosuppression of male dolphins in waters near Sarasota, Florida.[107] As discussed in chapter 1, toxicant loads quite possibly contributed to the mortality of at least 740 dolphins off the United States Atlantic coast[108] and calves receive a very high percentage (80 percent) of their mothers' toxicant loads, which may account for the rare survival of firstborn animals.[109] Unfortunately, the effects of toxicants at either the individual or population level have not been well assessed, so it is difficult to know what a particular toxicant load may mean. In fact, despite *correlations* between high tissue levels of chemical contaminants and certain reproductive, endocrinological, morphological, or other problems, there have been no instances in which exposure to toxicants has been *proven* to be the cause of death of any marine mammals.

There are other ways in which human activities can adversely affect dolphins.[110] For example, heavy boat traffic could affect dolphin distribution, behavior, and energetics.[111] Indeed, the effects of boats could be quite serious and obvious. For example, dolphins in Sarasota Bay, Florida, are struck by boats, especially around the time of July Fourth high-speed powerboat races.[112] Interestingly, in three of four instances where such strikes have been documented due to cuts inflicted on the dolphins, the animals were already compromised prior to the strike in some way (for example, scoliosis; inexperience).

Boat traffic can also induce short-term changes in swimming speed, diving, and distribution of animals, and scientists question whether long-term changes in behavior or habitat use might also result, with negative consequences for dolphin populations.[113]

The issue of noise pollution is complex and difficult to address. Boating activity described above is simply one of the many sources of underwater noise. There are several major sources of anthropogenic noise in marine environments: transportation, dredging and construction, oil and gas drilling and production, seismic exploration, sonars, explosions, and ocean science studies.[114] Each category of noise could potentially impact the abilities of certain marine mammals to communicate, detect predators or prey, and navigate. Very loud sounds could seriously and permanently damage marine mammal ears. It has even been suggested that sounds produced by human activities (for example, explosions) could shatter whale ears and kill them.

Although progress has been made of late, the effects of noise on marine mammals in general, and on bottlenose dolphins specifically, have been poorly studied to date.[115] Scientists note that "specific response thresholds have been determined for only a few combinations of species and noise type,

Fig. 86. Although collisions with boats occur less frequently with dolphins than with manatees, boats do strike dolphins, causing injury or death. This animal is affectionately known as Riptorn. Randall S. Wells, Chicago Zoological Society.

and they tend to be quite variable even within species,"[116] and that "tolerance of noise does not necessarily mean that noise has no deleterious effects."[117]

However, research on the issue has increased in recent years. Among other things, proposals to use extremely loud human-generated sounds as a means to assess global temperature change over time (the so-called ATOC—Acoustic Thermometry of Ocean Climate—or Heard Island experiments) have raised awareness and stimulated research about the issue.[118]

COMPETITION FOR RESOURCES

Dolphins may, as noted in chapter 1, take fish from nets or damage the nets themselves.[119] In such cases, fishermen have been observed or have been alleged to shoot the dolphins. The extent to which this occurs is unmeasured. On the other hand, regulation of commercial fishing effort may reduce competition from humans, actually permit dolphin prey species to rebound, and allow dolphin distribution and productivity to increase.[120]

In summary, perhaps more than any other species of marine mammal, the bottlenose dolphin has been used or otherwise affected by humans. In part because there is a lack of historical data, the individual, cumulative, and synergistic effects of interactions between people and dolphins have not been quantified. However, it is clear that most of our interactions with this and most other species have not been beneficial to the animals.

Plate 1. Four dolphins swimming. Flip Nicklin and Minden Pictures.

Plate 2. A dolphin starts to surface. Flip Nicklin and Minden Pictures.

Plate 3. Misha and Echo before their reintroduction to Tampa Bay. Randall S. Wells, Chicago Zoological Society.

Plate 4. Two dolphins, open-mouthed in shallow water. Flip Nicklin and Minden Pictures.

Plate 5. A view from overhead of dolphins swimming. Flip Nicklin and Minden Pictures.

Plate 6. A dolphin's face shows the famous "smile." Flip Nicklin and Minden Pictures.

Plate 7. A leaping adult male dolphin named Blackstripe Leadcrease. Randall S. Wells, Chicago Zoological Society.

Plate 8. Dolphins swimming. Randall S. Wells, Dolphin Biology Research Institute.

Plate 9. A dolphin calf leaps clear of the water. Kristi Fazioli, Dolphin Biology Research Institute.

Plate 10. Dolphins can play rough! William Carr, Dolphin Biology Research Institute.

Plate 11. Dolphins strand feeding in South Carolina. Flip Nicklin and Minden Pictures.

Plate 12. A group of dolphins surfacing. Flip Nicklin and Minden Pictures.

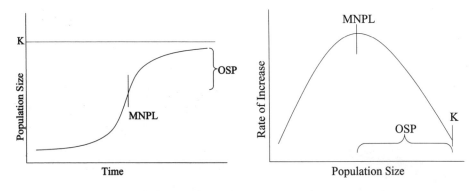

Fig. 87. Optimum sustainable population (OSP) for a particular stock is defined by the Marine Mammal Protection Act as the range of population sizes between the maximum net productivity level (MNPL) and the carrying capacity (K) of the environment. OSP can be represented graphically in different ways. Samantha D. Eide.

million animals. If all a manager knew about the direct harvest or incidental take in fishing nets of that species was that 2,000 animals a year were killed, the manager might be excused for not showing undue alarm. After all, 2,000 out of 1 million represents a reduction of only 0.2 percent, a level that is likely to be far less than the level of recruitment for a healthy species or population. However, lack of action would not be excusable if the following additional information were available: (1) of the 1 million total animals, about 900,000 occupy and interbreed in just one geographic area (that is, represent a single stock); (2) the other 100,000 animals exist in ten geographically and genetically isolated groups of animals (that is, ten separate stocks) of about 10,000 animals each; and (3) the take of 2,000 animals a year comes from just one of the small stocks. The more complete information on stock sizes and on locations of take would permit the manager to focus on an issue to prevent overexploitation, and perhaps extinction, of a particular stock for which the annual removal of 2,000 animals represented 20 percent of the population.

In the case of bottlenose dolphins, reliable population estimates are unavailable for most stocks or populations. We know that *Tursiops* is extremely abundant in certain large-scale geographic areas of the world: approximately 243,500 in the eastern tropical Pacific Ocean, nearly 317,000 in the northwestern Pacific Ocean, and up to 45,000 inshore of the 100 fathom contour in the Gulf of Mexico.[3] Breaking the abundance estimates in waters of the Gulf of Mexico down into units that could represent different stocks,

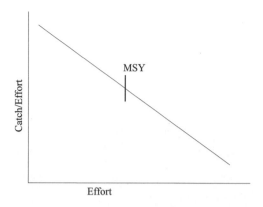

Fig. 88. Maximum sustainable yield (MSY) may be calculated in a variety of ways—all of which leave something to be desired. One way, shown here, reflects the occasional lack of use of biological data to calculate catch levels. Note that the axes incorporate economic measures, not biological data for the species in question. The use of MSY has contributed to overharvest of many species. Samantha D. Eide.

scientists have suggested the following: 3,554 dolphins in bays and sounds of the Gulf of Mexico; about 7,690 animals in coastal waters; and approximately 22,496 dolphins in waters of the continental shelf.[4]

Thus, there are several hundred thousand, and perhaps more than 1 million, bottlenose dolphins worldwide. As noted above, however, it would be dangerous to manage dolphins based on such numbers for several reasons. First, some populations of dolphins are quite small (for example, surveys suggest only a few tens to hundreds of dolphins in specific embayments in the southeastern United States).[5] In addition, the small populations may not mix extensively with other populations of dolphins—that is, they may be discrete stocks/management units. It has also been found that in some areas, such as the southwest coast of Britain,[6] small groups of bottlenose dolphins have reestablished residency after a relatively long period in which they were absent, and such small "founder groups" are particularly vulnerable. Finally, recall from chapter 2 that both molecular biologists and morphologists indicate that scientists are unclear regarding the status of the entire species, *Tursiops truncatus*, not to mention what constitutes a particular stock.[7] Thus, "it is not clear whether the considerable variability in morphology, habitat, feeding behavior, and social structure among populations reflects genuine phylogenetic separations or merely the ecological plasticity of a widely distributed single species."[8]

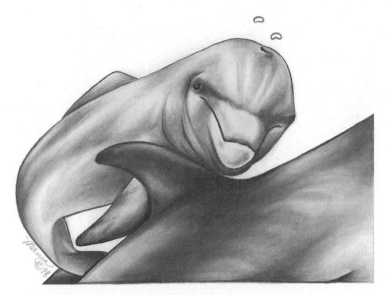

Fig. 89. A dolphin blowing bubbles. Marya Willis-Glowka.

Just as the Marine Mammal Protection Act encourages management of stocks or population stocks, the Endangered Species Act allows populations or stocks, not necessarily entire species, to be designated as threatened or endangered. For example, in 1997 the western stock of Steller sea lions was designated as endangered due to sustained and dramatic population declines, whereas the more stable eastern stock of the species continued to be classified as threatened.[9]

For conservation and management purposes, then, it is important to differentiate stocks of bottlenose dolphins and to determine how and how seriously individual stocks are impacted. Defining stocks, however, is not always as easy as it sounds.

The question of the discreteness of dolphin stocks came to a head following the 1987–88 die-off along the mid-Atlantic coast of the United States. As noted in chapter 1, a variety of potential causative agents were identified, the most recent being a morbillivirus.[10] More than 740 animals perished in the event, although the exact number of dead animals could not be determined because the number of unrecovered carcasses could not be estimated. However, scientists estimated that at least 50 percent of the "coastal migratory stock" of bottlenose dolphins between New Jersey and Florida perished in the die-off, and that this represented more than a tenfold increase in strandings in that coastal region.[11] As a result, the coastal migratory stock was considered to be below its optimum sustainable population, a finding that automatically caused the stock to be declared depleted under the provisions of the Marine Mammal Protection Act. This designation went into effect in April 1993.

The definition of a single "coastal migratory stock" hinged in part on perceptions about the timing and geographic scope of the die-off itself. One interpretation was that the die-off affected a group of animals that moved seasonally up and down the coast, affecting animals off the coast of Florida in cooler weather and those off the New Jersey coast, and even off Long Island, in warm months.[12] Two other stocks of dolphins along the mid-Atlantic coast were identified (an "offshore stock" and a "resident coastal stock"), but they were not considered to have been affected by the die-off and, hence, were neither recommended nor listed as depleted.[13] Especially in terms of differentiating the two coastal stocks, available scientific evidence was sparse.[14] Based on uncertainty regarding stock structure, some people and agencies questioned the appropriateness of declaring a stock of dolphins to be depleted off the Atlantic seaboard.

Fig. 90. Three dolphins swimming in the shallows. Flip Nicklin and Minden Pictures.

Fig. 91. Two dolphins swimming closely together. Flip Nicklin and Minden Pictures.

When a stock occupying waters of the United States is listed as depleted, the Marine Mammal Protection Act requires that a conservation plan be prepared. However, the National Marine Fisheries Service (the agency responsible for bottlenose dolphins and other cetaceans) found that "little is known regarding the biology, or the factors that affect the abundance, distribution or current population trends of the migratory stock,"[15] making it difficult to develop informed conservation guidelines or to judge when the stock might be de-listed. Finally, the service issued a contract to three independent scientists (Drs. D. A. Pabst, R. S. Wells, and A. J. Read) to develop a comprehensive bottlenose dolphin conservation plan by late 1999.

In 1994 amendments to the Marine Mammal Protection Act required the responsible federal agencies in charge of marine mammals (recall that, for dolphins this agency is the National Marine Fisheries Service) to do the following: (1) better define sizes and geographic ranges of stocks of marine mammals; (2) provide a minimum population estimate, current and maximum net productivity rates, and current population trends in size of stocks; (3) estimate the annual human-related mortality by source and location;

(4) calculate the maximum number of animals that can be removed annually due to human activities from each stock, a number called the potential biological removal, or PBR; and (5)designate stocks for which the actual takes exceed the PBR as "strategic stocks" and develop a take reduction plan.[16] At the outset, the key to accomplishing these imposing requirements is to be able to accurately define stocks. For bottlenose dolphins, this created real problems in many locations, especially along the U.S. Atlantic coast, where (as a great understatement!) "the current population delineations for bottlenose dolphins in the western Atlantic have not yet achieved this level of precision."[17]

Compounding the issue along the U.S. Atlantic coast and elsewhere is the fact that human activities, especially fishing, continue to remove tens of dolphins a year from inshore waters (see chapter 8); for example, in recent years human interactions have caused the death of at least 28 percent of all dolphins found stranded along the coast of North Carolina.[18] The questions must be addressed soon: Is take from certain dolphin stocks already exceeding PBR, and, if so, how can the take be reduced?

The questions of stock structure and discreteness are being addressed using a variety of research techniques.[19] One of the most obvious bits of evidence that animals come from separate stocks involves morphometrics, or analysis of anatomy of the individuals. This technique has been used by a number of scientists to help differentiate between inshore and offshore stocks of bottlenose dolphins in different areas of the world;[20] among other things, the former generally tend to be smaller and less robust than the latter.

Morphometric analyses have been conducted for some time, but some other techniques may provide better resolution to answer whether animals come from different stocks. Photo identification of individual dolphins (using naturally occurring marks or freeze branding) may provide important insight,[21] especially when results of a number of independent studies are combined into a central catalog, as is occurring in the southeastern United States. Such studies permit assessment of individual and group ranging patterns[22] and extent of migrations,[23] thereby facilitating an understanding of the extent to which adjacent or even geographically distant dolphins may mix.

Analysis at the molecular level (proteins or nuclear or mitchondrial genes) is also a powerful tool to differentiate populations or stocks of *Tursiops*.[24] In addition, scientists can sometimes infer that animals come from different stocks by comparing feeding habits, either by examination of gut contents[25] or by assessing the fats[26] or isotope ratios in body tissues;[27] the latter approaches are still being developed but appear to have immense potential in defining food habits, trophic levels, and perhaps stock discreteness. Another interesting, novel approach involves using toxicants or toxicant ratios in tissues to differentiate stocks;[28] this technique has been used to distinguish harbor porpoise stocks along the Pacific coast of the United States.[29]

To date, the available information and analyses thereof have been insufficient to document the extent to which bottlenose dolphins represent different stocks, or even different species or genera. In a recent review, scientists noted that (1) genetic differences exist between inshore and offshore dolphins in some oceans of the world; and (2) inshore groups of dolphins tend to be more genetically isolated than are offshore animals.[30] In light of both the efforts being made to address stock discreteness and the easy application of modern technology, it is likely that scientists will soon understand stock structure of bottlenose dolphins and thus be able to manage and conserve those stocks much better in the near future.

Conservation Strategies and Legislation

"The time has come to develop a different working relationship between people and natural resources."[1] The past century, in particular, has witnessed consequences, in terms of species extinctions and habitat destruction, of inappropriate use of natural resources. With the worldwide human population numbering over 5.5 billion and doubling approximately every forty years (or even twice that fast in some areas), it is especially important that new approaches, and even new ethics, be applied.[2]

Human population growth, however, is not the only issue. The world economy is expanding at an even more rapid pace, from about $4 trillion in output in 1950 to more than $20 trillion forty-five years later. A staggering example concerns economic growth in China, where the economy grew by 57 percent between 1991 and 1995, raising the average income of each of the 1.2 billion citizens by more than half.[3] The combination of a burgeoning population and poorly regulated or unregulated exploitation of natural resources provides a prescription for collapse of both ecosystems and of the human enterprises dependent on those ecosystems.

The importance of and the human effects on coastal and oceanic environments are enormous. In a document prepared in the United States for the 1998 International Year of the Ocean, federal scientists noted the following:

—the country has more than 95,000 miles of coastline and more than 3.4 million square miles of ocean within its territorial seas;

—in 1996, about $590 billion of goods, representing 41 percent of the total value of foreign trade by the United States, were transported on the ocean and involved United States ports;

—each resident of the country consumed, on average, fifteen pounds of fish and shellfish in 1997;

—18 percent of the oil and 27 percent of the natural gas in the United States are products of Outer Continental Shelf activities;

—180 million people visit coasts of the United States each year, and travel and tourism is "the largest and fastest growing segment of the U.S. service industry";

—marine algae contribute about 40 percent of the total global photosynthesis;

—one out of six people in the United States has a marine-related job;

—one-third of the country's GNP is produced in coastal areas;

—by the year 2025, 75 percent of the population of the United States will inhabit coastal areas;

—in 1998, 40 percent of the country's coastal and estuarine waters were neither swimmable nor fishable due to pollution; in 1996, bacterial contamination caused the closing of or advisories for bathing beaches on more than 2,500 occasions.[4]

The figures for the United States may be shocking, but they are not unrepresentative of what is happening worldwide. In fact, it has been suggested that "by 1989, all oceanic fisheries were being fished at or beyond capacity. Of the world's 15 leading oceanic fisheries, 13 are in decline."[5]

In the face of impacts of such enormity and diversity, how does one conserve species like the bottlenose dolphin, which occupy, to at least some extent, those coastal and estuarine waters most impacted by humans and their activities? The well-known zoologist and conservationist, George Schaller, observed that "conservation problems are social and economic, not scientific, yet biologists have traditionally been expected to solve them."[6] One should not take this statement to mean that scientists and scientific data about species are irrelevant to the conservation process; on the contrary good science is essential to permit appropriate conservation options to be chosen. Perhaps it would be simpler to observe that "management of . . .

species is typically a complex matter, involving constituencies with differing priorities and different courses of action."[7] A key would be to bring those constituencies together to discuss and seek solutions to problems.

Clearly, effective conservation of dolphins must take into account a number of factors associated with both the biology and habitat needs of the species and a huge array of human activities, including many on land. We describe some of the issues in chapters 1, 8, and 9 of this book. Given the complexity of the issue, we have arranged this chapter in sections that attempt to do the following: (1) discuss what conservation in general is and why it is important; (2) present approaches to conservation of marine mammals as a group; and (3) describe ingredients necessary to conserve bottlenose dolphins, specifically.

What Is Conservation?

The term *conservation* has been used by a variety of people to mean a variety of things. An early, useful interpretation stated that goals of conservation should include both the wise use of a resource and the maintenance of that resource for future use, an idea now associated with the popular term *sustainability*.[8] The same report suggested that "in its broad definition, it [conservation] includes management measures, and means the collection and application of biological information for the purposes of increasing and maintaining the number of animals within species and populations at some optimum level with respect to their habitat. Used in this way, conservation refers to the entire scope of activities that constitute a modern scientific resource program, including but not limited to research, census, law enforcement, habitat acquisition and improvement, and periodic or total protection, as well as regulated taking."[9]

Although this definition was quite useful for its time, it lacked an appreciation of the extent to which factors other than science play a role in marine mammal conservation, or indeed of conservation of any species. That issue is integral to more recent efforts which note that "an ideal relationship between humans and nature would safeguard the viability of all biota and the ecosystems of which they are a part and on which they depend, while allowing human benefit, for present and future generations, through various consumptive and nonconsumptive uses. The challenge is to determine the appropriate balance between resource and ecosystem use on one hand and the health and quality of human life on the other. But it must be remembered that human health and prosperity ultimately depend on healthy, functioning, and diverse ecosystems."[10]

Why Conserve Species?

In 1991, Dr. Daryl Domning published a short, articulate essay entitled "Why Save the Manatee?" The beauty of his paper is that his arguments apply equally well to other species, including bottlenose dolphins. In fact, due to the shared habitat of dolphins and manatees in some parts of the world, Domning's persuasive ideas may be particularly easily transferred to the bottlenose dolphin.

Domning describes seven reasons why manatees or dolphins should be protected.[11] In increasing order of importance, they can be summarized as follows:

1. Aesthetic benefits: People enjoy and are fascinated by them and feel that the world would be a far less interesting place without them.
2. Economic benefits: People can derive economic gain from their presence. For example, as noted in chapter 9, people who conduct dolphin watching cruises without harassing the animals can make money while they educate the public and cause little to no harm to the dolphins themselves.
3. Ecological benefits: In Domning's own words, "Although scientists recognize the interdependence of species within ecosystems, we do not yet understand all the ways that manatees [or dolphins] contribute."[12] In other words, a healthy dolphin population may indicate a healthy ecosystem.
4. Genetic and biomedical benefits: In this age of genetic engineering, we have found that genes or proteins in various species can provide enormous medical or other benefits to humans. Every time a species is lost, we play Russian roulette with our own future.
5. Spiritual benefits: As relatives, through evolution, of all other organisms, dolphins and humans are, in a sense, extended family. The term *biophilia* describes the natural affinity of many people for living organisms, an affinity demonstrated by the popularity of gardening, fishing, visiting zoological parks, and camping. The survival of other species provides benefits for our own mental state.

6. Stewardship: With great power come (or should come) great responsibility and accountability. Taking care to conserve living resources is a moral obligation, independent of whether those resources can or do provide any of the benefits for humans listed above.
7. Is there any excuse not to save dolphins?

Domning closes by wondering why, if there are so many reasons to save other species, our species has so much trouble actually doing it. He challenges current and future leaders to change the status quo in terms of how we treat other species, and he concludes by stating: "Like it or not, we will be judged by historians of the future, and judged to a great extent on our answer to one question: Are we willing to share our space with manatees and other species, even if it requires us to make sacrifices and limit the number of people who can live and play here? The politically easy answer to this question is the wrong answer."[13]

General Approaches to Marine Mammal Conservation

Although a number of authors have offered thoughts regarding conservation of marine mammals, a chapter by Meffe, Perrin, and Dayton provides an up-to-date "amalgamation and integration of biological, ecological, economic, sociological, political and institutional knowledge that must be brought to bear on the many issues facing marine mammal conservation."[14] It is important to note that their general principles, as outlined below, provide a general framework, not a specific set of criteria. Given both the uncertainty associated with ecological processes and the vast range of variables associated with human and natural activities in any particular location, conservation planning for any particular species or area must be carefully and appropriately tailored. The guiding principles to bear in mind as one approaches marine mammal conservation issues include the following:

1. The size of and resource consumption by the earth's expanding human population impair or prevent efforts to conserve marine mammals.
2. One can not effectively conserve marine mammal populations without knowledge of both the species itself and the ecosystem(s) of which it is a component, such that anthropogenic impacts do not exceed natural boundaries of variation. This principle can be addressed by a

combination of several approaches. First, manage total effects of activities on the ecosystem. Additionally, strive to identify and protect geographic areas, species, and processes that are especially important to conservation. People must also minimize the extent to which natural areas become fragmented and attempt to maintain natural processes at "normal" scales. The integrity of food webs must be maintained as well. Management should occur at the population or stock level, rather than at the level of the species, and maintaining genetic variability in populations should be a priority. Finally, people should attempt to understand nonlinearity of biological processes and critical thresholds and synergisms in biological systems.

3. Humans are components of ecosystems, and human interests (stakeholders) must be recognized and represented in conservation decisions. Several actions may be useful to promote this approach. Planners can create incentives by assigning property rights and decision making to the local or community level whenever possible. Regulators should ensure that both property rights and institutions consider and are consistent with conservation. We must try to minimize adverse impacts of conservation strategies and decisions on people whose livelihood is directly affected. People need to develop conflict resolution mechanisms. At the outset of negotiations, procedures and criteria to guide decision making must be set in place to avoid the possibility of undue influence by special interests. It is important to foster a system in which science and policy making can be done independently of the actual users of marine mammal resources. Both scientists and others involved in planning should understand that science is an important, but not the only, factor involved in effective conservation. Finally, we must strive to create institutions that have the appropriate temporal and spatial scales (that is, are consistent with ecological characteristics) and that are flexible, problem oriented, accountable, team oriented, interdisciplinary, and adaptive.

4. Assessment of a marine mammal resource and effects of its use should precede such use or restrictions thereof. Monitoring should accompany actual use. An especially important recommendation in terms of assessment, monitoring, and putting programs into effect is to use the precautionary principle, a proactive approach by which the "burden of proof" is placed on those who potentially benefit financially from

use of resources to demonstrate that their activities will not cause undue harm to those resources or the environment. This approach, sensible as it may seem, is often not followed. Rather it may be left to the government (using taxpayer money), for example, to demonstrate that a specific activity will cause unacceptable damage.[15] Another important but misunderstood aspect of conservation is that the potential consequences of ecological uncertainty must be recognized and incorporated into conservation planning. Finally, it should be obvious by now that it is vital to develop programs that are as inclusive, interdisciplinary, and consultative as possible at the outset.

5. It bears repeating—effective conservation must involve open and ongoing communication and targeted education. The communication process should ideally involve stakeholders, decision and policy makers, and the general public.

Underlying these several guidelines are three fundamental principles: the humility principle (recognizing our human limitations), the precautionary principle (moving cautiously and conservatively), and the reversibility principle (avoiding making irreversible changes).[16] As noted at the outset of this chapter, changes need to occur in *how* we deal with living resources, and these three simple principles capture values we should bear in mind as we attempt effective conservation and wise use of resources.

We expect that, for most readers, the preceding discussion has created the impression that effective conservation can be a hopelessly tangled web. How can an individual or group make a difference in terms of marine mammal conservation?[17] First, it is important to note that dedicated, knowledgeable individuals can and do make an enormous difference in conservation efforts; our favorite example of such an individual is the late Marjory Stoneman Douglas, whose book *The Everglades: River of Grass* and other personal endeavors were instrumental in catalyzing conservation of the Florida Everglades. In addition, people anxious to promote conservation should bear in mind several simple truisms, some of which have already been mentioned: (1) treat people honestly and sincerely, and attempt to understand their perspectives; (2) err on the side of too much communication rather than too little; (3) avoid seduction by technology—common sense and pragmatism are far more important than the latest (often expensive) technology; (4) create a values system that considers more than just monetary values; (5) be inclusive rather than exclusive; (6) be farsighted and conservative, especially when dealing with K-selected species; (7) shift the burden of proof onto the user; and (8) be reasonably patient—the problems we have today were not created overnight; neither will the solutions be immediate. On the other hand, excessive patience and tolerance of inertia can be deadly.[18]

Finally, we note that a lot of conservation principles are reactive and curative in nature—that is, they deal with ways to address or fix current problems. While this approach is necessary (we certainly understand that existing problems need to be addressed), we firmly believe that successful and cost-effective conservation needs to be built around proactive and preventative measures—that is, those that prevent damage in the first place. To do this requires, among other things, more farsighted, creative leadership and more predictable, long-term funding bases than have been available in the past.

Conserving Bottlenose Dolphins

Like other marine mammals in the United States, bottlenose dolphins are covered by provisions of the Marine Mammal Protection Act of 1972. The act begins by stating that certain marine mammal population stocks or species may be jeopardized by human activities; that these species and stocks "should not be permitted to diminish beyond the point at which they cease to be a significant functioning element of the ecosystem of which they are a part" (or below the optimum sustainable population level); that scientific knowledge about these animals is inadequate; that international, cooperative efforts to conserve marine mammals should be encouraged; and that the goal of marine mammal management should be to "obtain an optimum sustainable population keeping in mind the carrying capacity of the habitat."[19] As part of the act, provisions are made to punish individuals or groups that "take" (defined in chapter 1) marine mammals with fines of up to $20,000 and periods of incarceration up to one year in duration.

The idea of management to obtain optimum sustainable populations (OSP) is relatively new, and the Marine Mammal Protection Act of 1972, as the first law to endorse such an approach, was quite enlightened.[20] Historically, and to some extent even today, the approach to species management was to achieve maximum sustainable yield, or MSY.

Fig. 92. A dolphin peeks at the camera. Flip Nicklin and Minden Pictures.

Fig. 93. A leaping dolphin. Randall S. Wells, Chicago Zoological Society.

Semantics are very revealing. Optimum means best; maximum means most. Population is what is left in the wild; yield is what is taken from nature. Thus management with OSP as the goal tries to leave behind what is best, whereas managing for MSY tries to remove as much as possible. Both approaches attempt sustainability—to be achievable year after year.

Application of a maximum sustainable yield approach can decimate populations and species. In its worst form, MSY presents the following problems: (1) it can be calculated based on economic data more than on biological data (for example, demographic data for a population); (2) it is designed for species with high fecundity (that is, r-selected species; chapter 5), which can recover relatively easily from overharvest, but it is often merrily applied to K-selectors such as marine mammals, whose life history attributes prevent easy recovery; (3) it does not necessarily anticipate natural fluctuation, and when populations are at naturally low levels even r-selectors can be decimated (for example, Peruvian anchoveta);[21] (4) it is based on a single species approach, even though it is well known that changes in populations of target species affect food webs and ecosystem dynamics; (5) bycatch may often exceed take of target species (for example, bycatch levels approximately ten to fifteen times by weight that of the target catch by some shrimp trawlers);[22] and (6) animals "taken off the top" don't really matter to the health and well-being of populations. Altogether, MSY approaches management, especially of K-selected species' using assumptions that are anything but conservative—the result has been the regular overexploitation of species.

The use of an OSP approach is far more appropriate. Formulaically, one can consider that:

$$\text{OSP} = \text{MSY} + \begin{array}{c}\text{Biological} \\ \text{Data}\end{array} + \begin{array}{c}\text{Ecological} \\ \text{Data}\end{array} + \begin{array}{c}\text{Socioeconomic} \\ \text{Data}\end{array}$$

Thus, to implement an OSP plan (sometimes called a best-use plan), one must incorporate information about directed takes (MSY), about the biology of the target species, about the ecosystem occupied by the species, and about other socioeconomic activities in the area (both consumptive and nonconsumptive) besides directed take. The accumulation and integration of such diverse data solve the problems mentioned above with MSY.

The OSP approach is clearly more consistent than is MSY with modern species conservation efforts which bring together all the "stakeholders." Interestingly enough, MSY presumes that the best use of species is to harvest them. For OSP the best use of a species may involve zero harvest (for example, whale watching may be judged better for all parties concerned than whale harvesting).

If OSP is the wiser option for species conservation (especially for K-strategists for which conservatism is essential), why is MSY still used so frequently? There are two fundamental reasons: First, implementation of OSP requires a lot of data, which can be expensive and time consuming to accumulate and integrate. Second, in the absence of such data, economic interests that benefit people in the short term from take of a species may predominate. As time goes on, our knowledge of species biology, ecosystem function, and consumptive and nonconsumptive uses of resources will increase to the point where OSP can be implemented more and more frequently and effectively.

Bottlenose dolphins are automatically covered by the various specific provisions of the Marine Mammal Protection Act. However, as noted earlier (chapter 9), the so-called coastal migratory stock of dolphins along the south Atlantic coast of the United States was so severely reduced in size as a result of the 1987–88 die-off that it was declared "depleted" under the act. As a consequence, the National Marine Fisheries Service is required to develop a conservation plan for that stock.[23]

For bottlenose dolphins, the development and implementation of an effective conservation plan that includes all relevant stakeholders was hampered by several factors, among them a paucity of data on stocks (see chapter 9) and limited historical cooperation among the various concerned parties (for example, state and federal agencies, fishermen, scientists, conservationists). This situation stands in opposition to the more optimal one involving manatees in Florida,[24] in which a number of individuals, state and federal agencies, and other organizations have worked together to promote recovery of manatees and their habitat.

A tool that has been used with great success in the management of manatees and their habitat in Florida and that is being applied to management of certain Alaskan marine mammals is called Geographic Information Systems, or GIS.[25] A GIS involves computer hardware and software and a variety of geographically referenced data that can be displayed simultaneously to clarify areas where conflicts may exist between human activities and natural resources (for example, pupping locations for protected species; areas where coastal nutrients could be impacted). The beauty of GIS is that it provides a vehicle whereby non-experts (for example, legislators or other decision makers) can easily see where conflicts between human activities and conservation of natural resources may exist and take steps to minimize those conflicts.

The use of GIS for dolphins is still in its infancy. Although several groups have started using GIS in their dolphin research, at Eckerd College on the central west coast of Florida, interactive work between students and faculty doing marine mammalogy and computer science have permitted the development of a reasonably comprehensive GIS database that includes habitat features, locations and behaviors of dolphins, and locations of certain human activities.[26] Although a number of additional databases need to be added, the use of GIS for conservation of dolphins and their habitat is under way.

The 1994 amendments to the Marine Mammal Protection Act required that the National Marine Fisheries Service and the Fish and Wildlife Service develop an assessment for each stock of marine mammal found in waters of the United States. Originally, 145 stock assessments were done.[27] Nearly one-third of the 145 stocks were initially classified as strategic stocks.[28] Where such a designation is made and where fisheries are involved that frequently or occasionally kill or seriously injure dolphins,[29] a take reduction plan is required.

As we noted in chapter 9, stock discreteness in bottlenose dolphins is very uncertain; nonetheless, more than thirty stocks of *Tursiops* were designated as strategic stocks by the National Marine Fisheries Service. One stock, the coastal migratory stock along the southeastern coast of the United States, was automatically designated as strategic due to its depleted status following the 1987–88 epizootic. In at least some other cases, minimum abundance estimates for localized populations of dolphins were small enough that a single take caused the PBR level to be exceeded.

The take reduction planning process is the point at which science, policy, economics, sociology, and other forces become focused on conservation of dolphins. Specifically, teams should include members representing federal and state agencies, fishery management councils, fishery commissions, academic and scientific institutions or groups, environmental organizations, commercial or recreational fishermen, and appropriate native organizations—in other words, all the stakeholders. In addition, draft take reduction plans are to be published in the *Federal Register* for public review and comment. Assisting in the plan-development process by providing scientific data or insight are regional Scientific Review Groups—SRGs.

The Atlantic SRG has been the most actively involved in assessing status of and guiding conservation of bottlenose dolphins in the United States. Among other things, the SRG has pushed hard to clarify the ambiguity of dolphin stock structure. In addition, the SRG has worked hard to better identify those fisheries that occasionally or frequently kill or injure dolphins; in particular the Gulf of Mexico purse seine fishery for menhaden has recently been considered to be a more serious threat to bottlenose dolphins than was originally believed.[30] Another critical component to dolphin conservation articulated by the Atlantic SRG had to do with the proliferation of enterprises involving swimming with or feeding of dolphins by the public. As a result, the National Marine Fisheries Service developed better public awareness programs and added enforcement staff.

Despite some progress made by the Atlantic Scientific Review Group, there has not been a take reduction team formed for any of the thirty-plus strategic stocks of bottlenose dolphins in the United States. To be sure, the National Marine Fisheries Service has catalyzed the formation of such teams for other stocks of marine mammals whose status appears to be more precarious than is the case for most *Tursiops* stocks. However, the issues facing dolphin stocks in the United States and elsewhere are varied and, in some cases, expanding. They need to be addressed thoroughly and quickly.

The preceding discussion is centered on dolphin conservation and relevant legislation in the United States. There is also protective legislation in other parts of the world where bottlenose dolphins are found. The following discussion makes no attempt to be comprehensive (a discussion of all protective legislation in all countries where *Tursiops* exists would fill an entire additional book). We try simply to provide a little background for countries where the species has been well studied.

For example, in Australia, marine mammals are protected by a number of acts and regulations promulgated at the commonwealth, state, and territory levels, not to mention by the international treaties and agreements (for example, CITES) in which Australia is involved.[31] Within three nautical miles of the coast, dolphins are the responsibility of state conservation agencies, and from that point out to 200 miles offshore, they are protected, along with other marine mammals, under the commonwealth's National Parks and

Fig. 94. Swimming dolphins. Marya Willis-Glowka.

Wildlife Conservation Act of 1975. In addition, the Environment Protection and Biodiversity Conservation Bill of 1998 (also at the commonwealth level) applies to waters up to 200 nautical miles offshore and has implications for environmental impact assessments, conservation of biodiversity and, specifically, conservation of endangered species, and management of protected areas.[32]

The multiple authorities with jurisdiction over species such as dolphins are further illustrated by considering waters of the Great Barrier Reef, which are managed by the Great Barrier Reef Marine Park Authority and the

Queensland Department of Environment. The multiple levels of protection of marine mammals, including bottlenose dolphins, in Australia create a complexity that may actually hinder some conservation efforts, and "there is an obvious need for a more integrated and coordinated approach to the management of marine mammals in Australian waters."[33]

Under the authority of the National Parks and Wildlife Conservation Act, conservation plans may be prepared to provide protection to particular species or groups of species. Such plans include "The Action Plan for Cetaceans," published by Environment Australia's Endangered Species Program, and "The Plan for the Conservation and Management of Whales and Dolphins (Order Cetacea)," prepared by Queensland's Department of Environment.[34]

In the United Kingdom, bottlenose dolphins and other marine mammals are also covered by a number of acts, including the Wildlife and Countryside Act of 1981, which protects these species from taking and harassment. In addition, a European Union Habitats Directive extends protection of cetaceans to include some protection of their habitats.[35] Conservation of bottlenose dolphins, specifically, is "in a state of turmoil" as efforts are underway to create Special Areas for Conservation for bottlenose dolphins occupying Cardigan Bay, Wales, and Moray Firth, Scotland.[36] These locations encompass part of the range of the two largest known *Tursiops* populations in the United Kingdom.

In South Africa, another location where bottlenose dolphins have been studied well, protective legislation has also recently been revised. The Marine Living Resources Act of 1998 has specific provisions relevant to dolphins.[37] For example, except in cases where a permit is obtained, people may not collect, kill, attempt to kill, keep or maintain control over, possess, feed, or swim with a dolphin or porpoise. In addition, harassment or disturbance is forbidden, and these activities include driving a vessel through a school of dolphins or porpoises. Without a permit, possession of parts or products of these animals is also against the law. In fact, the primary way in which persons without permits may interact with dolphins or porpoises in South Africa involves helping beached, entangled, or entrapped animals.

It should be clear that dolphins are protected, to varying degrees and at least on paper, in various parts of the world. Although a number of chapters in this book have dealt to at least some extent with issues germane to conservation of dolphins around the world, we highlight here a couple of issues, one that is obvious and one more subtle. The obvious one is the need to identify habitat features essential to maintaining healthy dolphin populations and then to prevent those features from deteriorating. Pollution (via chemicals, discarded fishing gear, or noise), overfishing or other disruption of food webs, or simple disturbance can, either singly or cumulatively, prevent or at least hinder species conservation. Even species as plastic in their behaviors as the bottlenose dolphin need certain fundamental habitat attributes to remain intact for survival.

The less obvious ingredient in many species conservation programs involves captive facilities. As we discussed in chapter 8, the issue of captive maintenance of dolphins is quite controversial. However, zoological parks play an important role in the conservation of many species.[38] The only surviving members of some species exist in these parks; and for other species, the vast majority of the remaining animals survive in captivity as their natural habitat shrinks or disappears in the face of human intrusions. In the case of the golden lion tamarin (a type of primate), successful captive breeding programs have allowed reintroduction of animals into natural areas where danger of hunting and habitat destruction are minimal.

As we noted earlier, captive facilities provide opportunities to study aspects of species' biology that are difficult to assess in the wild. This is certainly the case with cetaceans such as the bottlenose dolphin. And it is also true that such knowledge can contribute to the successful conservation of free-ranging animals.

One benefit of captive maintenance of bottlenose dolphins that is particularly subtle relates to the extent to which knowledge of that species' biology and husbandry can contribute to conservation of other small odontocetes. For example, scientists considering the desirability of creating a captive breeding colony of the nearly extinct but poorly studied Yangtse River dolphin, or baiji, noted the utility of having extensive data on maintenance of the bottlenose dolphin.[39]

Certainly development of captive colonies of cetaceans is not the solution to their conservation. However, in the presence of high mortality in the wild and the deterioration or elimination of natural habitat, captivity may, in the short run, be the only hope some species have. Ultimately, of course, the answer is to maintain remaining natural areas and restore degraded areas so that no species in the future faces the choice of captivity or extinction.

Conclusion

In the United States, the species of cetacean that would come to mind for most people asked to name a marine mammal would probably be the bottlenose dolphin. Prominent in coastal waters and in oceanaria, and even the subject of television documentaries and the star of reruns of *Flipper,* the bottlenose is a species that most people assume we know well. It is also a species that most people assume is surviving well in the wild.

We have tried in this book to demonstrate that scientists do, in fact, know a lot about the bottlenose dolphin, but that important gaps in scientific knowledge of the species exist. We have also shown that not all bottlenose dolphins are equal—they look different, they occupy different habitats, and they are impacted by different human activities, some of which can be lethal.

Although survival of the bottlenose is certainly not jeopardized to the extent of some other cetaceans, such as right whales and the little baiji, we are concerned nonetheless about the bottlenose. It occupies waters where it is exposed to a variety of factors—noise, chemicals, physical disturbance, reduction of prey, entanglement in nets and fishing lines—that can debilitate animals or even kill them quickly and violently or slowly and insidiously. Unless we understand and mitigate the consequences of so many factors, the status of bottlenose dolphins, too, may become critical.

In a world where conservation issues tend to be addressed due to their perceived urgency, we worry that species not in desperate straits may be ignored until they, too, reach that level. Now is the time to create proactive, farsighted programs to conserve bottlenose dolphins and the ecosystems on which their survival depends. Unfortunately, history suggests that unless aggressive steps are taken to safeguard bottlenose dolphins or other species from pressures caused by humans, they may one day be the focus of paleontological rather than biological inquiry.

Glossary

aerobic: in the presence of oxygen; aerobic metabolism is much more efficient and productive energetically than is anaerobic (without oxygen present) metabolism.

altruism: behavior that can or does jeopardize survival of an individual for the benefit of others.

Animal and Plant Health Inspection Service (APHIS): Federal agency responsible for care and well-being of marine mammals (and other animals) in captivity; establishes and enforces standards and guidelines.

archeocetes: a primitive, extinct group of whales from which modern forms evolved.

axial: along the body's axis, or midline.

bends: a potentially lethal condition that arises in human divers from breathing air under conditions of elevated pressures; also called decompression sickness.

bradycardia: slowing of the heart rate (and metabolic rate) associated with diving in some animals.

carrying capacity (K): a measure of the number of organisms of a particular species that a particular environment can sustain; carrying capacity depends on a number of factors (food availability, predators, climate, etc.) and is not a constant.

cerebellum: a large region of the hindbrain that coordinates muscle movements and posture.

cerebrum: in humans and dolphins (among others), a large, convoluted region of the forebrain associated with memory, cognition, and "intelligence."

cetacean: any whale, dolphin, or porpoise.

community: a regional society of individuals that share ranges, social associates, and gene pools.

delphinid: a taxonomic group that includes the true dolphins, such as the bottlenose; the group also includes killer and pilot whales.

echolocation: the ability, possessed by bats and some cetaceans, to produce high-frequency clicks that can be detected and analyzed/interpreted when they bounce off objects; often equated to sonar.

encephalization quotient (EQ): a measure of the relative size of a species' brain; computed by comparing actual brain size to the expected brain size for a species of a particular body weight; an EQ over 1.0 signifies that a species has a larger than expected brain for its size.

endotherm: an animal that derives its body heat from internal sources (metabolism), rather than from external ones; often used interchangeably with the term *warm blooded*.

epimeletic: care-giving behavior.

eutherian: a placental mammal, such as humans.

fecundity: actual or potential reproductive output.

group (or school or herd): a number of individuals, usually of the same species, often engaged in similar activities or moving in the same general direction; may be stable over time or change composition over periods ranging from minutes to weeks.

growth layer groups (GLGs): layers in hard parts (teeth or bones) that can indicate age of individuals, once calibration of their deposition rate is known.

homeotherm: an animal that maintains a constant core body temperature.

home range: a well-defined area of regular use that provides for most, if not all, of an animal's needs.

hydrodynamic: having to do with changing forces that water or other fluids exert on an object; dolphins have a hydrodynamically favorable shape that allows them to minimize drag resulting from their movement through the water.

hyperosmotic: more concentrated than another solution; hyperosmotic urine is more concentrated than blood.

incidental take: the capture of a non-target species during harvest of a target species.

K-strategist: a species that has evolved attributes (adaptations) that facilitate maintenance of a stable population, the size of which hovers around the carrying capacity of the environment.

magnetite: iron-rich compound found in the brain of some cetaceans that some scientists hypothesize may provide some ability to navigate and orient using magnetic cues.

Marine Mammal Commission (MMC): the Federal agency with oversight for all marine mammal research, conservation, and enforcement activities in the United States.

Marine Mammal Protection Act (MMPA): primary legislation in the United States that focuses on understanding and conserving marine mammals; enacted in 1972; prohibits "taking" of marine mammals.

metanephric: the type of kidney found in mammals.

morbillivirus: a type of virus, similar to distemper virus in dogs and other pets; has decimated or contributed to the decimation of certain cetacean stocks.

myoglobin: respiratory pigment found in muscles; similar to hemoglobin in the blood; facilitates prolonged diving.

mysticete: a whale that, following birth, lacks teeth; instead, mysticetes possess baleen plates for filtering organisms from water.

National Marine Fisheries Service (NMFS): the primary federal agency charged with research, conservation, and enforcement of relevant laws for dolphins and most other marine mammals in waters of the United States.

odontocete: a so-called toothed whale, even though teeth do not necessarily protrude through the gums in females of some species; includes a variety of whales, dolphins, and porpoises.

optimum sustainable population (OSP): the goal, as stated in the Marine Mammal Protection Act, of maintaining marine mammal stocks at levels between their maximum net productivity level (MNPL) and the carrying capacity of the environment (K).

organochlorines: lipid-soluble toxicants, including PCBs and DDT, that can accumulate over time in blubber or other fat reserves.

perinatal: around the time of birth.

population: a group of organisms that occupies the same region and inter-breeds; a closed reproductive group.

porpoising: a behavior in which fast-swimming small cetaceans rapidly surface as they move forward, with much of their bodies appearing at the surface, and generally with much white water; this is done presumably to save energy by reducing drag.

phylogeny: evolutionary relationships among organisms.

primiparous: giving birth for the first time.

reniculate: the type of metanephric kidney found in dolphins and most other marine mammals; composed of a number of small, functionally discrete units.

rete: a network of small blood vessels or nerves.

r-strategist: a species that has evolved attributes (adaptations) that allow it to maximize rate of increase.

signature whistles: individually distinctive sounds produced by bottlenose dolphins to allow recognition of different individuals within a community and to help maintain group cohesion.

stock: basically the same as a population; a term established for wildlife management purposes.

subgroup: a distinct cluster of individuals within a group; often members are of similar age, sex, or reproductive condition.

take: defined in the Marine Mammal Protection Act to mean to harass, hunt, capture, or kill, or to attempt to harass, hunt, capture, or kill any marine mammal; prohibited under the Act.

telescoping: modifications (via elongation or overlapping) of some bones of the cetacean skull, resulting in a streamlined skull with the nares positioned to permit easy breathing while keeping most of the head submerged.

thermoregulation: maintenance of body temperature at the optimum level for an organism to survive.

toxicant: an anthropogenic chemical that can act as a poisonous agent.

toxin: a noxious or poisonous substance that is naturally produced.

viviparous: giving birth to live young.

Notes

1. A Crisis at the Turn of the Twenty-First Century?

1. Norris, "Marine Mammals and Man," 320.

2. Reeves and Mead, "Marine Mammals in Captivity."

3. Where the unmodified term *dolphin* is used in this book, it refers to the bottlenose dolphin, *Tursiops truncatus,* rather than to any of the many other species of small, toothed whales.

4. See DeMaster and Drevenak, "Survivorship Patterns in Captive Cetaceans," 297–311; and Small and DeMaster, "Acclimation to Captivity of Dolphins and Sea Lions," 510–19.

5. Of the dolphins known to be held in captivity, 416 are in facilities in the United States and 225 are in facilities outside that country. Information was provided by the National Marine Fisheries Service, personal communication to Reynolds.

6. See, for example, Brill and Friedl, "Reintroduction to the Wild for Marine Mammals," 1–16.

7. Gales and Waples, "Rehabilitation and Release of Bottlenose Dolphins," 49–59.

8. Ibid., 59.

9. The persons responsible for the unauthorized release, Richard O'Barry and Lloyd A. Good III, were found guilty of violating the Marine Mammal Protection Act and fined by federal court in 1999.

10. Marine Mammal Commission, *Annual Report to Congress 1996,* 214.

11. Described most fully by Bassos, "Reintroduction of Bottlenose Dolphins," 1–84; and Wells, Bassos-Hull, and Norris, "Experimental Return to the Wild of Two Dolphins," 51–71.

12. Wells, Bassos-Hull, and Norris, "Experimental Return to the Wild of Two Dolphins," 51–71.

13. Wilson, Thompson, and Hammond, "Skin Lesions and Physical Deformities," 243–47.

14. Lahvis et al., "Decreased Lymphocyte Responses in Dolphins," 67–72.

15. It is useful to distinguish between the terms *toxicant* and *toxin*. A toxicant is generally understood to be an anthropogenic (human-made) chemical that can act as a poisonous agent. A toxin is a noxious or poisonous substance that is naturally produced. Examples of toxicants are DDT and PCBs. Examples of toxins include brevetoxin and saxitoxin, which are produced by algae. Definitions are based on *Stedman's Medical Dictionary*, 1461–62.

16. There are a number of papers or chapters that discuss this phenomenon in a variety of marine mammal species; some especially useful references include Aguilar and Borrell, "Reproductive Transfer of Organochlorine Pollutants," 546–54; Boyd, Lockyer, and Marsh, "Reproduction in Marine Mammals," 218–86; and O'Shea, "Environmental Contaminants and Marine Mammals," 485–567.

17. Wells and Scott, "Bottlenose Dolphin," 149.

18. Vedder, "Organochlorine Pollutants in Milk," 1–35.

19. Kuss, "The Occurrence of PCBs and Chlorinated Contaminants in Dolphins," 1–100.

20. Cockcroft et al., "Organochlorines in Bottlenose Dolphins," 207–17.

21. Wells and Scott, "Bottlenose Dolphin," 152–53. Note that the interbirth interval may be slightly shorter or much longer than the three-year figure used in the text. Wells and Scott suggest a range of two to eleven years.

22. Ridgway and Reddy, "Organochlorines in Milk Collected at Varied Stages of Lactation," 609–14.

23. Stern et al., "PCBs and Other Organochlorine Contaminants in White Whales," 245–59.

24. O'Shea, "Environmental Contaminants and Marine Mammals," 485.

25. A series of studies on immune responses of harbor seals was done by De Swart, Ross, Reijnders, Osterhaus, and colleagues in the Netherlands. Among the papers worth consulting on the topic are De Swart et al., "Mitogen and Antigen Induced Cell Responses," 217–30; De Swart et al., "Impairment of Immunological Functions in Harbour Seals," 155–59; De Swart et al., "Impaired Immunity of Harbour Seals," 823–28; and Ross et al., "Contaminant-Induced Immunotoxicology in Harbour Seals," 157–69.

26. Safe, "PCBs and PBBs," 319–25.

27. O'Shea et al., "Organochlorine Pollutants in Small Cetaceans," 35–46.

28. DeLong, Gilmartin, and Simpson, "Premature Births in California Sea Lions," 1168–70.

29. O'Shea and Brownell, "California Sea Lion Populations and DDT Contamination," 159–64.

30. Subramanian et al., "Reductions in Testosterone Levels by PCBs in Dall's Porpoises," 643–46.

31. Reijnders, "Reproductive Failure in Common Seals," 456–57.

32. O'Shea, "Environmental Contaminants and Marine Mammals," 500–503.

33. De Guise, Lagace, and Beland, "Tumors in St. Lawrence Beluga Whales," 444–49.

34. Ibid., 444.

35. The 1982 event is described by O'Shea et al., "An Epizootic of Florida Manatees," 165–79. The 1996 die-off is best described by Bossart et al., "Brevetoxicosis in Manatees," 276–82, and Marine Mammal Commission, *Annual Report to Congress 1996*, 6–14.

36. Geraci, "Clinical Investigation of the 1987–88 Mass Mortality of Bottlenose Dolphins," 1–63.

37. Kuehl, Haebler, and Potter, "Chemical Residues in Dolphins," 1071–84.

38. Ibid., 1082.

39. Schulman et al., "Studies of Bottlenose Dolphins from the 1987–1988 Epizootic," 288–95.

40. Lipscomb et al., "Morbilliviral Disease in Bottlenose Dolphins," 567–71.

41. Duignan et al., "Morbillivirus Infections in Bottlenose Dolphins," 509.

42. Definition from *Stedman's Medical Dictionary*, 477.

43. Duignan et al., "Morbillivirus Infections in Bottlenose Dolphins," 499–515.

44. Ibid., 511.

45. Definition from *Stedman's Medical Dictionary*, 468.

46. Aguilar and Borrell, "Abnormally High Polychlorinated Biphenyl Levels in Striped Dolphins," 237–47.

47. Geraci et al., "Humpback Whales Fatally Poisoned by Dinoflagellate," 1885–98.

48. Aguilar, "Die-Off Strikes Mediterranean Monk Seals," 1–3.

49. Osterhaus, "Mediterranean Monk Seal Mortality Event," 2.

50. Regardless of the cause(s) of the die-off, the seals that died were a part of the largest population of this critically endangered species, which now may number only three hundred individuals worldwide (see Aguilar, "Die-Off Strikes Mediterranean Monk Seals," 1).

51. See, for example, Smayda, "Novel and Nuisance Phytoplankton Blooms," 29–40; and Henderson, "Red Tides," 62–68.

52. Henderson, "Red Tides," 62.

53. See Reynolds, "Interactions between Dolphins and Fisheries," 1–38.

54. Thayer and Rittmaster, "Marine Mammal Strandings in North Carolina," 50–52.

55. The term *take* is defined in the U.S. Marine Mammal Protection Act of 1972 to mean "to harass, hunt, capture or kill, or attempt to harass, hunt, capture or kill any marine mammal. The definition appears in: Marine Mammal Commission, *The Marine Mammal Protection Act of 1972 as Amended*, 7.

56. Marine Mammal Commission, *Annual Report to Congress 1996*, 98.

57. Wells, Hofmann, and Moors, "Entanglement and Mortality of Dolphins in Fishing Gear," 647–50.

58. The topic is reviewed by Boyd, Lockyer, and Marsh, "Reproduction in Marine Mammals,"218–86. Some of the seminal papers on the topic are by Lockyer; for example: "The Relationship between Body Fat, Food Resources, and Reproductive Energy," 343–

61; "The Role of Fat Reserves in Ecology of Fin and Sei Whales," 183–203; and "The Importance of Biological Parameters in Population Assessments," 22–31.

59. Eide, "Dolphin Distribution and the Florida State Ban on Commercial Netting," 1–57.

60. Ibid.; Eide and Reynolds, "Dolphin Abundance and Presence of Calves," 38.

61. Mahmoudi, "Status and Trends in the Mullet Fishery," 1–8.

62. Muller, "Status and Trends of Florida's Marine Resources," 1–40.

63. Marine Mammal Commission, *Annual Report to Congress 1996,* 29–30.

64. Swartzman and Hofman, "The Bering Sea and Antarctic Marine Ecosystems," 14, 26.

65. Marine Mammal Commission, *Annual Report to Congress 1996,* 19–20.

66. Polovina et al., "Consequences of a Climatic Event in the Central North Pacific, 15–21.

67. Information provided by Dr. Robert E. Hueter, Mote Marine Laboratory, personal communication to Reynolds.

68. Corkeron, Morris, and Bryden, "Interactions between Bottlenose Dolphins and Sharks," 109–13.

69. Urian et al., "An Analysis of Shark Bite Scars on Bottlenose Dolphins," 139.

70. Walsh et al., "Ray Encounters as a Mortality Factor in Bottlenose Dolphins," 154–62; and McLellan, Thayer, and Pabst, "Stingray Spine Mortality in a Bottlenose Dolphin," 98–101.

71. Estes et al., "Killer Whale Predation on Sea Otters Linking Oceanic and Nearshore Ecosystems," 475.

72. Dayton et al., "Sliding Baselines: Ghosts and Reduced Expectations in Kelp Forest Communities," 309–22.

2. Bottlenose Dolphins

1. For general reviews of cetacean systematics and characteristics, see Leatherwood and Reeves, *The Sierra Club Handbook of Whales and Dolphins,* 1–302; and Reynolds, Rommel, and Odell, "Marine Mammals of the World," 1–14.

2. The derivation of the scientific name comes from Rommel, "Osteology of the Bottlenose Dolphin," 38; and Wells and Scott, "Bottlenose Dolphin," 137–38.

3. Montagu, "Descriptions of a Species That Appears To Be New," 75–82.

4. Here and elsewhere in this book, we attempt to use terminology familiar to the layperson. The technical terms one would substitute for mammals such as dolphins or humans would include the following: *eutherian* = placental; *viviparous* means giving birth to live young; *endothermic* = warm blooded; and *homeothermic* means maintaining a constant body temperature.

5. Doria, "The Dolphin Rider," 33–51.

6. Ibid., 33.

7. Ibid., 33–51.

8. Varawa, *Mind in the Waters,* 31.

9. Alpers, *Dolphins. The Myth and the Mammal,* 1–268.

10. Lockyer, "Incidents Involving Wild, Sociable Dolphins, Worldwide," 337–53.

11. Care-giving behavior is termed *epimeletic*. Self- sacrificing behavior is called *altruistic*. An interesting paper by Connor and Norris ("Are Dolphins Reciprocal Altruists?" 358–74) speculates that reciprocal altruism (that is, the trading of altruistic acts by individuals at different times) exists among dolphins. There is no solid scientific evidence that true altruism (that is, self-destructive behavior done to benefit others) occurs in dolphins. Definitions of altruism and reciprocal altruism appear in Wilson, *Sociobiology: The New Synthesis,* 578, 593.

12. Lockyer, "Incidents Involving Wild, Sociable Dolphins, Worldwide," 337–353.

13. Ibid., 338.

14. Alpers, *Dolphins. The Myth and the Mammal,* 222–37.

15. Lockyer, "Incidents Involving Wild, Sociable Dolphins, Worldwide," 340.

16. Malins, "The Dolphin Is Not Like a 'Human with Flippers,'" 5, quoting from Lilly, *The Scientist: A Novel Autobiography.*

17. Lilly, *Lilly on Dolphins,* vii.

18. Caldwell and Caldwell, "Dolphins Communicate—But They Don't Talk," 25.

19. Awbry, "Communicating with Dolphins," 233.

20. Cato and Prochaska, "Porpoise Attacking Hooked Fish Irk and Injure Fishermen," 3B, 16B.

21. Ibid., 16B. For perspective it is worth noting that landings of Florida king mackerel (*Scomberomorus cavalla*) alone in 1977 (a year after Cato and Prochaska's paper appeared) exceeded $3.6 million in value (see Reynolds, "Interactions between Bottlenose Dolphins and Fisheries," 32).

22. Leatherwood, "Feeding Behavior of Bottlenose Dolphins," 1–16.

23. Lowery, *The Mammals of Louisiana,* 341 and 346; and Reynolds, "Interactions between Bottlenose Dolphins and Fisheries," 32.

24. Wells and Scott, "Bottlenose Dolphin," 149.

25. Barros and Odell, "Food Habits of Bottlenose Dolphins," 309–28.

3. Dolphin Evolution

1. See various chapters in Thewissen, *The Emergence of Whales. Evolutionary Patterns in the Origin of Cetacea,* 1–477.

2. Barnes, "The Fossil Record and Evolutionary Relationships of the Genus *Tursiops,*" 4–6.

3. Among modern adult whales, only the odontocetes possess teeth, although in some groups such as the beaked whales, the teeth may not protrude through the gums. It is worth noting that teeth were present in archeocetes and even in the adults of some extinct mysticetes, and that modern mysticetes possess tooth buds as fetuses.

4. Barnes, Domning, and Ray, "Studies on Fossil Marine Mammals," 15–53.

5. Flower, "On Whales, Present and Past," 466–513.

6. Barnes, "The Fossil Record and Evolutionary Relationships of the Genus *Tursiops,*" 4.

7. Van Valen, "Deltatheridae, a New Order of Mammals," 1–126; and Szalay, "Origin and Evolution of the Mesonychid Condylarth Feeding Mechanism," 703–20.

8. Barnes, "The Fossil Record and Evolutionary Relationships of the Genus *Tursiops*," 4.

9. A thorough, recent review is provided by Gatesy, "Molecular Evidence for the Phylogenetic Affinities of Cetacea," 63–112.

10. For example, see Heyning, "Sperm Whale Phylogeny Revisited," 596–613.

11. Interested readers may want to consult the following references on this timely topic: Milinkovitch, Orti, and Meyer, "Revised Phylogeny of Whales," 939–48; Hasegawa and Adachi, "Phylogenetic Position of Cetaceans," 710–17; and Shimamura et al., "Molecular Evidence That Whales Form a Clade within the Even-Toed Ungulates," 666–70.

12. Graur and Higgins, "Evidence for Inclusion of Whales within the Artiodactyla," 357–64.

13. See, for example, Gatesy, "DNA Support for a Cetacea/Hippopotamidae Clade," 537–543; and Nomura and Yasue, "Genetic Relationships among Hippopotamus, Whales, and Bovine," 526–27.

14. Bradley and Reynolds, "Marine Mammal Interleukin-2," in press.

15. See series of papers by Milinkovitch and colleagues: Milinkovitch, Orti, and Meyer, "Revised Phylogeny of Whales," 346–48; Milinkovitch, Meyer, and Powell, "Phylogeny of All Major Groups of Whales," 939–48; and Milinkovitch et al., "Phylogeny Reconstruction in Cetaceans," 1817–33.

16. Adachi and Hasegawa, "Phylogeny of Whales: Dependence of the Inference on Species Sampling," 178.

17. Thewissen and Hussain, "Underwater Hearing in Whales," 444–45.

18. Barnes, Domning, and Ray, "Studies on Fossil Marine Mammals," 18–19.

19. Barnes, "The Fossil Record and Evolutionary Relationships of the Genus *Tursiops*," 5.

20. Thewissen, Hussain, and Arif, "The Origin of Aquatic Locomotion in Whales," 210–12.

21. Thewissen and Fish, "Locomotor Evolution in the Earliest Cetaceans," 489.

22. Barnes, "The Fossil Record and Evolutionary Relationships of the Genus *Tursiops*," 5–6.

23. Barnes, Domning, and Ray, "Studies on Fossil Marine Mammals," 19.

24. Ibid., 25–26.

25. Ibid., 19.

26. Ibid., 25–26.

27. As noted above, the telescoping of the dolphin skull is described in chapter 4.

28. The use of common names for species can sometimes be very misleading. In some parts of the world, *Tursiops truncatus* is called the bottlenose porpoise, even though it is classified by systematists as a true dolphin (family Delphinidae) and not a porpoise (family Phocoenidae) at all. To further confound the layperson, a large marine teleost (bony fish), *Coryphaena* spp., is also called a dolphin; this situation can be par-

ticularly distressing to patrons of seafood restaurants who see "dolphin" on the menu and assume that they are being served bottlenose dolphin.

In any event, true porpoises can be distinguished from true dolphins by the following traits: body size (porpoises are generally small, whereas some delphinids, such as the killer whale, are large); tooth shape (flattened and spade-shaped in phocoenids, conical in dolphins); presence of a distinct "beak" (indistinct or absent in porpoises, more evident in dolphins); dorsal fin shape and size (small and triangular in porpoises, but large and falcate in most delphinids); and degree of skull asymmetry (more pronounced in delphinids).

Distinctive features of the various cetacean groups are discussed in a variety of references, including Reynolds, Rommel, and Odell, "Marine Mammals of the World," 1–14.

29. As will be discussed later in this chapter, a database is being developed that suggests a need to revise systematics of the genus *Tursiops*. Lacking such a revision, many authors have historically chosen to lump all animals designated as bottlenose dolphins into a single species, namely *Tursiops truncatus*. See Leatherwood and Reeves, "Bottlenose Dolphin and Other Toothed Cetaceans," 369–70; and Leatherwood and Reeves, *The Sierra Club Handbook of Whales and Dolphins*, 221.

30. Pilleri, "Second Record of *Tursiops osennae*," 23.

31. Barnes, "The Fossil Record and Evolutionary Relationships of the Genus *Tursiops*," 18.

32. Ibid., 3–26.

33. Wells and Scott, "Bottlenose Dolphin," 140.

34. Wells et al., "Northward Extension of the Range of Bottlenose Dolphins," 421–31.

35. Ferrero and Tsunoda, "First Record of a Bottlenose Dolphin from Washington State," 302–5.

36. Kenney, "Bottlenose Dolphins off the Northeastern United States," 369–86.

37. Distribution of bottlenose dolphins is summarized by Wells and Scott, "Bottlenose Dolphin," 139–40.

38. A couple of references that document well the offshore occurrence of bottlenose dolphins include Scott and Chivers, "Distribution of Bottlenose Dolphins in the Eastern Tropical Pacific Ocean," 387–402; and Mullin et al., "Cetaceans on the Upper Continental Slope in the Gulf of Mexico," 1–109.

39. See review by Hershkovitz, "Catalog of Living Whales," 47–56.

40. Wells and Scott, "Bottlenose Dolphin," 141.

41. Three references that document this phenomenon are Hersh and Duffield, "Distinction between Offshore and Coastal Bottlenose Dolphins," 129–39; Mead and Potter, "Natural History of Bottlenose Dolphins," 165–95; and Mead and Potter, "Two Populations of Bottlenose Dolphin off the Atlantic Coast," 31–44.

42. Recent, excellent references include Curry, "Phylogenetic Relationships among Bottlenose Dolphins," 1–138; Curry and Smith, "Phylogenetic Structure of the Bottlenose Dolphin," 227–47; and LeDuc, Perrin, and Dizon, "Phylogenetic Relationships among Delphinid Cetaceans," 619–48.

4. Function and Structure

1. Vogel and Wainwright, *A Functional Bestiary: Laboratory Studies about Living Systems*, 93.

2. Norris, *The Porpoise Watcher*, 201–14.

3. Note once again that use of common names for animals can be rather confusing. Regionally, people may casually refer to true dolphins (family Delphinidae) as either dolphins or porpoises. Hence, although Norris's book is entitled *The Porpoise Watcher*, the focus is on the bottlenose and other true dolphins. See distinctions between porpoises and dolphins in chapter 3 and in Reynolds, Rommel, and Odell, "Marine Mammals of the World," 10–12.

4. Schmidt-Nielsen, *Animal Physiology: Adaptation and Environment*, 249.

5. Interestingly, humans are also among the largest of all organisms, although people are obviously much smaller than most marine mammals. Our human perspective of the world is often biased by the fact that we are large. Gould (*Ever Since Darwin*, 171–98) contains some interesting observations about the consequences of human size.

6. See review by Pabst, Rommel, and McLellan, "The Functional Morphology of Marine Mammals," 17–22.

7. Schmidt-Nielsen, *Animal Physiology: Adaptations and Environment*, 192–97.

8. Several references provide excellent background regarding the morphology of marine mammals in general, or of bottlenose dolphins specifically. Rather than citing these references repeatedly throughout this chapter, we simply note that they provided the basis for many statements made in this chapter and we suggest that interested readers consult them. They include the following: For general anatomy of marine mammals, see Pabst, Rommel, and McLellan, "The Functional Morphology of Marine Mammals," 15–72. For a thorough overview of dolphin skeletal anatomy, see Rommel, "Osteology of the Bottlenose Dolphin," 29–49. For information on structure and function of sensory systems, see Wartzok and Ketten, "Marine Mammal Sensory Systems," 117–75. In other words, if readers find information in the text for which there is no specific citation, we suggest consulting these excellent overviews.

9. An excellent overview of marine mammal physiological adaptations appears in Elsner,"Living in Water: Solutions to Physiological Problems," 73–116. As with the various references used to describe dolphin anatomy, this reference served as the basis for much of the discussion of physiology; for the sake of brevity, we note here its extensive use but do not cite it every time it was used in the text.

10. Costa and Williams, "Marine Mammal Energetics," 184.

11. Lang and Norris, "Swimming Speed of a Bottlenose Dolphin," 588–90.

12. Williams, Friedl, and Haun, "The Physiology of Bottlenose Dolphins," 39.

13. See Cockcroft and Ross,"Age, Growth and Reproduction of Bottlenose Dolphins," 289–302; and Read et al., "Patterns of Growth in Wild Bottlenose Dolphins," 107–23.

14. Hersh, Odell, and Asper, "Sexual Dimorphism in Bottlenose Dolphins," 305–15.

15. Read et al., "Patterns of Growth in Wild Bottlenose Dolphins," 118.

16. Ibid., 120.

17. See the following references: Leatherwood and Reeves, *The Sierra Club Handbook*

of *Whales and Dolphins,* 221–25; Ross and Cockcroft, "Taxonomic Status of *Tursiops aduncus,*" 101–28; Hersh and Duffield, "Distinction between Offshore and Coastal Dolphins," 129–39; and Wells and Scott, "Bottlenose Dolphin," 141–44.

18. Leatherwood and Reeves, *The Sierra Club Handbook of Whales and Dolphins,* 221.

19. Ibid., 222.

20. Ibid., 227, 242.

21. Wells and Scott, "Bottlenose Dolphin," 141.

22. Ibid., 144.

23. Barros and Odell, "Food Habits of Bottlenose Dolphins," 309–28.

24. Pabst, Rommel, and McLellan, "The Functional Morphology of Marine Mammals," 17.

25. See, for example, Dellmann, *Veterinary Histology. An Outline Text Atlas,* 253–56; and Dellmann and Brown, *Textbook of Veterinary Histology,* 459–93.

26. The technique of scooping pieces of sloughed skin from the water for genetic analyses has become widely used. For example, see Clapham, Palsboll, and Mattila, "High-Energy Behaviors in Humpback Whales as a Source of Sloughed Skin," 213–20.

27. Hicks et al., "Epidermal Growth in the Bottlenose Dolphin," 61. For an excellent review of the structure and function of the epidermis of dolphins and other toothed whales, see: Geraci, St. Aubin, and Hicks, "The Epidermis of Odontocetes: A View from Within," 3–21.

28. Hicks et al., "Epidermal Growth in the Bottlenose Dolphin," 63.

29. Pabst, Rommel, and McLellan, "The Functional Morphology of Marine Mammals," 19.

30. Pabst, "The Subdermal Connective Tissue Sheath of Dolphins," 35.

31. Zimmer, "The Dolphin Strategy," 81.

32. Worthy and Edwards, "Factors Affecting Heat Loss in a Small Temperate Cetacean and a Small Tropical Cetacean," 432–42.

33. Koopman, Iverson, and Gaskin, "Blubber Fatty Acids of the Male Harbour Porpoise," 628–39.

34. Koopman, "Distribution of the Blubber of Harbor Porpoises," 260–70.

35. Fish and Hui, "Dolphin Swimming—A Review," 181.

36. Costa and Williams, "Marine Mammal Energetics," 185–86.

37. A study by Hertel, described by Costa and Williams, "Marine Mammal Energetics," 185–86.

38. Wells, "Marine Mammals of Sarasota Bay," 9.9.

39. See, for example, Wells, Scott, and Irvine, "Social Structure of Free-Ranging Bottlenose Dolphins," 247–305; and Urian et al., "Analysis of Shark Bite Scars," 139.

40. For example, see Lockyer, McConnell, and Waters, "Biochemical Composition of Fin Whale Blubber," 2561.

41. *Lipophilic* literally means lipid loving. Lipophilic chemicals, such as certain toxicants, are those that become sequestered in compartments of the body that are rich in lipids—fatty tissues. Thus, blubber becomes a region in dolphins where, over time, one might find high concentrations of the lipophilic organochlorines. On the other hand,

not all toxicants (for example, metals) are held in fatty tissues; they might preferentially be stored in the liver or other organs.

42. Zimmer, "The Dolphin Strategy," 83.

43. Hildebrand, *Analysis of Vertebrate Structure,* 434–38.

44. See Fish and Hui, "Dolphin Swimming—A Review," 181–95.

45. Pabst, "Axial Muscles and Connective Tissues of the Bottlenose Dolphin," 51–67; and Pabst, "Intramuscular Morphology and Tendon Geometry of Swimming Muscles of Dolphins," 159–70.

46. Pabst, "Axial Muscles and Connective Tissues of the Bottlenose Dolphin," 51–67.

47. Pabst, "Intramuscular Morphology and Tendon Geometry of Swimming Muscles of Dolphins," 159–70.

48. A number of sources of information provide insight into dolphin locomotion. Interested readers should check the following: Fish, "Power Output and Propulsive Efficiency of Swimming Dolphins," 179–83; Fish, "Hydrodynamic Design and Propulsive Mode," 79–101; Fish, "Kinematics and Hydrodynamics of Odontocete Cetaceans," 2867–77; Fish and Hui, "Dolphin Swimming—A Review," 181–95; Webb, "Vertebrate Aquatic Locomotion," 709–25; Williams et al., "Travel at Low Energetic Cost by Swimming and Wave-Riding Dolphins," 821–23.

49. Fish, "Power Output and Propulsive Efficiency of Swimming Dolphins," 179.

50. Costa and Williams, "Marine Mammal Energetics," 186.

51. See, for example, Au and Weihs, "Dolphins Save Energy by Leaping," 548–50; and Blake, "Energetics of Leaping Dolphins," 61–70.

52. An excellent overview appears in Costa and Williams, "Marine Mammal Energetics," 185–87.

53. Williams et al., "Travel at Low Energetic Cost by Swimming and Wave-Riding Dolphins," 821–23.

54. When people exercise hard, their muscles may operate for some time without the benefit of oxygen. The term for this state is anaerobic. Whereas metabolism with adequate oxygen available (aerobic metabolism) breaks down food molecules completely (e.g., aerobic breakdown of glucose produces carbon dioxide and water), anaerobic metabolism produces lactate or lactic acid, which can make overused muscles sore the next day. The more lactate one develops during hard exercise, the more the muscles have had to operate relatively inefficiently, without oxygen.

Thus, by examining post-exercise lactate levels, scientists can better understand the metabolic processes being used during exercise and, in turn, the potential stresses to an animal. Other physiological measures of energetic cost or stress, as mentioned in the text include heart and respiratory rates.

55. Woodcock and McBride, "Wave-Riding Dolphins," 215–17.

56. Unless otherwise indicated, information regarding skull and skeletal anatomy comes from Rommel, "Osteology of the Bottlenose Dolphin," 29–49; the other general source of information on skeletal anatomy is Pabst, Rommel, and McLellan, "The Functional Morphology of Marine Mammals," 26–33.

57. Wall, "Limb-Bone Density and Aquatic Habits in Mammals," 197–207.

58. Ibid., 58.

59. Before embarking on the next few paragraphs, readers may want to look at figure 29, which depicts the location of some of the skull bones in both the human and the dolphin. The main message of the text and the figure is how significantly the bones of a dolphin skull have become modified to accommodate an aquatic existence.

60. Miller, "Telescoping of the Cetacean Skull," 1–62.

61. Trees that lose their leaves seasonally are said to be deciduous, whereas trees that retain leaves year-round are nondeciduous. These familiar terms are also applied to teeth. Those that are not replaced, as in dolphins, are nondeciduous teeth.

62. Kooyman, Hammond, and Schroeder, "Bronchograms and Trachograms of Seals under Pressure," 82–84.

63. Some important recent and historical references that describe the anatomy of the sound-producing structures in dolphins include the following: Au, *The Sonar of Dolphins*, 81–95; Cranford, Amundin, and Norris, "The Odontocete Nasal Complex: Implications for Sound Production," 223–85; Evans and Maderson, "Mechanisms of Sound Production in Delphinid Cetaceans," 1205–13; and Mead, "Anatomy of the External Nasal Passages and Facial Complex in the Delphinidae," 1–72.

64. Purves and Pilleri, *Echolocation in Whales and Dolphins*, 53–66.

65. The bends, also called decompression sickness, results in human divers from breathing air under conditions of elevated pressures, as occurs at depth. When this occurs for too long a time period, gases such as nitrogen may be absorbed from the lungs into the blood, and subsequently into the body tissues during the dive. As ascent occurs and surrounding pressures decrease, the gases may diffuse from the tissues and expand to form bubbles that can create problems in various parts of the body, including the nervous system and joints. Dolphins and other marine mammals avoid the bends, at least in part due to collapse of the alveoli during deep dives. This prevents absorption of gases from the lungs during the dive. Thus, nitrogen has no opportunity to build up in the body tissues in the first place.

66. Ridgway, "The Central Nervous System of the Bottlenose Dolphin," 85.

67. For an excellent overview of both the microscopic and gross anatomy of the gastrointestinal tract, see Gaskin, "Form and Function in the Digestive Tract and Associated Organs in Cetacea," 313–45.

68. Ibid., 326.

69. Ibid., 319.

70. See ibid., and Brown, Bossart, and Reynolds, "Microscopic and Immunohistologic Anatomy of the Endocrine Pancreas," 291–96.

71. As with many other topics in this chapter, much of the information regarding cetacean circulatory systems comes from Pabst, Rommel, and McLellan, "The Functional Morphology of Marine Mammals," 45–51.

72. In addition to the general review of marine mammal anatomy noted above (note 68), see Viamonte et al., "Angiography in the Dolphin and Observations on Blood Sup-

ply to the Brain," 1225–49. A *rete* is a network of small blood vessels or nerve fibers. As we use the term here, we refer specifically to vascular retia. The term *rete mirabile* is also used specifically to indicate networks of blood vessels.

73. Nagel et al., "Rete Mirabile of Dolphin: Its Pressure-Damping Effect," 898–900.

74. Palmer and Weddell, "Structure, Innervation and Function of the Skin of the Dolphin," 555.

75. Here and elsewhere, the term *diffusion* is used. General readers may not appreciate all that diffusion does for organisms. The term describes the movement of molecules, ions, or particles toward a uniform distribution throughout the available volume. It can be perceived as a movement from areas of high concentration to areas of lower concentration. In day to day life, diffusion works, for example, when someone places a lump of sugar (high concentration) in a hot cup of coffee (where there is initially a low concentration of sugar). Even without stirring, the sugar molecules diffuse throughout the volume of coffee. So what is so remarkable? It can all happen without *any input of energy.* Thus, diffusion of oxygen and carbon dioxide in the lungs and blood—so necessary for life—happens automatically, with no energetic costs. Imagine how much energy you would spend if you had to invest energy moving every oxygen or carbon dioxide molecule into and out of the blood stream! The process of diffusion saves energy that organisms can invest otherwise—in growth, reproduction, acquisition of food, etc.

76. Harrison, "Blood-Supply of the Mammalian Testes," 340–41.

77. Some excellent references describing anatomical and physiological means by which testes in dolphins are kept cool are Pabst et al., "Thermoregulation of the Testes of the Dolphin," 221–26; Rommel et al., "Anatomical Evidence for a Countercurrent Heat Exchanger Associated with Dolphin Testes," 150–56; Rommel et al., "Temperature Regulation of the Testes of the Dolphin," 130–34.

78. For general readers, perhaps the best single reference dealing with thermoregulatory adaptations associated with reproductive organs (both male and female) in marine mammals is a very readable paper, Rommel, Pabst, and McLellan, "Reproductive Thermoregulation in Marine Mammals," 440–48.

79. Rommel, Pabst, and McLellan, "Functional Morphology of Vascular Plexuses Associated with the Cetacean Uterus," 538–46. As noted above, see also Rommel, Pabst, and McLellan, "Reproductive Thermoregulation in Marine Mammals," 440–48.

80. See review by Robeck et al., "Reproductive Biology of the Bottlenose Dolphin," 324.

81. Aside from the chapter by Pabst, Rommel, and McLellan (note 68), good reviews of marine mammal and/or dolphin reproductive anatomy exist in a number of references including: Robeck et al., "Reproductive Biology of the Bottlenose Dolphin," 321–36; and Boyd, Lockyer, and Marsh, "Reproduction in Marine Mammals."

82. Robeck et al., "Reproductive Biology of the Bottlenose Dolphin," 326–27.

83. The term for urine that is more concentrated than the blood of an animal is *hyperosmotic.* Mammalian kidneys are capable of producing hyperosmotic urine as a means by which to conserve water. However, mammalian kidneys can also produce copious, very dilute urine, termed hyposmotic, when the body's fluid intake has been high. Different species possess different abilities to concentrate their urine; as noted in the text,

desert rodents, which need to reduce loss of water as much as possible, are well known for their ability to produce extremely hyperosmotic urine.

84. See review by Elsner, "Living in Water, Solutions to Physiological Problems," 103–6.

85. Two papers that espouse this point of view are Vardy and Bryden, "The Kidney of *Leptonychotes weddelli*," 32; and Maluf and Gassman, "Kidneys of the Killerwhale," 42.

86. Hui, "Seawater Consumption and Water Flux in the Common Dolphin," 439.

87. A full and recent list of other studies of bottlenose dolphin anatomy appears in Wells and Scott, "Bottlenose Dolphin," 144–48.

88. Elsner, "Living in Water, Solutions to Physiological Problems," 74–95. As noted earlier (note 9), much of the information regarding dolphin or marine mammal physiology used in this chapter comes from Elsner's review. Statements made in the text for which no attribution is made come from that source.

89. Calculated based on Ridgway and Johnston, "Blood Oxygen and Ecology of Porpoises," 456–58.

90. Bryden and Lim, "Blood Parameters of the Elephant Seal," 139–48.

91. Elsner, "Living in Water, Solutions to Physiological Problems," 76.

92. See Ridgway, Scronce, and Kanwisher, "Respiration and Deep Diving in the Bottlenose Porpoise," 1651–54.

93. Ridgway and Howard, "Dolphin Lung Collapse and Intramuscular Circulation during Diving," 1182–83.

94. Elsner, Kenney, and Burgess, "Diving Bradycardia in the Dolphin," 407–8.

95. Williams , Freidl, and Haun, "The Physiology of Bottlenose Dolphins," 31–46.

96. Ridgway, Scronce, and Kanwisher, "Respiration and Deep Diving in the Bottlenose Porpoise," 1653.

97. Castellini, Costa, and Castellini, "Blood Glucose Distribution, Brain Size and Diving," 296.

98. Zimmer, "The Dolphin Strategy," 76.

99. Described by Zimmer, "The Dolphin Strategy," 76–77.

100. Williams et al., "Integrating Behavior and Energetics in Diving Marine Mammals," cited in Costa and Williams, "Marine Mammal Energetics," 190.

101. Ridgway, Scronce, and Kanwisher, "Respiration and Deep Diving in the Bottlenose Porpoise," 1651–1652.

102. Ibid., 1653.

103. Mohri et al., "Diving Patterns of Ama Divers," 137–43.

104. Noren et al., "Thermoregulation during Swimming and Diving in a Bottlenose Dolphin." 93–99. For a less technical description, see Zimmer, "The Dolphin Strategy," 77.

105. Zimmer, "The Dolphin Strategy," 77.

106. Noren et al., "Thermoregulation during Swimming and Diving in a Bottlenose Dolphin," 98–99.

107. Costa et al., "Oxygen Consumption and Thermoregulation in Bottlenose Dolphins," cited in Costa and Williams, "Marine Mammal Energetics," 182.

108. Costa and Williams, "Marine Mammal Energetics," 140.

109. Wells and Scott, "Bottlenose Dolphin," 140.

110. Costa et al., "Seasonal Changes in the Field Metabolic Rate of Bottlenose Dolphins," 37.

111. Costa and Williams, "Marine Mammal Energetics," 176–217.

112. Wartzok and Ketten, "Marine Mammal Sensory Systems," 117. Note that this reference is the source of much of the information used in this section of chapter 4.

113. Wartzok and Ketten, "Marine Mammal Sensory Systems," 148–51.

114. For example, see Ridgway, "The Central Nervous System of the Bottlenose Dolphin," 88–92.

115. Again, for a thorough review of the topic, refer to Wartzok and Ketten, "Marine Mammal Sensory Systems," 140–45.

116. Overviews of dolphin sounds and functions appear in the following: Wartzok and Ketten "Marine Mammal Sensory Systems," 125–33, and Tyack, "Communication and Cognition," 290–308. Also note that the upper frequency limit of signature whistles may exceed 24 kHz (Laela Sayigh, University of North Carolina at Wilmington, personal communication).

117. McCormick et al., "Sound Conduction in the Dolphin Ear," 1421.

118. Caldwell and Caldwell, "Individual Whistle Contours in Bottlenose Dolphins," 434–35.

119. At least two recent papers have provided a thorough review of the characteristics and functions of signature whistles. They are Caldwell, Caldwell, and Tyack, "Review of the Signature Whistle Hypothesis," 199–234, and Tyack, "Development and Social Functions of Signature Whistles in Bottlenose Dolphins," 21–46. The former report also considers other types of whistles that make up an individual animal's vocal repertoire.

120. Tyack, "Whistle Repertoires of Two Bottlenosed Dolphins," 251–57.

121. Janik and Slater, "Bottlenose Dolphin Signature Whistles Are Cohesion Calls," 829–36.

122. For example, see Sayigh et al., "Signature Whistles of Free-Ranging Bottlenose Dolphins," 247–60; Sayigh et al., "Sex Differences in Whistle Production," 171–77; Sayigh et al., "Individual Recognition in Wild Bottlenose Dolphins," 41–50.

123. Sayigh et al., "Sex Differences in Whistle Production," 171–77.

124. Ibid., 258.

125. Ibid., 176–77.

126. Sayigh et al., "Individual Recognition in Wild Bottlenose Dolphins," 47–48.

127. Tyack, "Communication and Cognition," 291.

128. Norris, "The Echolocation of Marine Mammals," 391–423.

129. Murchison, "Detection Range and Range Resolution of Echolocating Bottlenose Porpoise," 49.

130. Au, *The Sonar of Dolphins,* 81.

131. Norris and Möhl, "Can Odontocetes Debilitate Prey with Sound?" 85–104.

132. An excellent review is provided by Ackman and Lamothe, "Marine Mammals," 179–381.

133. Wartzok and Ketten, "Marine Mammal Sensory Systems," 139.

134. Much of the early work on this topic was done by Norris. Some of his papers include "The Evolution of Acoustic Mechanisms in Odontocete Cetaceans," 297–324; "Echolocation of Marine Mammals," 391–423, and "Peripheral Sound Processing in Odontocetes," 495–509.

135. Dral, "On the Retinal Anatomy of Cetacea," 86–87.

136. Osterberg, "Rods and Cones in the Human Retina," cited in Wartzok and Ketten, "Marine Mammal Sensory Systems," 150.

137. Simons and Huigen, "Colour Vision in Dolphins," 27–33, and Madsen and Herman, "Cetacean Vision and Visual Appearance," 111–12.

138. Ridgway, "The Central Nervous System of the Bottlenose Dolphin," 77. The term *fovea* is generally used to describe a depression or pit. In the retina, the fovea centralis is a depression where only cones are present. Since cones provide excellent visual acuity when abundant illumination is available, the presence of a fovea centralis is typically associated with organisms that are active in the daytime and have great vision.

139. Dral, "Aquatic and Aerial Vision in the Bottle-Nosed Dolphin," 510–13; and Dawson, Birndorf, and Perez, "Gross Anatomy and Optics of the Dolphin Eye," 1–12.

140. Morgane and Jacobs, "Comparative Anatomy of the Cetacean Nervous System," 120.

141. Nachtigall and Hall, "Taste Reception in the Bottlenose Dolphin," 147–48.

142. Donaldson, "The Tongue of the Bottlenosed Dolphin," 175–98.

143. Two important references on this topic are Klinowska, "Interpretation of UK Cetacean Stranding Data," 459–67, and Kirschvink, Dizon, and Westphal, "Geomagnetic Sensitivity in Cetaceans," 1–24.

144. Brabyn and Frew, "New Zealand Herd Stranding Sites Do Not Relate to Geomagnetic Topography," 195–207.

145. The membranes that cover and protect the central nervous system are called the meninges. Although this term may not be generally familiar, their inflammation is called *meningitis,* a word many people have heard. Magnetite in cetacean brains has been reported specifically from the tough, outer membrane called the dura mater. See Bauer et al., "Magnetoreception and Biomineralization of Magnetite in Cetaceans," 489–507.

146. Ridgway and Carder, "Tactile Sensitivity of the Bottlenose Dolphin," 163–79.

147. Samuels et al., "Gentle Rubbing among Bottlenose Dolphins," 58.

148. Wartzok and Ketten, "Marine Mammal Sensory Systems," 160–61.

149. Odell, "Southeastern United States Marine Mammal Stranding Network," 20.

5. Life History Strategies

1. This definition is by Lincoln, Boxshall, and Clark, *A Dictionary of Ecology, Evolution and Systematics,* as cited by Ricklefs, *Ecology,* 561.

2. Ricklefs, *Ecology,* 561.

3. Ibid., 560–80.

4. Bielsa, Murdich, and Labisky, "Species Profiles: Life Histories and Environmental Requirements," 1–21.

5. Reviews of r- vs. K-strategies appear in Pianka, "On r and K Selection," 592–97, and Ricklefs, *Ecology,* 577–79.

6. Reynolds and Odell, *Manatees and Dugongs,* 38.

7. Wells and Scott, "Bottlenose Dolphin," 149.

8. Excellent references on the technique are Hohn, "Reading between the Lines: Analysis of Age Estimation in Dolphins," 575–85, and Hohn et al., "Growth Layers in Teeth from Known-Age Dolphins," 315–42.

9. The topic of age determination in manatees is introduced and well discussed by Marmontel et al., "Age Determination in Manatees," 54–88; confirmed with larger sample size by Meghan Bolen, Florida Department of Environmental Protection, personal communication to Reynolds.

10. The term *epididymides* is the plural of *epididymis.* An epididymis is a highly convoluted duct that stores and conveys sperm from the testis to the vas deferens. The epididymis typically is closely adhered to the testis it drains.

11. Seminiferous tubules are the locations in the testes where sperm cells (spermatozoa) develop.

12. In the United States, stranded marine mammals have been handled by regional networks of trained individuals since 1977. The work of the various networks has been described in a few references, including Reynolds and Odell, *Marine Mammal Strandings in the United States,* 1–157.

13. Hernandez et al., "Age and Seasonality of Spermatogenesis in Manatees," 84–97.

14. Marmontel, "Age and Reproduction in Female Manatees," 98–119.

15. Wells and Scott, "Bottlenose Dolphin," 149.

16. Reynolds and Odell, *Manatees and Dugongs,* 52; Rathbun et al., "Reproduction in Free-Ranging Manatees," 146–47.

17. See reviews by Wells and Scott, "Bottlenose Dolphin," 148–57, for dolphins; and Reynolds and Odell, *Manatees and Dugongs,* 50–54, for manatees.

18. The terrible consequences have been described by a number of authors, including Mangel et al., "Principles for the Conservation of Wild Living Resources," 338–62.

19. Lockyer, "The Relationship between Body Fat, Food Resources, and Reproductive Energy Costs in Fin Whales," 343–61.

20. See reviews by Boyd, Lockyer, and Marsh, "Reproduction in Marine Mammals," 218–86, and Lockyer, "The Importance of Biological Parameters in Population Assessments," 22–31.

21. A female that gives birth to her first offspring is termed a *primiparous* female.

22. Wells, Scott, and Irvine, "The Social Structure of Free-Ranging Bottlenose Dolphins," 247–305.

23. Studies have suggested that, just because a male dolphin has reached its full adult size (that is, has reached physical maturity), it may not have acquired skills or behaviors that allow it to breed successfully. When it reaches the latter point and starts to father offspring, it is considered to have reached social maturity. The concept is considered

by Wells, Scott, and Irvine, "The Social Structure of Free-Ranging Dolphins," 247–305; Duffield and Wells, "Investigation of Social Unit Dynamics in *Tursiops truncatus*," 155–69; and Read et al., "Patterns of Growth in Wild Bottlenose Dolphins," 107–23.

24. Cockcroft and Ross, "Age, Growth and Reproduction of Bottlenose Dolphins," 289–302.

25. Kasuya et al., "Perinatal Growth in Delphinoids," 93.

26. Ibid., 90.

27. Mead and Potter, "Natural History of Bottlenose Dolphins," 183–86.

28. This topic is reviewed by a number of references, including the following: Perrin and Reilly, "Reproductive Parameters of Dolphins and Small Whales," 101, and Wells and Scott, "Bottlenose Dolphin," 151.

29. Data regarding South African dolphins come from Ross and Cockcroft, "Age, Growth, and Reproduction of Bottlenose Dolphins," 291; data for the southeastern United States are from Hohn, "Age Determination and Age-Related Factors in the Teeth of Bottlenose Dolphins," 45, and from Mead and Potter, "Natural History of Bottlenose Dolphins," 178; and data regarding Japanese dolphins are from Kasuya et al., "Perinatal Growth of Delphinoids," 89.

30. Smedley and Mann, "Maternal Investment in Bottlenose Dolphins," 15.

31. Wells, Boness and Rathbun, "Behavior," 372–75.

32. Wells and Scott, "Bottlenose Dolphin," 152.

33. For Shark Bay dolphins, see Smolker et al., "Sex Differences in Patterns of Association among Bottlenose Dolphins," 58; for Moray Firth dolphins, see Wilson, "The Ecology of Bottlenose Dolphins in the Moray Firth," 84.

34. The phenomenon of female dolphins carrying deceased calves has been described by many authors, including Fertl and Schiro, "Carrying of Dead Calves by Bottlenose Dolphins," 53–56. Readers should note, however, that dolphins have been reported to carry other objects as well, including small sharks for which the dolphins, presumably, feel no great affection! Thus, the best indicator of the strength of the mother-calf bond may simply be its duration.

35. Read et al., "Patterns of Growth in Wild Bottlenosed Dolphins," 118–20.

36. Wells and Scott, "Estimating Dolphin Population Parameters," 410.

37. Reviewed by Perrin and Reilly, "Reproductive Parameters of Dolphins and Small Whales," 106–7.

38. Wells and Scott, " Estimating Bottlenose Dolphin Population Parameters," 411.

39. Wells and Scott, "Bottlenose Dolphin," 154.

40. In other words, of a population of approximately one hundred dolphins, one would expect, on average, one death per year. Note that, for any particular age group in the population, mortality may differ considerably from that of the entire population.

41. Wells and Scott, "Estimating Bottlenose Dolphin Population Parameters," 412.

42. Hersh, Odell, and Asper, "Bottlenose Dolphin Mortality Patterns," 163.

43. Cockcroft, Cliff, and Ross, "Shark Predation on Indian Ocean Bottlenose Dolphins," 305–9.

44. Brewer, *The Science of Ecology*, 103–4.

45. Wells and Scott, "Bottlenose Dolphin," 153.

46. There are a number of papers that deal with shark attacks on dolphins. For example, see the following: for reports from Florida, Wood, Caldwell, and Caldwell, "Behavioral Interactions between Porpoises and Sharks, 264–77; Urian et al., "An Analysis of Shark Bite Scars on Wild Bottlenose Dolphins," 138; for reports from the mid-Atlantic coast of the United States, Mead and Potter, "Natural History of Bottlenose Dolphins," 177; for reports from Queensland, Australia, Corkeron, Morris, and Bryden, "Interactions between Bottlenose Dolphins and Sharks in Moreton Bay," 109–13; and for reports from South Africa, Cockcroft, Cliff and Ross, "Shark Predation on Indian Ocean Bottlenose Dolphins," 305–9.

47. Cockcroft, Cliff, and Ross, "Shark Predation on Indian Ocean Bottlenose Dolphins," 306.

48. Würsig and Würsig, "Behavior and Ecology of Bottlenose Dolphins in the South Atlantic," 407–8.

49. The two primary reports on this topic are Walsh et al., "Ray Encounters as a Mortality Factor in Bottlenose Dolphins," 154–62; and McLellan, Thayer, and Pabst, "Stingray Spine Mortality in a Bottlenose Dolphins," 98–101.

50. Wells and Scott, "Bottlenose Dolphin," 162.

51. See review by Howard, Britt, and Matsumoto, "Parasitic Diseases," 119–232.

52. Aspects of pilot whale life history, social behavior, and reproductive biology are covered by the following: Kasuya and Marsh, "Life History and Reproductive Biology of the Short-Finned Pilot Whale," 259–310, and Amos, "Use of Molecular Probes to Analyse Pilot Whale Pod Structure," 33–48.

53. Read and Hohn, "Life in the Fast Lane: The Life History of Harbour Porpoises," 423–40.

54. This theme appears in a number of books and papers. For an example with both examples of problems and some possible solutions, see Mangel et al., "Principles for the Conservation of Wild Living Resources," 338–62.

6. The Daily Lives of Dolphins

1. See, for example, Bartholomew, "The Evolution of Pinniped Polygyny," 546.

2. Weilgart, Whitehead, and Payne, "A Colossal Converence," 278–87.

3. The development and use of photo-identification techniques has been the basis of a number of studies of bottlenose dolphins. The technique is well described in references such as the following: Würsig and Würsig, "Bottlenose Porpoises in the South Atlantic," 348–59; Wells, Scott, and Irvine, "Social Structure of Free-Ranging Bottlenose Dolphins," 247–305; and Wells and Scott, "Estimating Bottlenose Dolphin Population Parameters," 407–15.

4. Although a number of studies fit this category (that is, pioneering work done only since 1950), interested readers may wish to look especially at the following references: Caldwell, "Evidence of Home Range of an Atlantic Bottlenose Dolphin," 304–5; Caldwell, Caldwell, and Siebenaler, "Observations on Captive and Wild Dolphins," 1–10; and Evans and Bastian, "Marine Mammal Communication," 425–76.

5. An admittedly incomplete list would include such people as Ken Norris, David and Melba Caldwell, Frank Essapian, Bill Evans, and Forrest Wood.

6. See, for example, the following: Irvine and Wells, "Attempts to Tag Bottlenosed Dolphins," 1–5; Irvine, Wells, and Scott, "Techniques for Tagging Small Cetaceans," 671–88; and Scott et al., "Tagging and Marking Studies on Small Cetaceans," 489–514.

7. A couple of good references include Irvine et al., "Movements and Activities of the Atlantic Bottlenose Dolphin," 671–88, and Mate et al., "Satellite-Monitored Movements and Dive Behavior," 452–63.

8. As noted in chapter 4, good references on this topic include Hohn, "Reading between the Lines: Analysis of Age Estimation in Dolphins," 575–85; and Hohn et al., "Growth Layers in Teeth from Bottlenose Dolphins," 315–42.

9. See Wells, Scott, and Irvine, "The Social Structure of Free-Ranging Bottlenose Dolphins," 255, and Robeck et al., "Reproductive Biology of the Bottlenose Dolphin," 326–28.

10. Hansen and Wells, "Bottlenose Dolphin Health Assessment," 5.

11. See, for example, Duffield and Wells, "The Combined Application of Chromosome, Protein, and Molecular Data for Investigation of Social Unit Dynamics," 155–69.

12. There have emerged a number of papers that describe behavior of bottlenose dolphins. Two among them that provide a good review are Shane, Wells, and Würsig, "Ecology, Behavior, and Social Organization of the Bottlenose Dolphin," 34–63; and Wells, "The Role of Long-Term Study in Understanding a Bottlenose Dolphin Community," 199–225.

13. It would be impractical to list the many books, book chapters, and articles written about bottlenose dolphins by the Caldwells. Among the publications that made important contributions are Caldwell, "Evidence of Home Range of an Atlantic Bottlenose Dolphin," 304–5; Caldwell and Caldwell, "Dolphins Communicate—But They Don't Talk," 23–27; Caldwell and Caldwell, The World of the Bottlenosed Dolphin, 1–157; Caldwell, Caldwell, and Siebenaler, "Captive and Wild Bottlenose Dolphins," 1–10; and Caldwell, Caldwell, and Tyack, "Review of the Signature Whistle Hypothesis," 199–234.

14. For definitions of terms, we use Wells, Boness, and Rathbun, "Behavior," 324–422. In fact, this source is excellent for a comparative review of marine mammal behaviors, including some interesting comparisons with behavior of terrestrial animals.

15. Among the many publications on this topic, we suggest interested readers consult especially the following: Wells, Scott, and Irvine, "The Social Structure of Free-Ranging Bottlenose Dolphins," 247–305, and Wells, "The Role of Long-Term Study in Understanding a Dolphin Community," 199–225.

16. Smolker et al., "Sex Differences in Patterns of Association among Indian Ocean Bottlenose Dolphins," 48–51.

17. See, for example, Wells, Scott, and Irvine, "The Social Structure of Free-Ranging Bottlenose Dolphins," 286; Wells, "The Role of Long-Term Study in Understanding a Dolphin Community," 218–20; and Scott, Wells, and Irvine, "A Long-Term Study of Bottlenose Dolphins," 241.

18. Wells, Scott, and Irvine, "The Social Structure of Free-Ranging Bottlenose Dolphins," 285.

19. See review by Caldwell, Caldwell, and Tyack, "Review of the Signature Whistle Hypothesis," 199–234.

20. Fundamental aspects of animal communication are discussed in a variety of references, including Wilson, *Sociobiology: The New Synthesis*, 176–241.

21. Recall that dolphins do not use olfaction.

22. Samuels et al., "Gentle Rubbing among Bottlenose Dolphins," 58.

23. Wells, "Reproductive Behavior and Hormonal Correlates in Spinner Dolphins," 465–72.

24. The phenomenon has been mentioned for both captive and free-ranging dolphins, most recently by Nguyen and Mann, "Sociosexual Development in Bottlenose Dolphin Calves," 11.

25. See Norris, *Dolphin Days*, 231–32, and Norris et al., *The Hawaiian Spinner Dolphin*, 278–80.

26. Good references on these topics include Tayler and Saayman, "Social Organization and Behaviour of Dolphins," 11–43; Norris, *The Porpoise Watcher*, 1–250; and Shane, Wells, and Würsig, "Ecology, Behavior, and Social Organization of the Bottlenose Dolphin," 34–63.

27. For descriptions of male consortships, see Connor, Smolker, and Richards, "Dolphin Alliances and Coalitions," 415–43, and Connor et al., "Patterns of Female Attractiveness in Bottlenose Dolphins," 37–69.

28. Scott, Wells, and Irvine, "A Long-Term Study of Bottlenose Dolphins," 241.

29. See Connor et al., "Patterns of Female Attractiveness in Bottlenose Dolphins," 50–53.

30. See Connor, Smolker, and Richards, "Dolphin Alliances and Coalitions," 427–28; and Connor et al., "Patterns of Female Attractiveness in Bottlenose Dolphins," 44–45. In at least one instance, chasing and fighting over a female by male dolphin alliances lasted over an hour.

31. Wilson, "The Ecology of Bottlenose Dolphins in the Moray Firth," 99–102.

32. Leks and other systems are described for marine mammals by Wells, Boness, and Rathbun, "Behavior," 324–422.

33. See review by Wells, Boness, and Rathbun, "Behavior," 367–68.

34. Moors, "Behavioral Patterns of Breeding Female Dolphins," 36.

35. Connor and Smolker, "'Pop' Goes the Dolphin," 643–62.

36. Saayman, Tayler, and Bower, "Diurnal Behavior Cycles in Bottlenose Dolphins," 222.

37. We again follow definitions used by Wells, Boness, and Rathbun, "Behavior," 324–422.

38. See Schroeder and Keller, "Artificial Insemination in Dolphins," 449. For a comparison, a review by Toppari et al., "Male Reproductive Health," 742–43, indicates that human males produce about 3×10^8 sperm per ejaculate, but that the number may be dropping, at least in some parts of the world, due to environmental xenoestrogens. Thus dolphins may possess about five orders of magnitude more sperm per ejaculate than do humans.

39. Duffield and Wells, "The Combined Application of Chromosome, Protein, and Molecular Data for Investigation of Social Dynamics," 167.

40. Tolley et al., "Sexual Dimorphism in Wild Bottlenose Dolphins," 1190–98.

41. Ibid.

42. Reddy et al., "Energy Requirements for the Bottlenose Dolphin," 26–31.

43. Wells, Boness and Rathbun, "Behavior," 373–74.

44. Essapian, "The Birth and Growth of a Porpoise," 395.

45. Wells, Boness, and Rathbun, "Behavior," 374.

46. Wells, Boness, and Rathbun, "Behavior," 374–75.

47. Ridgway et al., "Orphan Induced Lactation in *Tursiops*," 172–82.

48. Wells, Scott, and Irvine, "The Social Structure of Free-Ranging Bottlenose Dolphins," 297.

49. Interestingly enough, it has been shown in Shark Bay, Australia, that dolphin calves that are in poor condition may remain closer to their mothers than do calves that are in excellent shape. The closeness of the relationship affects age at weaning (which can range from almost three to nine years). This has been described by Smedley and Mann, "Maternal Investment in Bottlenose Dolphins," 15.

50. Care-giving behaviors in cetaceans, including dolphins, are reviewed by Caldwell and Caldwell, "Epimeletic (Care-Giving) Behavior in Cetacea," 755–89.

51. Mann and Smuts, "Allomaternal Care and Mother-Infant Separations in Wild Dolphins," 1097–113.

52. Wells, Boness, and Rathbun, "Behavior," 374.

53. Wells, "The Marine Mammals of Sarasota Bay," 9.10.

54. Wells, "Parental Investment Patterns of Wild Bottlenose Dolphins," 61.

55. Defined by Caldwell and Caldwell, "Epimeletic (Care-Giving) Behavior in Cetacea," 755; the Caldwells's definitions were followed by Wells, Boness, and Rathbun, "Behavior," 324–422, for their comprehensive overview.

56. Caldwell and Caldwell, "Epimeletic (Care-Giving) Behavior in Cetacea," 764–70.

57. Connor and Norris, "Are Dolphins Reciprocal Altruists?" 358–74.

58. Würsig and Würsig, "Behavior and Ecology of Bottlenose Porpoises," 410.

59. Würsig and Würsig, "Day and Night of the Dolphin," 64.

60. Wilson, *Sociobiology: The New Synthesis,* 165.

61. Ibid.

62. Tayler and Saayman, "The Social Organization and Behaviour of Dolphins and Baboons," 11–43.

63. Ibid., 28.

64. Ibid., 28.

65. Caldwell, "Home Range of an Atlantic Bottlenose Dolphin," 304–5.

66. Definition from Wilson, *Sociobiology: The New Synthesis,* 586.

67. Wells, "The Marine Mammals of Sarasota Bay," 9.6.

68. Scott, Wells, and Irvine, "A Long-Term Study of Bottlenose Dolphins," 237.

69. Bassos, "A Behavioral Assessment of the Reintroduction of Two Bottlenose Dolphins," 78.

70. Wells, "The Marine Mammals of Sarasota Bay," 9.6–9.10.

71. Wells et al., "Northward Extension of the Range of Bottlenose Dolphins," 421–31.

72. Reviewed by Wells, Boness, and Rathbun, "Behavior," 383.

73. A discussion of alternatives regarding stock structure of dolphins along the south Atlantic coast of the United States appears in Hohn, "Design for a Multiple-Method Approach to Determine Stock Structure," 2.

74. This idea was raised decades ago but remains unresolved. The idea appeared in Caldwell and Caldwell, *The World of the Bottlenosed Dolphin*, 62–71.

75. See Wells, Boness, and Rathbun, "Behavior," 374.

76. McBride and Hebb, "Behavior of the Captive Bottlenose Dolphin," 113.

77. Connor, Smolker, and Richards, "Aggressive Herding of Females by Male Bottle-nose Dolphins," 415–43.

78. Patterson et al., "Infanticide in Bottlenose Dolphins," 1167–70.

79. Barco et al., "Bottlenose Dolphin Calf Strandings," 3.

80. Ibid., 3.

81. Patterson et al., "Infanticide in Bottlenose Dolphins," 1169.

82. Barco et al., "Bottlenose Dolphin Calf Strandings," 3.

83. See the following: Green and Corkeron, "Attempt to Establish a Feeding Station for Bottlenose Dolphins," 127–28; and Corkeron, Bryden, and Hedstrom, "Feeding by Bottlenose Dolphins in Association with Trawling Operations," 333–35.

84. Würsig and Würsig, "Behavior and Ecology of the Bottlenose Dolphin," 410.

85. Described some time ago, and confirmed subsequently, by Caldwell and Caldwell, "Dolphins, Porpoises and Behavior," 16.

86. Samuels and Gifford, "A Quantitative Assessment of Dominance Relations among Bottlenose Dolphins," 70–99.

87. Scott and Chivers, "Distribution and Herd Structure of Bottlenose Dolphins," 394–97.

88. Benign or neutral interactions have been described in the literature. Possible epimeletic behavior by dolphins toward other marine mammal species is mentioned by Caldwell and Caldwell, "Epimeletic (Care-Giving) Behavior in Cetacea," 767–68.

89. This relationship has been reported by Saayman and Tayler, "The Socioecology of Humpback Dolphins," 209, and by Corkeron, "Behavioral Ecology of Inshore Dolphins in Moreton Bay," 290.

90. Herzing, "Underwater Behavior of Spotted Dolphins and Bottlenose Dolphins," 70.

91. Terry, "Behavior between *Sotalia fluviatilis guianensis* and *Tursiops truncatus*," 293.

92. See, for example: Jepson and Baker, "Bottlenosed Dolphins as a Possible Cause of Traumatic Injuries in Porpoises," 614–15, and Ross and Wilson, "Violent Interactions between Bottlenose Dolphins and Harbour Porpoises," 283–86.

93. Patterson et al., "Infanticide in Bottlenose Dolphins," 1169.

94. Reviewed by Leatherwood and Reeves, *The Sierra Club Handbook of Whales and Dolphins*, 224, and Reyes, "A Possible Case of Hybridism in Wild Dolphins," 305.

95. Leatherwood and Reeves, *The Sierra Club Handbook of Whales and Dolphins*, 224.

96. The topic is reviewed by Berube and Aguilar, "A New Hybrid and Implications of Hybridism," 82–99.

97. Cockcroft, Cliff, and Ross, "Shark Predation on Indian Ocean Bottlenose Dolphins," 308.

98. Corkeron, "Behavioral Ecology of Inshore Dolphins in Moreton Bay," 290.

99. Urian et al., "Analysis of Shark Bite Scars on Bottlenose Dolphins," 139.

100. Wood, Caldwell, and Caldwell, "Behavioral Interactions between Porpoises and Sharks," 265–66.

101. See, for example, Irvine, Wells, and Gilbert, "Conditioning an Atlantic Bottlenose Dolphin to Repel Sharks," 503–5, and Connor and Heithaus, "Approach by Great White Shark Elicits Flight in Dolphins," 602–6.

102. There is an old saying that if swimmers see dolphins nearby, it is safe to swim because there will be no sharks around; the reason, the legend goes, is that the dolphins will attack and scare away the sharks, thereby saving the hapless swimmers. An interesting quotation reflecting this attitude appears in Wood, Caldwell, and Caldwell, "Behavioral Interactions between Porpoises and Sharks, 265: "If a shark is sighted, the porpoises will circle him like a Comanche war party, moving in, one by one, to ram him with concrete hard noses and kill him by rupturing his organs."

In reality, the presence of dolphins may, indeed, sometimes be a good indicator that large sharks are absent—if the latter were around, the dolphins might detect them and hastily leave the area to escape being consumed! But not necessarily—sharks and dolphins are not infrequently observed in the same waters, sometimes feeding on the same fish schools.

103. Wood, Caldwell, and Caldwell, "Behavioral Interactions between Porpoises and Sharks," 270–71.

104. Essapian, "Birth and Growth of a Porpoise," 397.

105. Wood, Caldwell, and Caldwell, "Behavioral Interactions between Porpoises and Sharks," 268.

106. Walsh et al., "Ray Encounters as a Mortality Factor in Bottlenose Dolphins," 154–62.

107. Shane, Wells, and Würsig, "Ecology, Behavior, and Social Organization of the Bottlenose Dolphin," 50.

108. Food habits of bottlenose dolphins have been described or reviewed by a number of authors, including the following: Barros and Odell, "Food Habits of Bottlenose Dolphins," 309–28; and Barros and Wells, "Prey and Feeding Patterns of Bottlenose Dolphins," 1045–59.

109. This amazing behavior was briefly described decades ago by Hoese, "Dolphin Feeding out of Water in a Salt Marsh," 222–23. More recently, the behavior was documented more fully by Petricig, "Bottlenose Dolphins in Bull Creek, South Carolina," 102–69.

110. The phenomenon is well documented in various parts of the world. See, for example: Leatherwood, "Feeding Behavior of Bottle-Nosed Dolphins," 10–13; Shane,

Wells, and Würsig, "Ecology, Behavior, and Social Organization of the Bottlenose Dolphin," 54–55; and Corkeron, Bryden, and Hedstrom, "Feeding by Bottlenose Dolphins in Association with Trawling Operations," 329–36.

111. See Barros and Odell, "Food Habits of Bottlenose Dolphins," 324, and Barros and Wells, "Prey and Feeding Patterns of Bottlenose Dolphins," 1055.

112. Several references make this point. See Barros, "Feeding Ecology and Foraging Strategies of Bottlenose Dolphins," 217–28, and Barros and Odell, "Food Habits of Bottlenose Dolphins," 311.

113. Cockcroft and Ross, "Age, Growth, and Reproduction of Bottlenose Dolphins," 289.

114. Among the numerous papers on this topic, see the following: Leatherwood, "Feeding Behavior of Bottle-Nosed Dolphins," 10–16; Shane, Wells, and Würsig, "Ecology, Behavior, and Social Organization of the Bottlenose Dolphin," 50; and Shane, "Behavior and Ecology of the Bottlenose Dolphin," 250–51.

115. This behavior is described in different parts of the world by Irvine et al., "Movements and Activities of the Bottlenose Dolphin," 684–85, and Tayler and Saayman, "Social Organization and Behavior of Dolphins and Baboons," 17–18, 43.

116. Wells, Boness, and Rathbun, "Behavior," 359.

117. As noted above (note 109) see Hoese, "Dolphin Feeding out of Water in a Salt Marsh," 222–23, and Petricig, "Bottlenose Dolphins in Bull Creek, South Carolina," 102–69.

118. Petricig, "Bottlenose Dolphins in Bull Creek, South Carolina," 142.

119. Shane, Wells, and Würsig, "Ecology, Behavior, and Social Organization of the Bottlenose Dolphin," 50.

120. Harris, "Porpoises Feeding," 67.

121. Daniel Odell, Sea World, personal communication to Reynolds.

122. Wells, Boness, and Rathbun, "Behavior," 361.

123. Smolker et al., "Sponge-Carrying by Dolphins: A Foraging Specialization Involving Tool Use?" 454–65.

124. See Herzing, "Underwater Behavior of Spotted Dolphins and Bottlenose Dolphins," 71, and Rossbach and Herzing, "Benthic-Feeding Bottlenose Dolphins," 498–504.

125. Gunter, "Natural History of Bottlenose Dolphins, with Particular Reference to Food Habits," 275.

126. Leatherwood, "Feeding Behavior of Bottle-Nosed Dolphins," 10–13.

127. See two primary references: Norris and Möhl, "Can Odontocetes Debilitate Prey with Sound?" 85–104; and Zagaeski, "Some Observations on the Prey Stunning Hypothesis," 275–79.

128. Defined by Shane, Wells, and Würsig, "Ecology, Behavior, and Social Organization of the Bottlenose Dolphin," 47.

129. Ibid.

130. Ibid.

131. Note that dolphins in Texas and southwestern Florida tend to face into a current, perhaps to feed as described by Shane, "Behavior and Ecology of the Bottlenose Dolphin," 256.

132. Gruber, "Ecology of the Bottlenosed Dolphin in Matagorda Bay, Texas," 138–40.

133. Tayler and Saayman, "Social Organization and Behaviour of Dolphins and Baboons," 20.

134. Mate et al., "Satellite-Monitored Movements and Dive Behavior of a Bottlenose Dolphin," 460.

135. Hart, "Foraging Ecology and Behavior of Bottlenose Dolphins," 6.

136. Ibid., 103–8.

137. Ibid., 98.

138. Shane, "Behavior and Ecology of the Bottlenose Dolphin," 259.

139. Waples, "Activity Budgets of Free-Ranging Bottlenose Dolphins," 1–61.

140. Hanson and Defran, "Behaviour and Feeding Ecology of the Bottlenose Dolphin," 127.

141. Hansen, "California Coastal Bottlenose Dolphins," 415.

142. Waples, "Activity Budgets of Free-Ranging Bottlenose Dolphins," 13.

143. Ibid., 25–26.

144. Wells, "Why All the Blubbering?" 13.

145. Shane, "Behavior and Ecology of the Bottlenose Dolphin," 254.

146. Gruber, "Ecology of the Bottlenose Dolphin," 138–40.

147. For an overview applicable to bottlenose dolphins and other odontocetes, see Wells, Irvine, and Scott, "The Social Ecology of Inshore Odontocetes," 263–80.

148. Reviewed by Crook, Ellis, and Goss-Custard, "Mammalian Social Systems," 261–74.

149. See Shane, Wells, and Würsig, "Ecology, Behavior, and Social Organization of the Bottlenose Dolphin," 47.

150. Ibid., 44; Wilson, Thompson, and Hammond, "Habitat Use by Bottlenose Dolphins in the Moray Firth," 1368.

151. Wilson, Thompson, and Hammond, "Habitat Use by Bottlenose Dolphins in the Moray Firth," 1368.

152. Ibid., 1371.

153. The topic of different areas being used preferentially for different activities has been reviewed in several papers regarding Sarasota Bay dolphins. See for example: Wells, Irvine, and Scott, "The Social Ecology of Inshore Odontocetes," 280–310; Scott, Wells, and Irvine, "A Long-Term Study of Bottlenose Dolphins," 235–44; and Wells, "The Marine Mammals of Sarasota Bay," 9.6–9.11.

154. Wells, Boness, and Rathbun, "Behavior," 387.

155. A wonderful description of chimpanzee life appears in Jane Goodall's classic book, *The Chimpanzees of Gombe*. Although much of the book deals to some extent with behaviors of the animals and their relationships with one another, readers should consult especially chapter 8, "Relationships," 172–207.

7. Intelligence and Cognition

1. See Klinowska, "Brains, Behaviour and Intelligence," 21; and Tyack, "Communication and Cognition," 287.

2. Jerison, *Evolution of the Brain and Intelligence,* 387–95.

3. Ridgway, "The Central Nervous System of the Bottlenose Dolphin," 72. Note that this reference provided much of the material used in this chapter.

4. Slijper, *Whales,* 245. Interested readers should read Slijper's comments on this topic and examine his figure 127 (page 246), which graphically illustrates relationships between brain and body weights in a variety of species.

5. Klinowska, "Brains, Behaviour and Intelligence," 22.

6. See general descriptions provided in anatomical textbooks such as Gardner, Gray, and O'Rahilly, *Anatomy. A Regional Study of Human Structure,* 580–614.

7. The largest nerves in this region are cranial nerve V (trigeminal), cranial nerve VII (facial), and cranial nerve VIII (acoustic). Two good references that describe the structure and presumed importance of marine mammal cranial nerves are Ridgway, "The Central Nervous System of the Bottlenose Dolphin," 69–97, and Pabst, Rommel, and McLellan, "The Functional Morphology of Marine Mammals," 60–61.

8. Excellent references that discuss anatomy of the dolphin central nervous system are Morgane, Jacobs, and Galaburda, "Evolutionary Morphology of the Dolphin Brain," 5–29, and Ridgway, "The Central Nervous System of the Bottlenose Dolphin," 69–97. Comparative anatomy of cetacean nervous systems is described well by Morgane and Jacobs, "Comparative Anatomy of the Cetacean Nervous System," 117–224. For an even broader perspective that reviews the entire nervous system (brain, spinal cord, cranial nerves, peripheral nerves, and so forth) of marine mammals, see Pabst, Rommel, and McLellan, "The Functional Morphology of Marine Mammals," 56–60.

9. Ridgway, "The Central Nervous System of the Bottlenose Dolphin," 88.

10. Ibid., 75.

11. Ibid.

12. Ridgway and Brownson, "Relative Brain Sizes and Cortical Surface Areas of Odontocetes," 149.

13. Ridgway, "The Central Nervous System of the Bottlenose Dolphin," 75.

14. We refer to cortical layer IV. See Ridgway, "The Central Nervous System of the Bottlenose Dolphin," 75.

15. Ridgway, "The Central Nervous System of the Bottlenose Dolphin," 76.

16. Ibid., 79.

17. See ibid., 76, and elsewhere; and Pabst, Rommel, and McLellan, "The Functional Morphology of Marine Mammals," 56–60.

18. Ridgway, "The Central Nervous System of the Bottlenose Dolphin," 82.

19. Jacobs, Morgane, and McFarland, "The Anatomy of the Brain of the Bottlenose Dolphin," abstract, page 205.

20. Donaldson, "The Tongue of the Bottlenosed Dolphin," 181.

21. See Mead, "Anatomy of the External Nasal Passages and Facial Complex in the Delphinidae," 15, who commented that the nerve can even be mistaken for a tendon; and Ridgway, "The Central Nervous System of the Bottlenose Dolphin," 86.

22. Ridgway, "The Central Nervous System of the Bottlenose Dolphin," 77–78.

23. Ibid., 88.

24. Pabst, Rommel, and McLellan, "The Functional Morphology of Marine Mammals," 61.

25. Hunt, "The Role of Intelligence in Modern Society, 356–68.

26. Tyack, "Communication and Cognition," 287.

27. Gardner, *Frames of Mind: The Theory of Multiple Intelligences*, 3–11; 59–70.

28. Gould, *Ever Since Darwin*, 180.

29. Worthy and Hickie, "Relative Brain Size in Marine Mammals," 445–46.

30. Ibid., 445, emphasis added.

31. Gould, *Ever Since Darwin*, 180.

32. The topic is reviewed thoroughly by Worthy and Hickie, "Relative Brain Size in Marine Mammals," 445–59; and Pabst, Rommel, and McLellan, "The Functional Morphology of Marine Mammals."

33. The figure of 2.8 comes from a thorough assessment by Worthy and Hickie, "Relative Brain Size in Marine Mammals," 450. Dolphin EQ values that are much higher have been reported in the literature, including an astounding EQ value of 5.3 reported by Klinowska, "Brains, Behaviour and Intelligence," 24.

34. Jerison, *Evolution of the Brain and Intelligence*, 393. A lower EQ value of about 4.0 comes from Hofman, "Energy Metabolism, Brain Size and Longevity in Mammals," 500. Note that Marino, "A Comparison of Encephalization between Cetaceans and Primates," 235, indicates that the EQ_{72} value (an encephalization quotient she calculates in her paper) for humans approaches 3.0, whereas the same value for bottlenose dolphins is about 1.6.

35. Gould, *Ever Since Darwin*, 184–85.

36. Marino, "A Comparison of Encephalization between Cetaceans and Primates," 236–37.

37. Marino, "The Relationship between Gestation Length, Encephalization, and Body Weight in Odontocetes," 133.

38. Worthy and Hickie, "Relative Brain Size in Marine Mammals," 451.

39. Marino, "The Relationship between Gestation Length, Encephalization, and Body Weight in Odontocetes," 136.

40. Worthy and Hickie, "Relative Brain Size in Marine Mammals," 451–54.

41. Ridgway, "The Central Nervous System of the Bottlenose Dolphin," 88.

42. Ibid. Interestingly enough, bats have small EQs and small brains, even though they, like odontocetes, echolocate—see Worthy and Hickie, "Relative Brain Size in Marine Mammals," 452.

43. Worthy and Hickie, "Relative Brain Size in Marine Mammals," 450.

44. A table providing data on a variety of species appears in Worthy and Hickie, "Relative Brain Size in Marine Mammals," 450.

45. Tyack, "Communication and Cognition," 317–18.

46. For a review of chimpanzee alliances and coalitions, see de Waal, "Coalitions as Part of Reciprocal Relations in the Arnhem Chimpanzee Colony," 233–57. For a review of dolphins, see Connor, Smolker, and Richards, "Dolphin Alliances and Coalitions," 415–43. Both papers appear in a volume dealing with these topics in a range of animals.

47. See Connor, Smolker, and Richards, "Dolphin Coalitions and Alliances," 436–38; and Tyack, "Communication and Cognition," 317–18.

48. Metabolic cost is noted by the following: Worthy and Hickie, "Relative Brain Size in Marine Mammals," 450; and Ridgway, "The Central Nervous System of the Bottlenose Dolphin," 76–77.

49. Sokoloff, "Circulation and Energy Metabolism of the Brain," 394.

50. Hockett, "In Search of Jove's Brow," 284.

51. Herman, "Cognition and Language Competencies of Bottle-Nosed Dolphins," 221.

52. See Lilly, *Lilly on Dolphins,* 1–500.

53. The most comprehensive single source of information on dolphin cognition and communication, which attempts to shed light on dolphin attributes by comparing dolphins with other species, is by Schusterman, Thomas, and Wood, *Dolphin Cognition and Behavior: A Comparative Approach,* 1–393.

54. Tyack, "Communication and Cognition," 308.

55. Reviewed by Tyack, "Communication and Cognition," 309–14.

56. Lilly, *Lilly on Dolphins,* vii–viii.

57. Ibid., 148–63.

58. Tyack, "Communication and Cognition," 311.

59. Some excellent reviews appear in the following: Herman, "Cognitive Characteristics of Dolphins," 363–429; Herman, "Cognition and Language Competencies of Bottle-Nosed Dolphins," 221–52; and Herman, Richards, Wolz, "Comprehension of Sentences by Bottlenose Dolphins," 129–219.

60. For reviews of some training methods, see Defran and Pryor, "The Behavior and Training of Cetaceans in Captivity," 344–46; and Pryor, "Reinforcement Training as Interspecies Communication," 253–60.

61. Definitions from Tyack, "Communication and Cognition," 312–13.

62. Herman, "Cognition and Language Competencies of Bottle-Nosed Dolphins," 246.

63. Schusterman and Gisiner, "Animal Cognition in the Procrustean Bed of Linguistics," 3–18.

64. Herman, Richards, and Wolz, "Comprehension of Sentences by Bottlenose Dolphins," 129–219; and Herman, "Cognition and Language Competencies of Bottle-Nosed Dolphins," 211–52.

65. Schusterman, "Cognition and Intelligence of Dolphins," 138.

66. Tyack, "Communication and Cognition," 313.

67. Ibid., 314.

68. Ibid., 313.

69. Herman and Forestell, "Reporting Presence or Absence of Named Objects by a Dolphin," 667–81.

70. Herman, "Cognition and Language Competencies of Bottle-Nosed Dolphins," 225.

71. Tyack, "Communication and Cognition," 315.

72. Harley, Xitco, and Roitblat, "Echolocation, Cognition, and the Dolphin's World," 529–42.

73. Eisenberg, "Dolphin Behavior and Cognition," 268.

74. The waggle-dance of bees and other aspects of animal communication are discussed by Wilson, *Sociobiology: The New Synthesis,* 176–200.

75. Menzel, "How Can You Tell If an Animal Is Intelligent?" 167.

76. Tyack, "Communication and Cognition," 287.

8. Human Interactions with Dolphins

1. The issue of over-exploitation of BOTH target and non-target species is noted by a number of authors. For a review of the topic as it concerns bottlenose dolphins in the southeastern United States, see Reynolds, "Interactions between Dolphins and Fisheries," 1–38.

2. For example, see Busnel, "Symbiotic Relationship between Man and Dolphins," 112–31, and Pryor et al., "A Dolphin-Human Fishing Cooperative in Brazil, 77–82.

3. Pryor et al., "A Dolphin-Human Fishing Cooperative in Brazil," 80.

4. Ibid., 77–82.

5. Busnel, "Symbiotic Relationship between Man and Dolphins," 112–31.

6. Pryor et al., "A Dolphin-Human Fishing Cooperative in Brazil," 80.

7. Reeves and Mead, "Marine Mammals in Captivity," 412. This up-to-date and thorough reference forms the basis of much of the discussion of the issue of maintaining marine mammals in captivity. Unattributed statements in the text are from this source.

8. Besides the reference by Reeves and Mead (note 7), a good synopsis of the history of public display appears in Wells and Scott, "Bottlenose Dolphin," 163–64.

9. Collet and Duguy, "Les dauphins," 1–123, cited by Reeves and Mead, "Marine Mammals in Captivity," 413.

10. Leatherwood and Reeves, "Bottlenose Dolphin and Other Toothed Cetaceans," 382.

11. Klinowska, *Dolphins, Porpoises and Whales of the World. The IUCN Red Data Book,* 166.

12. See McBride, "Meet Mr. Porpoise," 16–29, and Caldwell and Caldwell, *The World of the Bottlenosed Dolphin,* 13.

13. National Marine Fisheries Service, personal communication to Reynolds, 1997.

14. Leatherwood and Reeves, " Bottlenose Dolphin and Other Toothed Cetaceans," 383.

15. Scott, "Management-Oriented Research on Bottlenose Dolphins," 624.

16. For excellent reviews of the topics of survival and acclimation of captive marine mammals, see the following references: DeMaster and Drevenak, "Survivorship Patterns in Captive Cetaceans," 297–311; Small and DeMaster, "Survival of Captive Marine Mammals," 209–26; and Small and DeMaster, "Acclimation to Captivity," 510–19.

17. Andrews, Duffield, and McBain. "Marine Mammal Management: Aiming at the Year 2000," 126.

18. Alison Kirk-Long, Marine Mammal Commission, personal communication to Reynolds, 1998.

19. Leatherwood and Reeves, *The Sierra Club Handbook of Whales and Dolphins,* 224.

20. Wells and Scott, "Bottlenose Dolphin," 164.

21. DeMaster and Drevenak, "Survivorship Patterns in Captive Cetaceans," 303.

22. Reeves and Mead, "Marine Mammals in Captivity," 418–19.

23. Here and elsewhere, as noted, our discussion of captivity relies to a large extent on Reeves and Mead, "Marine Mammals in Captivity," 419–25.

24. See the web page for the American Zoo and Aquarium Association: www.aza.org.

25. The poll was described by Ridgway, as cited in Reeves and Mead, "Marine Mammals in Captivity," 419.

26. Examples of publications dealing with these topics include the following: for cognition and "intelligence," see Herman, "Cognition and Language Competencies of Dolphins," 221–52; for aspects of physiology, consult Kanwisher and Ridgway, "The Physiological Ecology of Whales and Porpoises," 110–20; and for reproductive biology, see Robeck et al., "Reproductive Biology of the Bottlenose Dolphin," 321–36.

27. Wells and Scott, "Bottlenose Dolphin," 162. For a more comprehensive overview of diseases in dolphins and other marine mammals, see Dierauf, *The CRC Handbook of Marine Mammal Medicine*, 1–735.

28. Hansen and Wells, "Bottlenose Dolphin Health Assessment," 1–24.

29. For example, see Harley, Xitco, and Roitblat, "Echolocation, Cognition, and the Dolphin's World," 529–42.

30. Au, *The Sonar of Dolphins*, 271.

31. See, for example, the following: Shane, Wells, and Würsig, "Ecology, Behavior and Social Organization of the Bottlenose Dolphin," 45–50; Samuels and Gifford, "A Quantitative Assessment of Dominance Relationships among Dolphins," 70; and Saayman, Tayler, and Bower, "Diurnal Activity Cycles in Captive and Free-Ranging Dolphins," 228.

32. Samuels and Gifford, "A Quantitative Assessment of Dominance Relationships among Dolphins," 70.

33. Cited in Reeves and Mead, "Marine Mammals in Captivity," 421.

34. Quotation taken from Brownlee, "Ambassadors for Their Species," 7–19, as cited by Reeves and Mead, "Marine Mammals in Captivity," 421.

35. Wells, Bassos-Hull, and Norris, "Experimental Return to the Wild of Two Dolphins," 51–71.

36. Ibid.

37. See, for example, papers included in Reynolds and Odell, *Marine Mammal Strandings in the United States*, 1–157.

38. See, for example, the following papers: Geraci and Medway, "Simulated Field Blood Studies in the Bottle-Nosed Dolphin *Tursiops truncatus*. 2. Effects of Stress on Some Hematologic and Plasma Chemical Parameters," 29–33; Medway and Geraci, "Hematology of the Bottlenose Dolphin (*Tursiops truncatus*)," 1367–70; Medway and Geraci, "Simulated Blood Field Studies in the Bottle-Nosed Dolphin *Tursiops truncatus*. 1. Leucocyte Distribution between the Blood of Capillaries and Large Vessels," 239–41; and comprehensive review by Bossart and Dierauf," Marine Mammal Clinical Laboratory Medicine," 1–52.

39. See the following references for additional information: Brill and Friedl, "Reintroduction to the Wild as an Option for Managing Marine Mammals," 1–16, plus appen-

dices; St. Aubin, Geraci, and Lounsbury, "Rescue, Rehabilitation and Release of Marine Mammals," 1–65; and Reeves and Mead, "Marine Mammals in Captivity," 423–25, 428.

40. Reeves and Mead, "Marine Mammals in Captivity," 423–24.

41. See Perrin and Brownell, "Report of the Workshop," 7, 21–22; and Kaiya and Xing-duan, *Baiji. The Yangtze River Dolphin and Other Endangered Animals of China,* 79–87.

42. Wilson, Thompson, and Hammond, "Skin Lesions and Physical Deformities in Dolphins in Moray Firth," 243–47.

43. Reeves and Mead, "Marine Mammals in Captivity," 422.

44. See Scott, "Management-Oriented Research on Dolphins," 623–39. Quotas established under the rule appear on page 634.

45. Scott, "Management-Oriented Research on Dolphins," 624.

46. See DeMaster and Drevenak, "Survivorship Patterns in Three Species of Cetaceans," 297–311; and Small and DeMaster, "Survival in Captive Marine Mammals," 209–26.

47. Small and DeMaster, "Survival in Captive Marine Mammals," 225.

48. Duffield and Wells, "Wild and Oceanarium *Tursiops* Populations," 28–39.

49. DeMaster and Drevenak, "Survivorship Patterns in Three Species of Cetaceans," 303.

50. Barstow, "Non-Consumptive Utilization of Whales," 161.

51. Alison Kirk-Long, Marine Mammal Commission, personal communication to Reynolds, 1998.

52. Samuels and Spradlin, "Quantitative Behavioral Study of Dolphins in Swim-with-the-Dolphin Programs," 538–42.

53. Ibid., 540.

54. Ibid.

55. See de O. Santos, "Lone Sociable Bottlenose Dolphin in Brazil: Human Fatality and Management," 355–56; and review by Samuels and Spradlin, "Quantitative Behavioral Study of Dolphins in Swim-with-the-Dolphin Programs," 538.

56. Shane, Tepley, and Costello, "Life-Threatening Contact between a Woman and a Pilot Whale," 335.

57. Samuels and Spradlin, "Quantitative Behavioral Study of Dolphins in Swim-with-the-Dolphin Programs," 540.

58. See the following: Nathanson et al., "Effectiveness of Short-Term Dolphin Assisted Therapy," 90–100; Nathanson, "Long-Term Effectiveness of Dolphin-Assisted Therapy for Children," 22–32.

59. Nathanson, "Long-Term Effectiveness of Dolphin-Assisted Therapy for Children," 30.

60. Nathanson, "Using Dolphins to Increase Cognition of Mentally Retarded Children," 233.

61. Marino and Lilienfeld, "Dolphin-Assisted Therapy: Flawed Data, Flawed Conclusions," 194–200.

62. Marine Mammal Commission, *Annual Report to Congress 1997,* 200.

63. For example, in the 1991 court case, *Strong* v. *United States,* operators of dolphin-feeding ventures argued that the activity should be permitted. The courts disagreed, as described in Marine Mammal Commission, *Annual Report to Congress 1992,* 189–91.

64. Marine Mammal Commission, *Annual Report to Congress 1998,* 198.

65. Orams, Hill, and Baglioni, "'Pushy' Behavior in a Wild Dolphin Feeding Program," 107.

66. This point of view is espoused by Wilson, "Review of Dolphin Management at Monkey Mia," 5. Note, however, that Perrine, "Jojo: Rogue Dolphin?" 41, suggests pollution as the culprit responsible for low survival of juveniles.

67. Marine Mammal Commission, *Annual Report to Congress 1992,* 189.

68. S. Murphy, "Impact of Commercial Dolphin Feeding Operations," 93–95, provides some specific data regarding the economic and other impacts of dolphin feeding in South Carolina, and T. Murphy, "Feeding Bottlenose Dolphins in South Carolina," 95–97, summarizes potential positive and negative impacts of the activity there. In the latter study, Murphy listed eleven possible problems and only four possible benefits.

69. See Barstow, "Non-Consumptive Utilization of Whales," 155–63.

70. National Marine Fisheries Service, personal communication to Reynolds, 1998.

71. Marine Mammal Commission, *Annual Report to Congress 1997,* 200.

72. See various papers included in Lindberg and Hawkins, *Ecotourism: A Guide for Planners and Managers,* 1–175.

73. The National Marine Fisheries Service is responsible for cetaceans and most pinnipeds (seals, sea lions, and fur seals), and the U.S. Fish and Wildlife Service for manatees, sea otters, polar bears, and walruses.

74. The process by which permit applications are reviewed and permits approved is thoroughly described in various Marine Mammal Commission Annual Reports.

75. Level B harassment is defined as activities that have only short-term and/or relatively inconsequential effects on marine mammals. For definitions of terms used in the Marine Mammal Protection Act, see Marine Mammal Commission, *The Marine Mammal Protection Act of 1972 as Amended,* 6–9.

76. U.S. Navy, SPAWAR, "The U.S. Navy Marine Mammal Program," 1–8.

77. See, for example, the many references by Ridgway and his colleagues listed in the bibliography of this book.

78. U.S. Navy, SPAWAR, "The U.S. Navy Marine Mammal Program," 1–8.

79. See review by Mead, "Report on the Former Net Fisheries for *Tursiops truncatus,*" 1155–62.

80. Radcliffe, "Whales and Porpoises as Food," 1–10.

81. See the following references: Tomilin, *Mammals of the U.S.S.R. and Adjacent Countries,* 548; Berkes, "Turkish Dolphin Fisheries," 163–67; and Wells and Scott, "Bottlenose Dolphin," 164.

82. See Berkes, "Turkish Dolphin Fisheries," 166, and Leatherwood and Reeves, *The Sierra Club Handbook of Whales and Dolphins,* 224.

83. Wells and Scott, "Bottlenose Dolphin," 164.

84. References on this topic are as follows: For Peru, Read et al., "Exploitation of Small Cetaceans in Coastal Peru," 53–70; for Sri Lanka, West Africa, and Venezuela, Leatherwood and Reeves, *The Sierra Club Handbook of Whales and Dolphins,* 224; and for Japan, Miyazaki, "Catch Records of Cetaceans off the Coast of the Kii Peninsula,"

74–75; and Kasuya, "Fishery-Dolphin Conflict in the Iki Island Area," 261–63 and 267–68.

85. Wells and Scott, "Bottlenose Dolphin," 164.

86. Bottlenose dolphins were taken by this fishery, but in relatively small numbers.

87. See Marine Mammal Commission, *Annual Report to Congress 1995*, 3–5. For the actual language of the Marine Mammal Protection Act, see Marine Mammal Commission, *The Marine Mammal Protection Act of 1972 as Amended*, 67–80.

88. Papers describing this take of both bottlenose dolphins and other species include Harwood et al., "Incidental Catch of Small Cetaceans in a Gillnet Fishery," 555–59; Northridge, "World Review of Interactions between Marine Mammals and Fisheries," 130; and Northridge, "An Updated World Review of Interactions between Marine Mammals and Fisheries," 36–37.

89. The topic of fisheries interactions and regulations developed to address such interactions appears in recent Marine Mammal Commission annual reports and in the National Marine Fisheries Service, "Marine Mammal Protection Act of 1972 Annual Report," 20–24.

90. Reynolds, "Interactions between Dolphins and Fisheries," 1–38.

91. See National Marine Fisheries Service, "The 1998 List of Fisheries," 4–5.

92. Ibid.

93. See Wells and Scott, "Gear Entanglement for Dolphins near Sarasota, Florida," 629; and Wells, Hofmann, and Moors, "Entanglement and Mortality of Dolphins in Recreational Fishing Gear," 647–50.

94. Mann, Smolker, and Smuts, "Responses to Calf Entanglement in Dolphins," 100–106.

95. Ibid., 105. Similar conclusions regarding susceptibility of young animals to entanglement have been reached by Wells and Scott, "Gear Entanglement for Dolphins near Sarasota, Florida," 629.

96. For a review of the issue and possible solutions, see Goodson, "Developing Deterrent Devices to Reduce Mortality of Small Cetaceans," 211–36.

97. Kraus et al., "Acoustic Alarms Reduce Porpoise Mortality," 525.

98. See Goodson and Mayo, "Interactions between Dolphins and Passive Acoustic Deterrents," 365–79; and Goodson, "Developing Deterrent Devices to Reduce Mortality of Small Cetaceans," 224–31.

99. 1995 Florida Statute, Art. 10, sec. 16.

100. See Bannister, "Incidental Catches of Small Cetacea off Australia," 506; and Cockcroft, "Dolphin Catches in the Natal Shark Nets," 44–51.

101. Peddemors, Cockcroft, and Wilson, "Incidental Dolphin Mortality in the Natal Shark Nets: A Preliminary Report on Prevention Measures," 129–37.

102. Ross et al., "Population Estimates for Bottlenose Dolphins in Natal and Transkei Waters," 128; and Cockcroft, "Dolphin Catches in the Natal Shark Nets," 49.

103. For dolphin-related injuries and mortality associated with watercraft, see Wells and Scott, "Seasonal Incidence of Boat Strikes on Dolphins," 475–80. For an overview of this problem for manatees, see Reynolds and Odell, *Manatees and Dugongs*, 55–57.

104. See Wells and Scott, "Bottlenose Dolphin," 165.

105. Perrine, "Jojo: Rogue Dolphin?" 41.

106. See O'Shea et al., "Organochlorine Pollutants in Small Cetaceans," 38, 44.

107. Lahvis et al., "Decreased Lymphocyte Response in Free-Ranging Bottlenose Dolphins," 70.

108. Kuehl, Haebler, and Potter, "Chemical Residues in Dolphins," 1082.

109. Cockcroft et al., "Organochlorines in Bottlenose Dolphins," 214.

110. A review of causes of disturbance to cetaceans appears in Richardson, "Documented Disturbance Reactions," 241–324.

111. Wells and Scott, "Seasonal Incidence of Boat Strikes on Dolphins," 479.

112. Ibid., 475–80.

113. Janik and Thompson, "Changes in Surfacing Patterns of Dolphins in Response to Boat Traffic," 597–602.

114. Greene and Moore, "Man-Made Noise," 101–58.

115. See reviews by Richardson and Würsig, "Significance of Responses and Noise Impacts," 387–424; and Richardson and Würsig, "Influences of Man-Made Noise and Other Human Actions on Cetacean Behavior," 183–209.

116. Richardson and Würsig, "Influences of Man-Made Noise and Other Human Actions on Cetacean Behavior," 183.

117. Ibid., 204.

118. See review by Richardson, "Documented Disturbance Reactions," 241–324.

119. A number of references describe interactions between commercial fishing activities and bottlenose dolphins. Several sources are Lowery, *The Mammals of Louisiana and Its Adjacent Coastal Waters*, 344; Cato and Prochaska, "Porpoise Attacking Hooked Fish Irk and Injure Fishermen," 3B, 16B; Leatherwood and Reeves, "Bottlenose Dolphin and Other Toothed Cetaceans," 382; and Reynolds, "Interactions between Bottlenose Dolphins and Fisheries," 1–38.

120. Eide and Reynolds, "Bottlenose Dolphin Abundance and the Florida State Ban on Netting," 38.

9. The Stock Question

1. Marine Mammal Commission, "Marine Mammal Protection Act of 1972 as Amended," 7.

2. Ibid., 5.

3. See review by Wells and Scott, "Bottlenose Dolphin," 140–41.

4. Blaylock and Hoggard, "Bottlenose Dolphin Abundance," 5.

5. Scott, "Management-Oriented Research on Bottlenose Dolphins," 627–28.

6. Wood, "Movement of Bottlenose Dolphins around the Coast of Britain," 162.

7. The molecular perspective appears in Curry and Smith, "Phylogeographic Structure of the Bottlenose Dolphin," 227–47; the morphological side of the issue is in Mead and Potter, "Natural History of Bottlenose Dolphins," 166, and in Mead and Potter, "Recognizing Two Populations of the Bottlenose Dolphin," 31–44.

8. Curry and Smith, "Phylogeographic Structure of the Bottlenose Dolphin," 228.

9. Marine Mammal Commission, *Annual Report to Congress 1997*, 59.

10. Lipscomb et al., "Morbilliviral Disease in Bottlenose Dolphins," 567–71.

11. Scott, Burn, and Hansen, "The Dolphin Die-Off," 821.

12. See Scott, Burn, and Hansen, "The Dolphin Die-Off," 819–20; and Hohn, "Design for a Multiple-Method Approach to Determine Stock Structure of Bottlenose Dolphins," 1.

13. Scott, Burn, and Hansen, "The Dolphin Die-Off," 820.

14. Hohn, "Design for a Multiple-Method Approach to Determine Stock Structure of Bottlenose Dolphins," 1.

15. Wang, Payne, and Thayer, "Coastal Stock(s) of Atlantic Bottlenose Dolphin," v.

16. See various annual reports of the Marine Mammal Commission for discussions of the amendments and how the agencies have progressed in dealing with their mandates.

17. Hohn, "Design for a Multiple-Method Approach to Determine Stock Structure of Bottlenose Dolphins," 1.

18. Thayer and Rittmaster, "Marine Mammal Strandings in North Carolina," 79.

19. Hohn, "Design for a Multiple-Method Approach to Determine Stock Structure of Bottlenose Dolphins," 1–11.

20. For dolphins off South Africa, see Ross, "The Taxonomy of Bottlenosed Dolphins," 136–94; for animals off the Pacific coast of South America, consult van Waerebeek et al., "Bottlenose Dolphins from South America"; and for morphometric analyses of dolphins in the northwestern Atlantic, see Hersh and Duffield, "Distinction between Offshore and Coastal Dolphins," 129–39; Mead and Potter, "Natural History of Bottlenose Dolphins," 165–95; and Mead and Potter, "Recognizing Two Populations of the Bottlenose Dolphin," 31–44.

21. See, for example, Wells's doctoral dissertation, "Structural Aspects of Dolphin Societies," 1–200, as well as many of the publications of his research group in Sarasota.

22. Wells, "Structural Aspects of Dolphin Societies," 112–13.

23. See, for example, Würsig, "Occurrence and Group Organization of Bottlenose Porpoises," 354–55.

24. Among the references interested readers should consult on this topic are the following: Duffield and Wells, "Population Structure of Bottlenose Dolphins: Genetic Studies," 1–16; Dowling and Brown, "Population Structure of the Bottlenose Dolphin as Determined by Analysis of Mitochondrial DNA," 138–55; Curry and Smith, "Phylogeographic Structure of the Bottlenose Dolphin," 227–47; and LeDuc, Perrin, and Dizon, "Phylogenetic Relationships among Delphinid Cetaceans," 619–48.

25. For example, see Barros and Odell, "Food Habits of Bottlenose Dolphins," 309–28. Other references are cited in chapter 6.

26. An exciting technique has been developed to investigate feeding habits of organisms by assessing their fatty acids. The assessment of so-called fatty acid signatures has been done extensively by S. J. Iverson and her colleagues. See, for example, Iverson, Arnould, and Boyd, "Milk Fatty Acid Signatures Indicate Shifts in Diet," 188–97.

27. See review by Bowen and Siniff, "Distribution, Population Biology, and Feeding Ecology of Marine Mammals," 451–56.

28. Reviewed by Aguilar, "Using Organochlorine Pollutants to Discriminate Marine Mammal Populations," 242–62.

29. See Calambokidis and Barlow, "Chlorinated Hydrocarbon Concentrations and Their Use for Describing Population Discreteness in Harbor Porpoises," 101–10.

30. Curry and Smith, "Phylogeographic Structure of the Bottlenose Dolphin," 241.

10. Conservation Strategies and Legislation

1. Mangel et al., "Principles for the Conservation of Wild Living Resources," 339.

2. Norse, *Global Marine Biological Diversity*, 151.

3. Brown, "The Acceleration of History," 3.

4. *Year of the Ocean Discussion Papers*, iii–v.

5. Brown, "The Acceleration of History," 5.

6. The quotation by Schaller appears in Clark, Reading, and Clarke, *Endangered Species Recovery*, 6.

7. Quotation by Michael E. Soule, cited in Clark, Reading, and Clarke, *Endangered Species Recovery*, 1.

8. Holt and Talbot, "New Principles for the Conservation of Wild Living Resources," 6–33.

9. Ibid., 21.

10. Meffe, Perrin, and Dayton, "Marine Mammal Conservation," 437.

11. Domning, "Why Save the Manatee?" 168–73.

12. Ibid., 169.

13. Ibid., 173.

14. Meffe, Perrin, and Dayton, "Marine Mammal Conservation," 437. Note that this chapter borrowed heavily from Mangel et al., "Principles for the Conservation of Wild Living Resources," 338–62.

15. The importance of placing the burden of proof on the user for fisheries management is discussed by Dayton, "Reversal of the Burden of Proof in Fisheries Management," 821–22.

16. Meffe and Carroll, *Principles of Conservation Biology*, 546.

17. For a reference that cites successful programs to conserve manatees or other living resources as examples and then provides suggestions for ways to "make a difference," see Reynolds, "Efforts to Conserve the Manatees," 287–89.

18. Reynolds, "Efforts to Conserve the Manatees," 289.

19. The text of the Marine Mammal Protection Act, including definitions of terms, appears in Marine Mammal Commission, "Marine Mammal Protection Act of 1972 as Amended," 5–107.

20. Hofman, "The Marine Mammal Act: A First of Its Kind Anywhere," 25.

21. Idyll, "The Anchovy Crisis," 22–29.

22. Alverson et al., "A Global Assessment of Fisheries Bycatch and Discards," 32–33.

23. As an aside, we note that under the Endangered Species Act of 1973, the agencies responsible for species or stocks designated as endangered or threatened must develop Recovery Plans, which are generally similar in scope and intent to conservation plans required for stocks or species designated as depleted under the Marine Mammal Protection Act. Bottlenose dolphins are not considered endangered or threatened in the United States and are, thus, not covered by provisions of the Endangered Species Act.

24. See Reynolds and Gluckman, "Protection of West Indian Manatees in Florida," 1–85; and Reynolds and Odell, *Manatees and Dugongs,* 134–44 and 161–65.

25. For information on GIS development for manatees in Florida, see Reynolds and Haddad, "GIS as an Aid to Managing Habitat for Manatees," 1–57. For similar perspectives regarding Alaskan marine mammals, see Hoover-Miller, "Use of GIS to Facilitate Conservation of Marine Mammals," 1–55.

26. See, for example, the following: Eide et al., "Assessment and Habitat Use of Bottlenose Dolphins," 9; Forys et al., "Field Application of Technology to Assist Research on Dolphins," 68–70; Thoms et al., "The Use of Geographic Information Systems to Relate Behavior of Dolphins and Environmental Parameters," 134.

27. Marine Mammal Commission, *Annual Report to Congress 1997,* 95.

28. Strategic stocks are those for which direct, human-caused mortality exceeds the calculated potential biological removal (PBR) level, or those currently or likely to be listed as depleted under the Marine Mammal Protection Act, or threatened or endangered under the Endangered Species Act.

29. These are the so-called category I or category II fisheries; see chapter 8.

30. National Marine Fisheries Service, personal communication to Reynolds, 1998.

31. Bryden, Marsh, and Shaughnessy, *Dugongs, Whales, Dolphins and Seals. A Guide to the Sea Mammals of Australasia,* 159–64.

32. Frances Michaelis, Senate Committee on the Environment, Canberra, Australia, personal communication to Reynolds, 1998.

33. Bryden, Marsh, and Shaughnessy, *Dugongs, Whales, Dolphins and Seals. A Guide to the Sea Mammals of Australasia,* 164.

34. Ibid., 163–64.

35. Simon Northridge, Sea Mammals Research Unit, St. Andrews, Scotland, personal communication to Reynolds, 1998.

36. Ben Wilson, personal communication to Reynolds, 1998.

37. *South Africa Government Gazette,* "Marine Living Resources Act," 40.

38. Reynolds and Odell, *Manatees and Dugongs,* 161–65.

39. Ames, "Saving Some Cetaceans May Require Breeding in Captivity," 746–49.

Bibliography

Ackman, R. G., and F. Lamothe. "Marine Mammals," 179–381. In R. G. Ackman, ed., *Marine Biogenic Lipids, Fats and Oils.* Vol. 2. Boca Raton, Fla.: CRC Press, 1989.

Adachi, J., and M. Hasagawa. "Letter to the Editor. Phylogeny of Whales: Dependence of the Inference on Species Sampling." *Molecular Biology and Evolution* 12, no. 1 (1995): 177–79.

Aguilar, A. "Using Organochlorine Pollutants to Discriminate Marine Mammal Populations: A Review and Critique of the Methods." *Marine Mammal Science* 3, no. 3 (1987): 242–62.

———. "Die-off Strikes the Western Sahara Population of Mediterranean Monk Seals." *Marine Mammal Society Newsletter* 5, no. 3 (1997): 1–3.

Aguilar, A., and A. Borrell. "Abnormally High Polychlorinated Biphenyl Levels in Striped Dolphins (*Stenella coeruleoalba*) Affected by the 1990–1992 Mediterranean Epizootic." *The Science of the Total Environment* 154 (1994): 237–47.

———. "Reproductive Transfer and Variation of Body Load of Organochlorine Pollutants with Age in Fin Whales (*Balaenoptera physalus*)." *Archives of Environmental Contamination and Toxicology* 27 (1994): 546–54.

Alpers, A. *Dolphins: The Myth and the Mammal.* Boston, Mass.: Houghton Mifflin Co., 1961.

Alverson, D. L., M. H. Freeberg, S. A. Murawski, and J. G. Pope. "A Global Assessment of Fisheries Bycatch and Discards." *Food and Agriculture Organization Fisheries Technical Paper* 339 (1994): 1–233.

Ames, M. H. "Saving Some Cetaceans May Require Breeding in Captivity." *Bioscience* 41 (1991): 746–49.

Amos, W. "Use of Molecular Probes to Analyse Pilot Whale Pod Structure: Two Novel Analytical Approaches." *Symposium of the Zoological Society of London* 6 (1993): 33–48.

Andrews, B. F., D. A. Duffield and J. F. McBain. "Marine Mammal Management: Aiming at Year 2000." *IBI Reports*, no. 7 (1997): 125–30.

Au, W. W. L. *The Sonar of Dolphins*. New York: Springer-Verlag, 1993.

Au, D., and D. Weihs. "At High Speeds Dolphins Save Energy by Leaping." *Nature* (London) 284 (1980): 548–50.

Awbry, F. T. "Communicating with Dolphins." *Marine Mammal Science* 2, no. 3 (1986): 233–35.

Bannister, J. L. "Incidental Catches of Small Cetacea off Australia." *Reports of the International Whaling Commission* 27 (1977): 506.

Barco, S. G., W. A. McLellan, D. A. Pabst, D. G. Dunn, W. J. Walton, H. Fearnbach, and W. M. Swingle. "Virginia Atlantic Bottlenose Dolphin (*Tursiops truncatus*) Calf Strandings: Dramatic Rise in Numbers and Emergence of Traumatic Deaths," 3. In S. A. Rommel et al., eds., *Proceedings of the Sixth Annual Atlantic Coastal Dolphin Conference*, 1–3, Sarasota, Fla., May 1998.

Barnes, L. G. "The Fossil Record and Evolutionary Relationships of the Genus *Tursiops*," 3–26. In S. Leatherwood and R. R. Reeves, eds., *The Bottlenose Dolphin*. New York: Academic Press, 1990.

Barnes, L. G., D. P. Domning, and C. E. Ray. "Status of Studies on Fossil Marine Mammals." *Marine Mammal Science* 1, no. 1 (1985): 15–53.

Barros, N. B. "Feeding Ecology and Foraging Strategies of Bottlenose Dolphins on the Central East Coast of Florida." Ph.D. diss., University of Miami, 1993.

Barros, N. B., and D. K. Odell. "Food Habits of Bottlenose Dolphins in the Southeastern United States," 309–28. In S. Leatherwood and R. R. Reeves, eds., *The Bottlenose Dolphin*. New York: Academic Press, 1990.

Barros, N. B., and R. S. Wells. "Prey and Feeding Patterns of Resident Bottlenose Dolphins (*Tursiops truncatus*) in Sarasota Bay, Florida." *Journal of Mammalogy* 79, no. 3 (1998): 1045–59.

Barstow, R. "Non-Consumptive Utilization of Whales." *Ambio* 15 (1986): 155–63.

Bartholomew, G. A. "A Model for the Evolution of Pinniped Polygyny." *Evolution* 24 (1970): 546–59.

Bassos, M. K. "A Behavioral Assessment of the Reintroduction of Two Bottlenose Dolphins." Master's thesis, University of California, Santa Cruz, 1993.

Bauer, G. B., M. Fuller, A. Perry, J. R. Dunn, and J. Zoeger. "Magnetoreception and Biomineralization of Magnetite in Cetaceans," 489–507. In J. L. Kirschvink, D. S. Jones, and B. J. MacFadden, eds., *Magnetite Biomineralization and Magnetoreception in Living Organisms: A New Biomagnetism*. New York: Plenum Press, 1985.

Berkes, F. "Turkish Dolphin Fisheries." *Oryx* 14, no. 2 (1977): 163–67.

Bérubé, M., and A. Aguilar. "A New Hybrid between a Blue Whale, *Balaenoptera musculus*, and a Fin Whale, *B. physalus:* Frequency and Implications of Hybridism." *Marine Mammal Science* 14, no. 1 (1998): 82–98.

Bielsa, L. M., W. H. Murdich, and R. F. Labisky. "Species Profiles: Life Histories and Environmental Requirements of Coastal Fishes and Invertebrates (South Florida)."

U.S. Department of the Interior, Fish and Wildlife Service Report FWS/OBS-82/11.17 (1983): 21pp.

Blake, R. W. "Energetics of Leaping Dolphins and Other Aquatic Animals." *Journal of the Marine Biological Association of the United Kingdom* 63 (1983): 61–70.

Blaylock, R. A., and W. Hoggard. "Preliminary Estimates of Bottlenose Dolphin Abundance in Southern U.S. Atlantic and Gulf of Mexico Continental Shelf Waters." *NOAA Technical Memorandum* NMFS-SEFSC-356 (1994): 1–10.

Bossart, G. D., D. G. Baden, R. Y. Ewing, B. Roberts, and S. D. Wright. "Brevetoxicosis in Manatees (*Trichechus manatus latirostris*) from the 1996 Epizootic: Gross, Histologic, and Immunohistochemical Features." *Toxicologic Pathology* 26, no. 2 (1998): 276–82.

Bossart, G. D., and L. A. Dierauf. "Marine Mammal Clinical Laboratory Medicine," 1–52. In L. A. Dierauf, ed., *CRC Handbook of Marine Mammal Medicine: Health, Disease, and Rehabilitation*. Boca Raton, Fla.: CRC Press, 1990.

Bowen, W. D., and D. B. Siniff. "Distribution, Population Biology, and Feeding Ecology of Marine Mammals," 423–85. In J. E. Reynolds III and S. A. Rommel, eds., *Biology of Marine Mammals*. Washington, D.C.: Smithsonian Institution Press, 1999.

Boyd, I. L., C. Lockyer, and H. Marsh. "Reproduction in Marine Mammals," 218–86. In J. E. Reynolds III and S. A. Rommel, eds., *Biology of Marine Mammals*. Washington, D.C.: Smithsonian Institution Press, 1999.

Brabyn, M., and R. V. C. Frew. "New Zealand Herd Stranding Sites Do Not Relate to Geomagnetic Topography." *Marine Mammal Science* 10 (1994): 195–207.

Bradley, W. G., and J. E. Reynolds III. "Isolation, Cloning, Sequencing and Expression of Marine Mammal Interleukin-2." In C. J. Pfeiffer, ed., *Cell and Molecular Biology of Marine Mammals*. Melbourne, Fla.: Krieger Publishing Co., in press.

Brewer, R. *The Science of Ecology*. Philadelphia, Pa.: Saunders College Publishing, 1988.

Brill, R. L., and W. A. Friedl. "Reintroduction to the Wild as an Option for Managing Navy Marine Mammals." Biosciences Division, Naval Command, Control and Ocean Surveillance Center, Technical Report 1549 (1993): 1–16, appendix.

Brown, E. K., G. D. Bossart, and J. E. Reynolds III. "The Microscopic and Immunohistologic Anatomy of the Endocrine Pancreas of Pygmy and Dwarf Sperm Whales (Kogiidae)." *Marine Mammal Science* 4, no. 4 (1988): 291–96.

Brown, L. H. "The Acceleration of History," 3–20. In L. R. Brown et al., eds., *State of the World 1996*. New York: W. W. Norton and Co., 1996.

Brownlee, S. "Ambassadors for Their Species." *Pacific Discovery* 39, no. 4 (1986): 7–19.

Bryden, M. M., and G. H. K. Lim. "Blood Parameters of the Southern Elephant Seal (*Mirounga leonina*) in Relation to Diving." *Comparative Biochemistry and Physiology* 28 (1969): 139–48.

Bryden, M., H. Marsh, and P. Shaughnessy. *Dugongs, Whales, Dolphins and Seals: A Guide to the Sea Mammals of Australasia*. St. Leonards, New South Wales, Australia: Allen and Unwin, 1998.

Busnel, R. G. "Symbiotic Relationship between Man and Dolphins." *Transactions of the New York Academy of Sciences* 35 (1973): 112–31.

Calambokidis, J., and J. Barlow. "Chlorinated Hydrocarbon Concentrations and Their Use for Describing Population Discreteness in Harbor Porpoises from Washington, Oregon, and California," 101–10. In J. E. Reynolds III and D. K. Odell, eds., *Marine Mammal Strandings in the United States. Proceedings of the Second Marine Mammal Stranding Workshop, Miami, Florida, December 3–5, 1987*. NOAA Technical Report NMFS 98, 1991.

Caldwell, D. K. "Evidence of Home Range of an Atlantic Bottlenose Dolphin." *Journal of Mammalogy* 36 (1955): 304–5.

Caldwell, D. K., and M. C. Caldwell. "Dolphins, Porpoises and Behavior." *Underwater Naturalist* 4, no. 2 (1967): 14–19.

———. "Dolphins Communicate—But They Don't Talk." *Naval Research Review* 25, Nos. 6–7 (1972): 23–27.

———. *The World of the Bottlenosed Dolphin*. Philadelphia, Pa.: J. B. Lippincott Co., 1972.

Caldwell, M. C., and D. K. Caldwell. "Individualized Whistle Contours in Bottlenosed Dolphins (*Tursiops truncatus*)." *Science* 207 (1965): 434–35.

———. "Epimeletic (Care-Giving) Behavior in Cetacea," 755–89. In K. S. Norris, ed., *Whales, Dolphins, and Porpoises*. Berkeley: University of California Press, 1966.

Caldwell, M. C., D. K. Caldwell, and J. B. Siebenaler. "Observations on Captive and Wild Atlantic Bottlenosed Dolphins, *Tursiops truncatus*, in the Northeastern Gulf of Mexico." *Los Angeles County Museum of Natural History Contributions in Science* 91 (1965): 1–10.

Caldwell, M. C., D. K. Caldwell, and P. L. Tyack. "Review of the Signature-Whistle Hypothesis for the Atlantic Bottlenose Dolphin," 199–234. In S. Leatherwood and R. R. Reeves, eds., *The Bottlenose Dolphin*. New York: Academic Press, 1990.

Castellini, M. A., D. P. Costa, and J. M. Castellini. "Blood Glucose Distribution, Brain Size and Diving in Small Odontocetes." *Marine Mammal Science* 8, no. 3 (1992): 294–98.

Cato, J. C., and F. J. Prochaska. "Porpoise Attacking Hooked Fish Irk and Injure Florida Fishermen." *National Fisherman* 56, no. 9 (1976): 3B and 16B.

Clapham, P. J., P. J. Palsboll, and D. K. Mattila. "High-Energy Behaviors in Humpback Whales as a Source of Sloughed Skin for Molecular Analysis." *Marine Mammal Science* 9, no. 2 (1993): 213–20.

Clark, T. W., R. P. Reading, and A. L. Clarke, eds. *Endangered Species Recovery. Finding the Lessons, Improving the Process*. Washington, D.C.: Island Press, 1994.

Cockcroft, V. G. "Dolphin Catches in the Natal Shark Nets." *South African Tydskr. Natuurnav* 20, no. 2 (1990): 44–51.

Cockcroft, V. G., G. Cliff, and G. J. B. Ross. "Shark Predation on Indian Ocean Bottlenose Dolphins, *Tursiops truncatus* off Natal, South Africa." *South African Journal of Zoology* 24, no. 4 (1989): 305–9.

Cockcroft, V. G., A. C. Dekock, D. A. Lord, and G. J. B. Ross. "Organochlorines in Bottlenose Dolphins, *Tursiops truncatus*, from the East Coast of South Africa." *South African Journal of Marine Science* 8 (1989): 207–17.

Cockcroft, V. G., and G. J. B. Ross. "Age, Growth and Reproduction of Bottlenose Dolphins *Tursiops truncatus* from the East Coast of Southern Africa." *Fishery Bulletin* 88, no. 2 (1990): 289–302.

Collet, A., and R. Duguy. "Les dauphins: Historique et biologie." *Science et Découvertes,* Monaco: Le Rocher, 1987.

Connor, R. C., and M. R. Heithaus. "Approach by Great White Shark Elicits Flight Response in Bottlenose Dolphins." *Marine Mammal Science* 12, no. 4 (1996): 602–6.

Connor, R. C., and K. S. Norris. "Are Dolphins Reciprocal Altruists?" *American Naturalist* 119, no. 3 (1982): 358–74.

Connor, R. C., A. F. Richards, R. S. Smolker, and J. Mann. "Patterns of Female Attractiveness in Indian Ocean Bottlenose Dolphins." *Behaviour* 133 (1996): 37–69.

Connor, R. C., and R. A. Smolker. "'Pop' Goes the Dolphin: A Vocalization Male Bottlenose Dolphins Produce during Consortships." *Behaviour* 133 (1996): 643–62.

Connor, R. C., R. A. Smolker, and A. F. Richards. "Aggressive Herding of Females by Coalitions of Male Bottlenose Dolphins (*Tursiops* sp.)," 415–43. In A. H. Harcourt and F. B. M. De Waal, eds., *Coalitions and Alliances in Humans and Other Animals.* Oxford: Oxford University Press, 1992.

Corkeron, P. J. "Aspects of the Behavioral Ecology of Inshore Dolphins *Tursiops truncatus* and *Sousa chinensis* in Moreton Bay, Australia," 285–94. In S. Leatherwood and R. R. Reeves, eds., *The Bottlenose Dolphin.* San Diego, Calif.: Academic Press, 1990.

Corkeron, P. J., M. M. Bryden, and K. E. Hedstrom. "Feeding by Bottlenose Dolphins in Association with Trawling Operations in Moreton Bay, Australia," 329–36. In S. Leatherwood and R. R. Reeves, eds., *The Bottlenose Dolphin.* San Diego, Calif.: Academic Press, 1990.

Corkeron, P. J., R. J. Morris, and M. M. Bryden. "Interactions between Bottlenose Dolphins and Sharks in Moreton Bay." *Aquatic Mammals* 13, no. 3 (1987): 109–13.

Costa, D. P., S. D. Feldcamp, J. P. Schroeder, W. Friedl, and J. Haun. "Oxygen Consumption and Thermoregulation in Bottlenose Dolphins." Abstract, Thermal Physiology Satellite Symposium IUPS, Tromso, Norway, 1989.

Costa, D. P., and T. M. Williams. "Marine Mammal Energetics," 176–217. In J. E. Reynolds III and S. A. Rommel, eds., *Biology of Marine Mammals,* Washington, D.C.: Smithsonian Institution Press, 1990.

Costa, D. P., G. A. J. Worthy, R. W. Wells, A. Read, M. Svott, B. Irvine, and D. Waples. "Seasonal Changes in the Field Metabolic Rate of Bottlenose Dolphins." *Proceedings of the 10th Biennial Conference on the Biology of Marine Mammals,* Galveston, Tex., 1993.

Cranford, T. W., M. Amundin, and K. S. Norris. "Functional Morphology and Homology in the Odontocete Nasal Complex: Implications for Sound Generation." *Journal of Morphology* 228 (1996): 223–85.

Crook, J. H., J. E. Ellis, and J. D. Goss-Custard. "Mammalian Social Systems: Structure and Function." *Animal Behaviour* 24 (1976): 261–74.

Curry, B. E. "Phylogenetic Relationships among Bottlenose Dolphins (Genus *Tursiops*) in a Worldwide Context." Ph.D. diss., Texas A & M University, 1997.

Curry, B. E., and J. Smith. "Phylogeographic Structure of the Bottlenose Dolphin

(*Tursiops truncatus*): Stock Identification and Implications for Management," 227–47. In A. E. Dizon, S. J. Chivers, and W. F. Perrin, eds., *Molecular Genetics of Marine Mammals.* Lawrence, Kans.: Special Publication no. 3, Society for Marine Mammalogy, 1997.

Darwin, C. R. *On the Origin of Species by Means of Natural Selection.* London: 1859.

Dawson, W. W., L. A. Birndorf and J. M. Perez. "Gross Anatomy and Optics of the Dolphin Eye (*Tursiops truncatus*)." *Cetology* 10 (1972): 1–12.

Dayton, P. K. "Reversal of the Burden of Proof in Fisheries Management." *Science* 279 (1998): 821–22.

Dayton, P. K., M. J. Tegner, P. B. Edwards, and K. L. Riser. "Sliding Baselines, Ghosts, and Reduced Expectations in Kelp Forest Communities." *Ecological Applications* 8, no. 2 (1998): 309–22.

Defran, R. H., and K. Pryor. "The Behavior and Training of Cetaceans in Captivity," 319–62. In L. M. Herman, ed., *Cetacean Behavior: Mechanisms and Functions.* New York: Wiley-Interscience, 1980.

De Guise, S., A. Lagace and P. Beland. "Tumors in St. Lawrence Beluga Whales (*Delphinapterus leucas*)." *Veterinary Pathology* 31 (1994): 444–49.

Dellmann, H. *Veterinary Histology: An Outline Text Atlas.* Philadelphia, Pa.: Lea and Febiger, 1971.

Dellmann, H., and E. M. Brown. *Textbook of Veterinary Histology.* Philadelphia, Pa.: Lea and Febiger, 1976.

DeLong, R. L., W. G. Gilmartin, and J. G. Simpson. "Premature Births in California Sea Lions: Association with High Organochlorine Pollutant Residue Levels." *Science* 181 (1973): 1168–71.

Demaster, D. P., and J. K. Drevenak. "Survivorship Patterns in Three Species of Captive Cetaceans." *Marine Mammal Science* 4, no. 4 (1988): 297–311.

De O. Santos, M. C. "Lone Sociable Bottlenose Dolphin in Brazil: Human Fatality and Management." *Marine Mammal Science* 13, no. 2 (1997): 355–56.

De Swart, R. L., R. M. G. Kluten, C. J. Huizing, E. J. Vedder, P. J. H. Reijnders, I. K. G. Visser, F. G. C. M. Uytdehaag, A. D. M. E. Osterhaus. "Mitogen and Antigen Induced B Cell and T Cell Responses of Peripheral Blood Mononuclear Cells from the Harbour Seal (*Phoca vitulina*)." *Veterinary Immunology and Immunopathology* 37 (1993): 217–30.

De Swart, R. L., P. S. Ross, E. J. Vedder, H. H. Timmerman, S. H. Heisterkamp, H. Van Loveren, J. G. Vos, P. J. H. Reijnders, and A. D. M. E. Osterhaus. "Impairment of Immunological Functions in Harbour Seals (*Phoca vitulina*) Feeding on Fish from Polluted Coastal Waters." *Ambio* 23 (1994): 155–59.

De Swart, R. L., P. S. Ross, J. G. Vos, and A. D. M. E. Osterhaus. "Impaired Immunity in Harbour Seals (*Phoca vitulina*) Exposed to Bioaccumulated Environmental Contaminants: Review of a Long-Term Feeding Study." *Environmental Health Perspectives* 104, Suppl. 4 (1996): 823–28.

De Waal, F. B. M. "Coalitions as Reciprocal Relations in the Arnhem Chimpanzee

Colony," 233–57. In A. H. Harcourt and F. B. M. De Waal, eds., *Coalitions and Alliances in Humans and Other Animals.* Oxford: Oxford University Press, 1992.

Dierauf, L. A. *CRC Handbook of Marine Mammal Medicine: Health, Disease, and Rehabilitation.* Boca Raton, Fla.: CRC Press, 1990.

Domning, D. P. "Why Save the Manatee?" 167–73. In J. E. Reynolds III and D. K. Odell. *Manatees and Dugongs.* New York: Facts on File, 1991.

Donaldson, B. J. "The Tongue of the Bottlenosed Dolphin," 175–98. In R. J. Harrison, ed., *Functional Anatomy of Marine Mammals.* New York: Academic Press, 1977.

Doria, C. "The Dolphin Rider," 33–51. In J. Mcintyre, *Mind in the Waters.* New York: Charles Scribner's Sons, 1974.

Dowling, T. E., and W. M. Brown. "Population Structure of the Bottlenose Dolphin (*Tursiops truncatus*) as Determined by Restriction Endonulease Analysis of Mitochondrial DNA." *Marine Mammal Science* 9, no. 2 (1993): 138–55.

Dral, A. D. G. "Aquatic and Aerial Vision in the Bottle-Nosed Dolphin." *Journal of Sea Research* 5 (1972): 510–13.

———. "On the Retinal Anatomy of Cetacea," 86–87. In R. J. Harrison, ed., *Functional Anatomy of Marine Mammals.* New York: Academic Press, 1977.

Duffield, D. A., and R. S. Wells. "Population Structure of Bottlenose Dolphins: Genetic Studies of Bottlenose Dolphins along the Central West Coast of Florida." Contract Report to National Marine Fisheries Service, Southeast Fisheries Center, Contract no. 45-WCNF-5-00366, 1986.

———. "A Discussion on Comparative Data of Wild and Oceanarium *Tursiops* Populations," 28–39. In N. F. Hecker, ed., *Proceedings of the 18th International Marine Animal Trainers Association Conference,* November 4–9, 1990, Chicago.

———. "The Combined Application of Chromosome, Protein and Molecular Data for Investigation of Social Unit Dynamics in *Tursiops truncatus*," 155–69. In A. R. Hoelzel, ed., *Genetic Ecology of Whales and Dolphins.* Cambridge, Eng.: Reports of the International Whaling Commission Special Issue No. 13, 1991.

Duignan, P. J., C. House, D. K. Odell, R. S. Wells, L. J. Hansen, M. T. Walsh, D. J. St. Aubin, B. K. Rima, and J. R. Geraci. "Morbillivirus Infection in Bottlenose Dolphins: Evidence for Recurrent Epizootics in the Western Atlantic and Gulf of Mexico." *Marine Mammal Science* 12, no. 4 (1996): 499–515.

Eide, S. D. "Correlations between Bottlenose Dolphin (*Tursiops truncatus*) Distribution and Presence of Calves in Boca Ciega Bay, Florida, and the Florida State Ban of Commercial Netting." Senior thesis, Eckerd College, St. Petersburg, Fla., 1998.

Eide, S. D., M. E. Bolen, S. Carlson, S. M. Doty, E. A. Forys, J. M. Morris, J. L. Odell, K. A. Thoms, and J. E. Reynolds III. "Assessment and Habitat Use of Bottlenose Dolphins, *Tursiops truncatus*, in Boca Ciega Bay, Florida." *Proceedings of the 5th Annual Atlantic Coastal Dolphin Conference,* April 4–6, 1997, Wilmington, NC.

Eide, S. D., and J. E. Reynolds III. "Correlations between Bottlenose Dolphin (*Tursiops truncatus*) Abundance and Presence of Calves in Boca Ciega Bay, Florida, and the Florida State Ban on Commercial Netting." *Proceedings of the World Marine Mammal Science Conference,* January 20–24, 1998, Monaco.

Eisenberg, J. F. "Dolphin Behavior and Cognition: Evolutionary and Ecological Aspects," 261–70. In R. J. Schusterman, J. A. Thomas, and F. G. Wood, eds., *Dolphin Cognition and Behavior: A Comparative Approach.* Hillsdale, N.J.: Lawrence Erlbaum Associates, 1986.

Elsner, R. "Living in Water, Solutions to Physiological Problems," 73–116. In J. E. Reynolds III and S. A. Rommel, eds., *Biology of Marine Mammals.* Washington, D.C.: Smithsonian Institution Press, 1999.

Elsner, R., D. W. Kenney, and K. Burgess. "Diving Bradycardia in the Trained Dolphin." *Nature* 212 (1966): 407–8.

Essapian, F. S. "The Birth and Growth of a Porpoise." *Natural History* (November 1953): 392–99.

Estes, J. A., M. T. Tinker, T. M. Williams, and D. F. Doak. "Killer Whale Predation on Sea Otters Linking Oceanic and Nearshore Ecosystems." *Science* 282 (1998): 473–76.

Evans, W. E., and J. Bastian. "Marine Mammal Communication: Social and Ecological Factors," 425–76. In H. T. Andersen, ed., *The Biology of Marine Mammals.* New York: Academic Press, 1969.

Evans, W. E., and P. Maderson. "Mechanisms of Sound Production in Delphinid Cetaceans: A Review and Some Anatomical Considerations." *American Zoologist* 13, no. 4 (1973): 1205–13.

Ferrero, R. C., and L. M. Tsunoda. "First Record of a Bottlenose Dolphin (*Tursiops truncatus*) in Washington State." *Marine Mammal Science* 5, no. 3 (1989): 302–5.

Fertl, D., and A. Schiro. "Carrying of Dead Calves by Free-Ranging Texas Bottlenose Dolphins (*Tursiops truncatus*)." *Aquatic Mammals* 20, no. 1 (1989): 53–56.

Fish, F. E. "Power Output and Propulsive Efficiency of Swimming Bottlenose Dolphins (*Tursiops truncatus*)." *Journal of Experimental Biology* 185 (1993): 179–93.

———. "Influences of Hydrodynamic Design and Propulsive Mode on Mammalian Swimming Energetics." *Australian Journal of Zoology* 42 (1993): 79–101.

———. "Comparative Kinematics and Hydrodynamics of Odontocete Cetaceans: Morphological and Ecological Correlates with Swimming Performance." *Journal of Experimental Biology* 201 (1998): 2867–77.

Fish, F. E., and C. A. Hui. "Dolphin Swimming—A Review." *Mammal Reviews* 21, no. 4 (1991): 181–95.

Flower, W. H. "On Whales, Present and Past and Their Probable Origin." *Proceedings of the Zoological Society of London* (1883): 466–513.

Forys, E. A., E. L. Gallizzi, J. E. Reynolds III, S. M. Doty, and S. D. Eide. "Field Application of Technology to Assist Photo-Identification Research on Bottlenose Dolphins in the Tampa Bay Florida Area," 68–70. In S. A. Rommel, J. E. Reynolds III, and R. S. Wells, eds., *Proceedings of the 6th Annual Atlantic Coastal Dolphin Conference,* May 1–3, 1998, Sarasota, Fla.

Gales, N., and K. Waples. "The Rehabilitation and Release of Bottlenose Dolphins from Atlantis Marine Park, Western Australia." *Aquatic Mammals* 19, no. 2 (1993): 49–59.

Gardner, E., D. J. Gray, and R. O'Rahilly. *Anatomy: A Regional Study of Human Structure.* Philadelphia, Pa.: W. B. Saunders Co., 1975.

Gardner, H. *Frames of Mind: The Theory of Multiple Intelligences.* New York: Basic Books, 1983.

Gaskin, D. E. "Form and Function in the Digestive Tract and Associated Organs in Cetacea, with a Consideration of Metabolic Rates and Specific Energy Budgets." *Oceanography and Marine Biology Annual Review* 16 (1978): 313–45.

———. *The Ecology of Whales and Dolphins.* London: Heinemann, 1982.

Gatesy, J. "More DNA Support for a Cetacea/Hippopotamidae Clade: The Blood-Clotting Protein Gene Fibrinogen." *Molecular Biology and Evolution* 14, no. 5 (1997): 537–43.

———. "Molecular Evidence for the Phylogenetic Affinities of Cetacea," 63–112. In J. G. M. Thewissen, ed., *The Emergence of Whales. Evolutionary Patterns in the Origin of Cetacea.* New York: Plenum Press, 1998.

Geraci, J. R. "Clinical Investigation of the 1987–88 Mass Mortality of Bottlenose Dolphins along the U.S. Central and South Atlantic Coast." Final Report to the National Marine Fisheries Service, U.S. Navy (Office of Naval Research), and Marine Mammal Commission, 1989.

Geraci, J. R., D. M. Anderson, R. J. Timperi, D. J. St. Aubin, G. A. Early, J. H. Prescott, and C. A. Mayo. "Humpback Whales (*Megaptera novaeangliae*) Fatally Poisoned by Dinoflagellate Toxin." *Canadian Journal of Fisheries and Aquatic Sciences* 46 (1989): 1895–98.

Geraci, J. R., and W. Medway. "Simulated Field Blood Studies in the Bottle-Nosed Dolphin *Tursiops truncatus.* 2. Effects of Stress on Some Hematologic and Plasma Chemical Parameters." *Journal of Wildlife Diseases* 9 (1973): 29–33.

Geraci, J. R., D. J. St. Aubin, and B. D. Hicks. "1. The Epidermis of Odontocetes: A View from Within," 3–21. In M. M. Bryden and R. J. Harrison, eds., *Research on Dolphins.* Oxford, Eng.: Clarendon Press, 1986.

Goodall, J. *The Chimpanzees of Gombe: Patterns of Behavior.* Cambridge, Mass.: The Belknap Press of Harvard University Press, 1986.

Goodson, A. D. "Developing Deterrent Devices Designed to Reduce the Mortality of Small Cetaceans in Commercial Fishing Nets." *Marine and Freshwater Behaviour and Physiology* 29 (1997): 211–36.

Goodson, A. D., and R. H. Mayo. "Interactions between Free-Ranging Dolphins (*Tursiops truncatus*) and Passive Acoustic Gill-Net Deterrent Devices," 365–79. In R. A. Kastelein, J. A. Thomas, and P. E. Nachtigall, eds., *Sensory Systems of Aquatic Mammals.* Woerden, The Netherlands: De Spil Publishers, 1995.

Gould, S. J. "Sizing Up Human Intelligence," 179–86. In *Ever Since Darwin: Reflections in Natural History.* New York: W. W. Norton and Co., 1977.

Graur, D., and D. S. Higgins. "Molecular Evidence for the Inclusion of Cetaceans within the Order Artiodactyla." *Molecular Biology and Evolution* 11, no. 3 (1994): 357–64.

Green, A., and P. J. Corkeron. "An Attempt to Establish a Feeding Station for Bottlenose Dolphins (*Tursiops truncatus*) on Moreton Island, Queensland, Australia. *Aquatic Mammals* 17, no. 3 (1991): 125–29.

Greene, C. R., Jr., and S. E. Moore. "Man-Made Noise," 101–58. In W. J. Richardson et al., eds., *Marine Mammals and Noise*. San Diego, Calif.: Academic Press, 1995.

Gruber, J. A. "Ecology of the Atlantic Bottlenosed Dolphin (*Tursiops truncatus*) in the Pass Cavallo Area of Matagorda Bay, Texas." Master's thesis, Texas A & M University, 1981.

Gunter, G. "Contributions to the Natural History of the Bottlenose Dolphins, *Tursiops truncatus* (Montague [*sic*]), on the Texas Coast, with Particular Reference to Food Habits." *Journal of Mammalogy* 23, no. 3 (1942): 267–76.

Hansen, L. J. "California Coastal Bottlenose Dolphins," 403–20. In S. Leatherwood and R. R. Reeves, eds., *The Bottlenose Dolphin*. San Diego, Calif.: Academic Press, 1990.

Hansen, L. J., and R. S. Wells. "Bottlenose Dolphin Health Assessment: Field Report on Sampling Near Beaufort, North Carolina, during July 1995." Final Report to the National Marine Fisheries Service, U.S. Navy (Office of Naval Research), and Marine Mammal Commission, 1996.

Hanson, M. T., and R. H. Defran. "The Behaviour and Feeding Ecology of the Pacific Coast Bottlenose Dolphin, *Tursiops truncatus*." Aquatic Mammals 19 (1993): 127–42.

Harley, H. E., M. J. Xitco Jr., and H. L. Roitblat. "Echolocation, Cognition, and the Dolphin's World," 529–42. In R. A. Kastelein, J. A. Thomas, and P. E. Nachtigall, eds., *Sensory Systems of Aquatic Mammals*. Woerden, The Netherlands: De Spil Publishers, 1995.

Harris, J. C. "Porpoises Feeding." *Life* 5 (1938): 67.

Harrison, R. G. "The Comparative Anatomy of the Blood-Supply of the Mammalian Testis." *Proceedings of the Zoological Society of London* 119 (1948): 325–44.

Hart, K. D. "Foraging Ecology and Behavior of Atlantic Bottlenose Dolphins (*Tursiops truncatus*) in the Indian River Lagoon, Florida." Ph.D. diss., Florida Institute of Technology, 1997.

Harwood, M. B., K. J. McNamara, and G. R. V. Anderson. "Incidental Catch of Small Cetaceans in a Gillnet Fishery in Northern Australian Waters." *Reports of the International Whaling Commission* 34 (1984): 555–59.

Hasagawa, M., and J. Adachi. "Phylogenetic Position of Cetaceans Relative to Artiodactyls: Reanalysis of Mitochondrial and Nuclear Sequences." *Molecular Biology and Evolution* 13, no. 5 (1996): 710–17.

Heimlich-Boran, J. R. "Social Organization of the Short-Finned Pilot Whale, *Globicephala macrorhynchus*, with Special Reference to the Comparative Social Ecology of Delphinids." Ph.D. diss., University of Cambridge, 1993.

Henderson, D. "Red Tides." *Scientific American* (August 1994): 62–68.

Herman, L. M. "Cognitive Characteristics of Dolphins," 363–429. In L. M. Herman, ed., *Cetacean Behavior: Mechanisms and Functions*. New York: Wiley-Interscience, 1980.

———. "Cognition and Language Competencies of Bottle-Nosed Dolphins," 221–52. In R. J. Schusterman, J. A. Thomas, and F. G. Wood, eds., *Dolphin Cognition and Behavior: A Comparative Approach*. Hillsdale, N.J.: Lawrence Erlbaum Associates, 1986.

Herman, L. M., and P. H. Forestell. "Reporting Presence or Absence of Named Objects by a Language-Trained Dolphin." *Neuroscience and Biobehavioral Reviews* 9 (1985): 667–81.

Herman, L. M., D. G. Richards and J. P. Wolz. "Comprehension of Sentences by Bottlenosed Dolphins." *Cognition* 16 (1984): 129–219.

Hernandez, P., J. E. Reynolds III, H. Marsh, and M. Marmontel. "Age and Seasonality in Spermatogenesis of Florida Manatees," 84–97. In T. J. O'Shea, B. B. Ackerman, and H. F. Percival, eds., *Population Biology of the Florida Manatee*. Washington, D.C.: U.S. Department of the Interior, National Biological Service Information and Technology Report 1, 1995.

Hersh, S. L., and D. A. Duffield. "Distinction between Northwest Atlantic Offshore and Coastal Bottlenose Dolphins Based on Hemoglobin Profile and Morphometry," 129–39. In S. Leatherwood and R. R. Reeves, eds., *The Bottlenose Dolphin*. New York: Academic Press, 1990.

Hersh, S. L., D. K. Odell, and E. D. Asper. "Bottlenose Dolphin Mortality Patterns in the Indian/Banana River System of Florida," 155–64. In S. Leatherwood and R. R. Reeves, eds., *The Bottlenose Dolphin*. New York: Academic Press, 1990.

———. "Sexual Dimorphism in Bottlenosed Dolphins from the East Coast of Florida." *Marine Mammal Science* 6, no. 4 (1990): 305–15.

Hershkovitz, P. "Catalog of Living Whales." *Smithsonian Institution, U.S. National Museum Bulletin* 246 (1966): 259pp.

Hertel, H. *Structure, Form, Movement*. New York: Reinhold, 1966.

Herzing, D. L. "Vocalizations and Associated Underwater Behavior of Free-Ranging Atlantic Spotted Dolphins, *Stenella frontalis*, and Bottlenose Dolphins, *Tursiops truncatus*." *Aquatic Mammals* 22 (1996): 61–79.

Heyning, J. E. "Sperm Whale Phylogeny Revisited: Analysis of the Morphological Evidence." *Marine Mammal Science* 13, no. 4 (1997): 596–613.

Hicks, B. D., D. J. St. Aubin, J. R. Geraci, and W. R. Brown. "Epidermal Growth in the Bottlenose Dolphin, *Tursiops truncatus*." The *Journal of Investigative Dermatology* 85 (1985): 60–63.

Hildebrand, M. *Analysis of Vertebrate Structure*, 4th ed. New York: John Wiley and Sons, 1995.

Hockett, C. F. "In Search of Jove's Brow." *American Speech* 53 (1978): 243–313.

Hoese, H. D. "Dolphin Feeding out of Water in a Salt Marsh." *Journal of Mammalogy* 52 (1971): 222–23.

Hofman, M. A. "Energy Metabolism, Brain Size, and Longevity in Mammals." *Quarterly Review of Biology* 58, no. 4 (1983): 495–512.

Hofman, R. J. "The Marine Mammal Act: A First of Its Kind Anywhere." *Oceanus* 32, no. 1 (1989): 21–28.

Hohn, A. A. "Age Determination and Age Related Factors in the Teeth of Western North Atlantic Bottlenose Dolphins." *Scientific Reports of the Whales Research Institute* 32 (1980): 575–85.

———. "Reading between the Lines: Analysis of Age Estimation in Dolphins," 575–85.

In S. Leatherwood and R. R. Reeves, eds., *The Bottlenose Dolphin*. New York: Academic Press, 1990.

———. "Design for a Multiple-Method Approach to Determine Stock Structure of Bottlenose Dolphins in the Mid-Atlantic." NOAA Technical Memorandum NMFS-SEFSC-401, 1997.

Hohn, A. A., M. D. Scott, R. S. Wells, J. C. Sweeney, and A. B. Irvine. "Growth Layers in Teeth from Known-Age, Free Ranging Bottlenose Dolphins." *Marine Mammal Science* 5, no. 4 (1989): 315–42.

Holt, S. J., and L. M. Talbot. "New Principles for the Conservation of Wild Living Resources." *Wildlife Monographs* 43, no. 2 (1978): 6–33.

Hoover-Miller, A. "Assessment of Possible Use of a Cooperative/Coordinated Geographic Information System (GIS) to Facilitate Access to, and Integration and Analysis of, Data Bearing upon the Conservation of Marine Mammals in Alaska." National Technical Information Service Publication PB93–128429, 1992.

Howard, E. B., J. O. Britt Jr., and G. K. Matsumoto. "Parasitic Diseases," 119–232. In E. B. Howard, ed., *Pathobiology of Marine Mammal Diseases*. Vol. 1. Boca Raton, Fla.: CRC Press, 1983.

Hui, C. A. "Seawater Consumption and Water Flux in the Common Dolphin *Delphinus delphis*." *Physiological Zoology* 54, no. 4 (1981): 430–40.

Hunt, E. "The Role of Intelligence in Modern Society." *American Scientist* 83, no. 4 (1995): 356–68.

Idyll, C. P. "The Anchovy Crisis." *Scientific American* 228 (1973): 22–29.

Irvine, A. B., M. D. Scott, R. S. Wells, and J. H. Kaufmann. "Movements and Activities of the Atlantic Bottlenose Dolphin, *Tursiops truncatus,* near Sarasota, Florida. *Fishery Bulletin* 79 (1981): 671–88.

Irvine, A. B., and R. S. Wells. "Results of Attempts to Tag Atlantic Bottlenosed Dolphins (1972)." *Cetology* 13 (1972): 1–5.

Irvine, A. B., R. S. Wells, and P. W. Gilbert. "Conditioning an Atlantic Bottle-Nosed Dolphin, *Tursiops truncatus,* to Repel Various Species of Sharks." *Journal of Mammalogy* 54, no. 2 (1973): 503–5.

Irvine, A. B., R. S. Wells, and M. D. Scott. "An Evaluation of Techniques for Tagging Small Odontocete Cetaceans." *Fishery Bulletin* 79 (1982): 671–88.

Iverson, S. J., J. P. Y. Arnould, and I. L. Boyd. "Milk Fatty Acid Signatures Indicate Both Major and Minor Shifts in Diet of Lactating Antarctic Fur Seals." *Canadian Journal of Zoology* 75 (1997): 188–97.

Jacobs, M. S., P. J. Morgane, and W. L. McFarland. "The Anatomy of the Brain of the Bottlenose Dolphin (*Tursiops truncatus*). Rhinic Lobe (Rhinencephalon) I. The Paleocortex." *Journal of Comparative Neurology* 141, no. 2 (1971): 205–72.

Janik, V. M., and P. J. B. Slater. "Context-Specific Use Suggests That Bottlenose Dolphin Signature Whistles Are Cohesion Calls." *Animal Behaviour* 56 (1998): 829–38.

Janik, V. M., and P. M. Thompson. "Changes in Surfacing Patterns of Bottlenose Dolphins in Response to Boat Traffic." *Marine Mammal Science* 12, no. 4 (1996): 597–602.

Jefferson, T. A., S. Leatherwood, and M. C. Webber. *Marine Mammals of the World. FAO*

Species Identification Guide. Rome: United Nations Environment Programme, Food and Agriculture Organization of the United Nations, 1993.

Jepson, P. D., and J. R. Baker. "Bottlenosed Dolphins (*Tursiops truncatus*) as a Possible Cause of Acute Traumatic Injuries in Porpoises (*Phocoena phocoena*)." *Veterinary Record* 143 (1998): 614–15.

Jerison, H. J. *Evolution of the Brain and Intelligence.* New York: Academic Press, 1973.

Kaiya, Z., and Z. Xingduan. *Baiji: The Yangtze River Dolphin and Other Endangered Animals of China.* Washington, D.C.: Stone Wall Press, 1991.

Kanwisher, J. W., and S. H. Ridgway. "The Physiological Ecology of Whales and Porpoises." *Scientific American* 248, no. 6 (1983): 110–20.

Kasuya, T. "Fishery-Dolphin Conflict in the Iki Island Area of Japan," 253–72. In J. R. Beddington et al., eds., *Marine Mammals and Fisheries.* London: George Allen and Unwin, 1985.

Kasuya, T., and H. Marsh. "Life History and Reproductive Biology of the Short-Finned Pilot Whale, *Globicephala macrorhynchus,* off the Pacific Coast of Japan," 259–310. In W. F. Perrin, R. L. Brownell, and D. P. Demaster, eds., *Reproduction in Whales, Dolphins, and Porpoises.* Cambridge, Eng.: Reports of the International Whaling Commission, Special Issue No. 6, 1984.

Kasuya, T., T. Tobayama, T. Saiga, and T. Kataoka. "Perinatal Growth of Delphinoids: Information from Aquarium Reared Bottlenose Dolphins and Finless Porpoises." *Scientific Reports of the Whales Research Institute* 37 (1986): 85–97.

Kenney, R. D. "Bottlenose Dolphins off the Northeastern United States," 369–86. In S. Leatherwood and R. R. Reeves, eds., *The Bottlenose Dolphin.* New York: Academic Press, 1990.

Kirschvink, J. L., A. E. Dizon, and J. A. Westphal. "Evidence from Strandings for Geomagnetic Sensitivity in Cetaceans." *Journal of Experimental Biology* 120 (1986): 1–24.

Klingener, N. "Activist Tries to Free Dolphins, But the Mammals Choose to Stay." *Miami Herald,* June 7, 1995, 1B–2B.

Klinowska, M. "Interpretation of UK Cetacean Stranding Records." *Report of the International Whaling Commission* 35 (1985): 459–67.

———. *Dolphins, Porpoises and Whales of the World. The IUCN Red Data Book.* Cambridge, Eng.: International Union for the Conservation of Nature and Natural Resources, 1991.

———. "Brains, Behaviour and Intelligence in Cetaceans," 21–26. In *Essays on Whales and Man,* Lofoten, Norway: High North Alliance, 1993.

Koopman, H. N. "Topographical Distribution of the Blubber of Harbor Porpoises (*Phocoena phocoena*)." *Journal of Mammalogy* 79, no. 1 (1998): 260–70.

Koopman, H. N., S. J. Iverson, and D. E. Gaskin. "Stratification and Age-Related Differences in Blubber Fatty Acids of the Male Harbour Porpoise (*Phocoena phocoena*)." *Journal of Comparative Physiology B* 165 (1996): 628–39.

Kooyman, G. L., D. D. Hammond, and J. P. Schroeder. "Bronchograms and Trachograms of Seals Under Pressure." *Science* 169 (1970): 82–84.

Kraus, S. D., A. J. Read, A. Solow, K. Baldwin, T. Spradlin, E. Anderson, and J. Williamson. "Acoustic Alarms Reduce Porpoise Mortality." *Nature* 388 (1997): 525.

Kuehl, D. W., R. Haebler, and C. Potter. "Chemical Residues in Dolphins from the U.S. Atlantic Coast Including Atlantic Bottlenose Obtained during the 1987/88 Mass Mortality." *Chemosphere* 22, no. 11 (1991): 1071–84.

Kuss, K. M. "The Occurrence of PCBs and Chlorinated Pesticide Contaminants in Bottlenose Dolphins (*Tursiops truncatus*) in a Resident Community: Comparison with Age, Gender, and Birth Order." Master's thesis, NOVA Southeastern University, 1991.

Lahvis, G. P., R. S. Wells, D. W. Kuehl, J. L. Stewart, H. L. Rhinehart, and C. S. Via. "Decreased Lymphocyte Responses in Free-Ranging Bottlenose Dolphins (*Tursiops truncatus*) Are Associated with Increased Concentrations of PCBs and DDT in Peripheral Blood." *Environmental Health Perspectives* 103, no. 4 (1995): 67–72.

Lang, T. G., and K. S. Norris. "Swimming Speed of a Pacific Bottlenose Dolphin." *Science* 151 (1966): 588–90.

Leatherwood, S. "Some Observations of Feeding Behavior of Bottle-Nosed Dolphins (*Tursiops truncatus*) in the Northern Gulf of Mexico and (*Tursiops cf. T. gilli*) off Southern California, Baja California, and Nayarit, Mexico." *Marine Fisheries Review* 37, no. 9 (1975): 1–16.

Leatherwood, S., and R. R. Reeves. "Bottlenose Dolphin *Tursiops truncatus* and Other Toothed Cetaceans," 369–414. In J. A. Chapman and G. A. Feldhamer, eds., *Wild Mammals of North America. Biology, Management, and Economics.* Baltimore, Md.: Johns Hopkins University Press, 1982.

———. *The Sierra Club Handbook of Whales and Dolphins.* San Francisco: Sierra Club Books, 1983.

Leduc, R. G., W. F. Perrin, and A. E. Dizon. "Phylogenetic Relationships among Delphinid Cetaceans Based on Full Cytochrome B Sequences." *Marine Mammal Science* 15, no. 3 (1999): 619–48.

Lilly, J. C. The *Mind of the Dolphin: A Nonhuman Intelligence.* New York: Doubleday, 1967.

———. *Lilly on Dolphins.* New York: Anchor Press, Doubleday, 1975.

———. *The Scientist: A Novel Autobiography.* New York: J. P. Lippincott Co., 1978.

Lincoln, R. J., G. A. Boxshall, and P. F. Clark. *A Dictionary of Ecology, Evolution and Systematics.* Cambridge: Cambridge University Press, 1982.

Lindberg, K., and D. E. Hawkins, eds. *Ecotourism: A Guide for Planners and Managers.* North Bennington, Vt.: Ecotourism Society, 1993.

Lipscomb, T. P., F. Y. Schulman, D. Moffett, and S. Kennedy. "Morbilliviral Disease in Atlantic Bottlenose Dolphins (*Tursiops truncatus*) from the 1987–1988 Epizootic." *Journal of Wildlife Diseases* 30, no. 4 (1994): 567–71.

Lockyer, C. "The Relationship between Body Fat, Food Resources, and Reproductive Energy Costs in North Atlantic Fin Whales (*Balaenoptera physalus*)." *Symposia of the Zoological Society of London* 57 (1987): 343–61.

———. "Evaluation of the Role of Fat Reserves in Relation to the Ecology of North

Atlantic Fin and Sei Whales," 183–203. In A. C. Huntley, D. P. Costa, G. A. J. Worthy, and M. A. Castellini, eds., *Approaches to Marine Mammal Energetics.* Lawrence, Kans.: Society for Marine Mammalogy, Special Publication No. 1, 1987.

———. "The Importance of Biological Parameters in Population Assessments with Special Reference to Fin Whales from the N.E. Atlantic." *North Atlantic Studies* 2, no. 1–2 (1990): 22–31.

———. "Review of Incidents Involving Wild, Sociable Dolphins, Worldwide," 337–53. In S. Leatherwood and R. R. Reeves, eds., *The Bottlenose Dolphin.* New York: Academic Press, 1990.

Lockyer, C. H., L. C. McConnell, and T. D. Waters. "The Biochemical Composition of Fin Whale Blubber." *Canadian Journal of Zoology* 62 (1984): 2553–62.

Lowery, G. H. *The Mammals of Louisiana and Its Adjacent Waters.* Baton Rouge: Louisiana State University Press, 1974.

Madsen, C. J., and L. M. Herman. "Social and Ecological Correlates of Cetacean Vision and Visual Appearance," 101–47. In L. M. Herman, ed., *Cetacean Behavior: Mechanisms and Functions.* New York: Wiley Interscience, 1980.

Mahmoudi, B. "Status and Trends in the Florida Mullet Fishery and an Update on Stock Assessment." Unpublished Report, Florida Department of Environmental Protection, Marine Research Institute, 1997.

Malins, D.C. "The Dolphin Is Not Like a 'Human with Flippers.'" *Cetus* 6, no. 1 (1986): 5–8.

Maluf, N. S. R., and J. J. Gassman. "Kidneys of the Killerwhale and Significance of Reniculism." *Anatomical Record* 250 (1998): 34–44.

Mangel, M., et al. "Principles for the Conservation of Wild Living Resources." *Ecological Applications* 6, no. 2 (1996): 338–62.

Mann, J., R. A. Smolker, and B. B. Smuts. "Responses to Calf Entanglement in Free-Ranging Bottlenose Dolphins." *Marine Mammal Science* 11, no. 1 (1995): 100–106.

Mann, J., and B. B. Smuts. "Natal Attraction: Allomaternal Care and Mother-Infant Separations in Wild Bottlenose Dolphins." *Animal Behaviour* 55 (1998): 1097–113.

Marine Mammal Commission. *Annual Report to Congress 1992.* Washington, D.C., 1993.

———. *Annual Report to Congress 1993.* Washington, D.C., 1994.

———. *The Marine Mammal Protection Act of 1972 as Amended.* Washington, D.C., 1995.

———. *Annual Report to Congress 1995.* Washington, D.C., 1996.

———. *Annual Report to Congress 1996.* Washington, D.C., 1997.

———. *Annual Report to Congress 1997.* Washington, D.C., 1998.

———. *Annual Report to Congress 1998.* Washington, D.C., 1999.

Marino, L. "The Relationship between Gestation Length, Encephalization, and Body Weight in Odontocetes." *Marine Mammal Science* 13, no. 1 (1997): 133–38.

———. "A Comparison of Encephalization between Odontocete Cetaceans and Anthropoid Primates." *Brain, Behavior and Evolution* 51 (1998): 230–38.

Marino, L., and S. Lilienfeld. "Dolphin-Assisted Therapy: Flawed Data, Flawed Conclusions." *Anthrozoos* 11, no. 4 (1998): 194–200.

Marmontel, M. "Age and Reproduction in Female Florida Manatees," 98–119. In T. J. O'Shea, B. B. Ackerman, and H. F. Percival, eds., *Population Biology of the Florida*

Manatee. Washington, D.C.: U.S. Department of the Interior, National Biological Service Information and Technology Report 1, 1995.

Marmontel, M., T. J. O'Shea, H. I. Kochman, and S. R. Humphrey. "Age Determination in Manatees Using Growth-Layer-Group Counts in Bone." *Marine Mammal Science* 12, no. 1 (1996): 54–88.

Mate, B. R., K. A. Rossbach, S. L. Nieukirk, R. S. Wells, A. B. Irvine, M. D. Scott, and A. J. Read. "Satellite-Monitored Movements and Dive Behavior of a Bottlenose Dolphin (*Tursiops truncatus*) in Tampa Bay, Florida." *Marine Mammal Science* 11, no. 4 (1996): 452–63.

McBride, A. F. "Meet Mr. Porpoise." *Natural History* 45 (1940): 16–29.

McBride, A. F., and D. O. Hebb. "Behavior of the Captive Bottlenose Dolphin, *Tursiops truncatus*." *Journal of Comparative Physiology and Psychology* 41 (1948): 111–23.

McCormick, J. G., E. G. Wever, J. Palin, and S. H. Ridgway. "Sound Conduction in the Dolphin Ear." *Journal of the Acoustical Society of America* 48 (1970): 1418–28.

McLellan, W. A., V. G. Thayer, and D. A. Pabst. "Stingray Spine Mortality in a Bottlenose Dolphin, *Tursiops truncatus,* from North Carolina Waters." *Journal of the Elisha Mitchell Scientific Society* 112, no. 2 (1996): 98–101.

Mead, J. G. "Anatomy of the External Nasal Passages and Facial Complex in the Delphinidae (Mammalia: Cetacea)." *Smithsonian Contributions to Zoology* 207 (1975): 1–72.

———. "Preliminary Report on the Former Net Fisheries for *Tursiops truncatus* in the Western North Atlantic." *Journal of the Fisheries Research Board of Canada* 32 (1975): 1155–62.

Mead, J. G., and C. W. Potter. "Natural History of Bottlenose Dolphins along the Central Atlantic Coast of the United States," 165–95. In S. Leatherwood and R. R. Reeves, eds., *The Bottlenose Dolphin*. New York: Academic Press, 1990.

———. "Recognizing Two Populations of the Bottlenose Dolphin (*Tursiops truncatus*) off the Atlantic Coast of North America—Morphologic and Ecologic Considerations." *IBI Reports* 5 (1995): 31–44.

Medway, W., and J. R. Geraci. "Hematology of the Bottlenose Dolphin (*Tursiops truncatus*)." *American Journal of Physiology* 207, no. 6 (1964): 1367–70.

———. "Simulated Field Blood Studies in the Bottle-Nosed Dolphin *Tursiops truncatus*. 1. Leucocyte Distribution between the Blood of Capillaries and Large Vessels." *Journal of Wildlife Diseases* 8 (1972): 239–41.

Meffe, G. K., and C. R. Carroll. *Principles of Conservation Biology*. Sunderland, Mass.: Sinauer Associates, 1994.

Meffe, G. K., W. F. Perrin, and P. K. Dayton. "Marine Mammal Conservation: Guiding Principles and Their Implementation," 437–54. In J. R. Twiss and R. R. Reeves, eds., *Conservation and Management of Marine Mammals*. Washington, D.C.: Smithsonian Institution Press, 1999.

Menzel, E. W., Jr. "How Can You Tell If an Animal Is Intelligent?" 167–82. In R. J. Schusterman, J. A. Thomas, and F. G. Wood, eds., *Dolphin Cognition and Behavior: A Comparative Approach*. Hillsdale, N.J.: Lawrence Erlbaum Associates, 1986.

Milinkovitch, M. C., M. Bérubé, and P. J. Palsbøll. "Cetaceans Are Highly Derived Artio-dactyls," 113–31. In J. G. M. Theiwissen, ed., *The Emergence of Whales: Evolutionary Patterns in the Origin of Cetacea.* New York: Plenum Press, 1998.

Milinkovitch, M. C., R. G. Leduc, J. Adachi, F. Farnir, M. Georges, and M. Hasegawa. "Effects of Character Weighting and Species Sampling on Phylogeny Reconstruction: A Case Study Based on DNA Sequence Data in Cetaceans." *Genetics* 144 (1996): 1817–33.

Milinkovitch, M. C., A. Meyer, and J. R. Powell. "Phylogeny of All Major Groups of Cetaceans Based on DNA Sequences from Three Mitochondrial Genes." *Molecular Biology and Evolution* 11, no. 6 (1994): 939–48.

Milinkovitch, M. C., G. Orti, and A. Meyer. "Revised Phylogeny of Whales Suggested by Mitchondrial Ribosomal DNA Sequences." *Nature* 361 (1993): 346–48.

Miller, G. S. "Telescoping of the Cetacean Skull." *Smithsonian Miscellaneous Collection* 76, no. 5 (1923): 1–62.

Miyazaki, N. "Catch Records of Cetaceans off the Coast of the Kii Peninsula." *Memoirs of the National Science Museum, Tokyo* 13 (1980): 69–82.

Mohri, M., R. Torii, K. Nagaya, K. Shiraki, R. Elsner, H. Takeuchi, Y. S. Park, and S. K. Hong. "Diving Patterns of Ama Divers of Hegura Island, Japan." *Undersea and Hyperbaric Medicine* 22 (1995): 137–43.

Montagu, G. "Description of a Species of *Delphinus* Which Appears To Be New." *Memoirs of the Wernerian Natural History Society* 3 (1821): 75–82.

Moors, T. L. "Is a 'Ménage à Trois' Important in Dolphin Mating Systems? Behavioral Patterns of Breeding Female Bottlenose Dolphins." Master's thesis, University of California, Santa Cruz, 1997.

Morgane, P. J., and J. S. Jacobs. "Comparative Anatomy of the Cetacean Nervous System," 117–224. In R. J. Harrison, ed., *Functional Anatomy of Marine Mammals.* Vol. 1. New York: Academic Press, 1972.

Morgane, P. J., M. S. Jacobs, and A. Galaburda. "Evolutionary Morphology of the Dolphin Brain," 5–29. In R. J. Schusterman, J. A. Thomas, and F. G. Wood, eds., *Dolphin Cognition and Behavior: A Comparative Approach.* Hillsdale, N.J.: Lawrence Erlbaum Associates, 1986.

Muller, R. "Status and Trends of Florida's Marine Resources." Memorandum to Russell S. Nelson, Director, Florida Marine Fisheries Commission, 1998.

Mullin, K., W. Hoggard, C. Roden, R. Lohoefner, C. Rogers, and B. Taggart. "Cetaceans on the Upper Continental Slope in the North-Central Gulf of Mexico." Minerals Management Service OCS Study MMS 91-0027, 1991.

Murchison, A. E. "Detection Range and Range Resolution of Echolocating Bottlenose Porpoise (*Tursiops truncatus*)," 43–70. In R. G. Busnel and J. F. Fish, eds., *Animal Sonar Systems.* NATO ASI Series A28, 1980.

Murphy, S. "Apparent Impact of Commercial Dolphin Feeding Operations on Bottlenose Dolphins in South Carolina," 93–95. In K. R. Wang, P. M. Payne, and V. G. Thayer, compilers, "Coastal Stock(s) of Atlantic Bottlenose Dolphin: Status Review and Management. Proceedings and Recommendations from a Workshop Held in

Beaufort, North Carolina, 13–14 September 1993." NOAA Technical Memorandum NMFS-OPR-4, 1994.

Murphy, T. "Some Thoughts on the Practice of Feeding Bottlenose Dolphins in South Carolina—Another Perspective," 95–97. In K. R. Wang, P. M. Payne, and V. G. Thayer, compilers, "Coastal Stock(s) of Atlantic Bottlenose Dolphin: Status Review and Management. Proceedings and Recommendations from a Workshop Held in Beaufort, North Carolina, 13–14 September 1993." NOAA Technical Memorandum NMFS-OPR-4, 1994.

Nachtigall, P. E., and R. W. Hall. "Taste Reception in the Bottlenosed Dolphin." *Acta Zoologica Fennica* 172 (1984): 147–48.

Nagel, E. L., P. J. Morgane, W. L. McFarland, and A. E. Galliano. "Rete Mirabile of Dolphins: Its Pressure-Damping Effect on Cerebral Circulation." *Science* 161 (1968): 898–900.

Nathanson, D. E. "Using Atlantic Bottlenose Dolphins to Increase Cognition of Mentally Retarded Children," 233–42. In P. Lovibond and P. Wilson, eds., *Clinical and Abnormal Psychology.* North Holland: Elsevier Science Publishers, 1989.

———. "Long-Term Effectiveness of Dolphin-Assisted Therapy for Children with Severe Disabilities." *Anthrozoos* 11, no. 1 (1998): 22–32.

Nathanson, D. E., D. De Castro, H. Friend, and M. McMahon. "Effectiveness of Short-Term Dolphin Assisted Therapy for Children with Severe Disabilities." *Anthrozoos* 10, nos. 2–3 (1997): 90–100.

National Marine Fisheries Service. "The 1998 List of Fisheries." *MMPA Bulletin* no. 12 (1998): 4–5.

———. *Marine Mammal Protection Act of 1972 Annual Report. January 1, 1997 to December 31, 1997.* Silver Spring, Md.: U.S. Department of Commerce, 1998.

Nguyen, D., and J. Mann. "Sociosexual Development in Bottlenose Dolphin Calves." Proceedings of the Seventh Annual Atlantic Coastal Dolphin Conference, Virginia Beach, Va., March 19–21, 1999.

Nomura, O., and H Yasue. "Genetic Relationships among Hippopotamus, Whales, and Bovine Based on SINE Insertion Analysis." *Mammalian Genome* 10 (1999): 526–27.

Noren, D. P., T. M. Williams, P. Berry, and E. Butler. "Thermoregulation during Swimming and Diving in Bottlenose Dolphins, *Tursiops truncatus.*" *Journal of Comparative Physiology B* 169 (1999): 93–99.

Norris, K. S. "The Evolution of Acoustic Mechanisms in Odontocete Cetaceans," 297–324. In E. T. Drake, ed., *Evolution and Environment,* New Haven, Conn.: Yale University Press, 1968.

———. "The Echolocation of Marine Mammals," 391–423. In H. T. Andersen, ed., *The Biology of Marine Mammals.* New York: Academic Press, 1969.

———. *The Porpoise Watcher.* New York: W. W. Norton and Co., 1974.

———. "Marine Mammals and Man," 320–38. In H. P. Brokaw, ed., *Wildlife and America. Contributions to an Understanding of American Wildlife and Its Conservation.* Washington, D.C.: U.S. Government Printing Office, 1978.

————. "Peripheral Sound Processing in Odontocetes," 495–509. In R. G. Busnel and J. F. Fish, eds., *Animal Sonar Systems*. New York: Plenum Press, 1980.

————. *Dolphin Days*. New York: W. W. Norton and Co., 1991.

————. "Looking at Captive Dolphins," 293–303. In K. Pryor and K. S. Norris, eds., *Dolphin Societies: Discoveries and Puzzles*. Berkeley: University of California Press, 1991.

Norris, K. S., and B. Möhl. "Can Odontocetes Debilitate Prey with Sound?" *American Naturalist* 122, no. 1 (1983): 85–104.

Norris, K. S., B. Würsig, R. S. Wells, and M. Würsig. *The Hawaiian Spinner Dolphin*. Berkeley: University of California Press, 1994.

Norse, E. A. *Global Marine Biological Diversity*. Washington, D.C.: Island Press, 1993.

Northridge, S. P. "World Review of Interactions between Marine Mammals and Fisheries." *FAO Technical Paper* 251 (1984): 1–190.

————. "An Updated World Review of Interactions between Marine Mammals and Fisheries." *FAO Technical Paper* 251, Suppl. 1 (1991): 1–58.

Odell, D. K. "Distribution and Abundance of Marine Mammals in South Florida: Preliminary Results." *University of Miami Sea Grant Special Publication* 5 (1976): 203–12.

————. "A Review of the Southeastern United States Marine Mammal Stranding Network: 1978–1987," 19–23. In J. E. Reynolds III and D. K. Odell, eds., *Marine Mammal Strandings in the United States. NOAA Technical Report* NMFS 98, 1991.

Orams, M. B., G. J. E. Hill, and A. J. Baglioni Jr. "'Pushy' Behavior in a Wild Dolphin Feeding Program at Tangalooma, Australia." *Marine Mammal Science* 12, no. 1 (1996): 107–17.

O'Shea, T. J. "Environmental Contaminants and Marine Mammals," 485–563. In J. E. Reynolds III and S. A. Rommel, eds., *Biology of Marine Mammals*. Washington, D.C.: Smithsonian Institution Press, 1999.

O'Shea, T. J., and R. L. Brownell Jr. "California Sea Lion (*Zalophus californianus*) Populations and Σ DDT Contamination." *Marine Pollution Bulletin* 36, no. 2 (1998): 159–64.

O'Shea, T. J., R. L. Brownell Jr., D. R. Clark Jr., W. A. Walker, M. L. Gay, and T. G. Lamont. "Organochlorine Pollutants in Small Cetaceans from the Pacific and South Atlantic Oceans, November 1968–June 1976." *Pesticides Monitoring Journal* 14, no. 2 (1980): 35–46.

O'Shea, T. J., G. B. Rathbun, R. K. Bonde, C. D. Buergelt, and D. K. Odell. "An Epizootic of Florida Manatees Associated with a Dinoflagellate Bloom." *Marine Mammal Science* 7, no. 2 (1991): 165–79.

Osterberg, G. "Topography of the Layer of Rods and Cones in the Human Retina." *Acta Ophthalmologica* Suppl. 6 (1935): 1–102.

Osterhaus, A. D. M. E. "Mediterranean Monk Seal Mortality Event." *Marine Mammal Society Newsletter* 5, no. 4 (1997): 2.

Pabst, D. A. "Axial Muscles and Connective Tissues of the Bottlenose Dolphin," 51–67. In S. Leatherwood and R. R. Reeves, eds., *The Bottlenose Dolphin*. New York: Academic Press, 1990.

———. "Intramuscular Morphology and Tendon Geometry of the Epaxial Swimming Muscles of Dolphins." *Journal of Zoology, London* 230 (1993): 159–70.

———. "Morphology of the Subdermal Connective Tissue Sheath of Dolphins: A New Fibre-Wound, Thin-Walled, Pressurized Cylinder Model for Swimming Vertebrates." *Journal of Zoology, London* 238 (1996): 35–52.

Pabst, D. A., S. A. Rommel, and W. A. McLellan. "Functional Anatomy of Marine Mammals," 15–72. In J. E. Reynolds III and S. A. Rommel, eds., *Biology of Marine Mammals.* Washington, D.C.: Smithsonian Institution Press, 1999.

Pabst, D. A., S. A. Rommel, W. A. McLellan, T. M. Williams, and T. K. Rowles. "Thermoregulation of the Intra-Abdominal Testes of the Bottlenose Dolphin (*Tursiops truncatus*) during Exercise." *Journal of Experimental Biology* 198 (1995): 221–26.

Palmer, E., and G. Weddell. "The Relationship between Structure, Innervation and Function of the Skin of the Bottlenose Dolphin (*Tursiops truncatus*)." *Proceedings of the Zoological Society of London* 143, no. 4 (1964): 553–68.

Patterson, I. A. P., R. J. Reid, B. Wilson, K. Grellier, H. M. Ross, and P. M. Thompson. "Evidence for Infanticide in Bottlenose Dolphins: An Explanation for Violent Interactions with Harbour Porpoises." *Proceedings of the Royal Society of London B* 265 (1998): 1167–70.

Peddemors, V. M., V. G. Cockcroft, and R. B. Wilson. "Incidental Dolphin Mortality in the Natal Shark Nets: A Preliminary Report on Prevention Measures," 129–37. In S. Leatherwood and G. P. Donovan, eds., *Cetaceans and Cetacean Research in the Indian Ocean Sanctuary.* United Nations Environment Programme, *Marine Mammal Technical Report* 3, 1991.

Perrin, W. F., and R. L. Brownell, eds. "Report of the Workshop," 1–22. In W. F. Perrin, R. L. Brownell Jr., Zhou Kaiya, and Liu Jiankang, eds., *Biology and Conservation of the River Dolphins.* Occasional Papers of the IUCN Species Survival Commission, no. 3, 1991.

Perrin, W. F., R. L. Brownell, and D. P. Demaster, eds. *Reproduction in Whales, Dolphins and Porpoises.* Reports of the International Whaling Commission, Special Issue No. 6, 1984.

Perrin, W. F., and S. B. Reilly. "Reproductive Parameters of Dolphins and Small Whales of the Family Delphinidae," 97–133. In W. F. Perrin, R. L. Brownell, and D. P. Demaster, eds., *Reproduction in Whales, Dolphins and Porpoises.* Reports of the International Whaling Commission, Special Issue No. 6, 1984.

Perrine, D. "Jojo: Rogue Dolphin?" *Sea Frontiers* 36, no. 2 (1991): 32–41.

Petricig, R. O. "Bottlenose Dolphins (*Tursiops truncatus*) in Bull Creek, South Carolina." Ph.D. diss., University of Rhode Island, 1995.

Pianka, E. R. "On r and K Selection." *American Naturalist* 104 (1970): 592–97.

Pilleri, G. "Second Record of *Tursiops osennae* (Cetacea, Delphinidae) in a Pliocene Horizon of the Romagna Apennines, Central Italy, and the Phylogeny of *Tursiops*." *Investigations on Cetacea* 17 (1985): 11–30.

Polovina, J. J., G. T. Mitchum, N. E. Graham, M. P. Craig, E. E. Demartini, and E. N. Flint.

"Physical and Biological Consequences of a Climate Event in the Central North Pacific." *Fisheries Oceanography* 3, no. 1 (1994): 15–21.

Pryor, K. "Reinforcement Training as Interspecies Communication," 253–60. In R. J. Schusterman, J. A. Thomas, and F. G. Wood. *Dolphin Cognition and Behavior: A Comparative Approach.* Hillsdale, N.J.: Lawrence Erlbaum Associates, 1986.

Pryor, K., J. Lindbergh, S. Lindbergh, and R. Milano. "A Dolphin-Human Fishing Cooperative in Brazil." *Marine Mammal Science* 6, no. 1 (1990): 77–82.

Purves, P. E., and G. E. Pilleri. *Echolocation in Whales and Dolphins.* New York: Academic Press, 1983.

Radcliffe, L. "Whales and Porpoises as Food." *Economic Circular No. 38.* Washington, D.C.: Bureau of Fisheries, Department of Commerce, 1918.

Rathbun, G. B., J. P. Reid, R. K. Bonde, and J. A. Powell. "Reproduction in Free-Ranging Florida Manatees," 135–56. In T. J. O'Shea, B. B. Ackerman, and H. F. Percival, eds., *Population Biology of the Florida Manatee.* U.S. Department of the Interior, National Biological Service, Information and Technology Report 1, 1995.

Read, A. J., and A. A. Hohn. "Life in the Fast Lane: The Life History of Harbour Porpoises from the Gulf of Maine." *Marine Mammal Science* 11 (1995): 423–40.

Read, A. J., K. Van Waerebeek, J. C. Reyes, J. S. McKinnon, and L. C. Lehman. "The Exploitation of Small Cetaceans in Coastal Peru." *Biological Conservation* 46, no. 1 (1988): 53–70.

Read, A. J., R. S. Wells, A. A. Hohn, and M. D. Scott. "Patterns of Growth in Wild Bottlenose Dolphins, *Tursiops truncatus.*" *Journal of Zoology, London* 231 (1993): 107–23.

Reddy, M., T. Kamolnick, C. Curry, and D. Skaar. "Energy Requirements for the Bottlenose Dolphin (*Tursiops truncatus*) in Relation to Sex, Age, and Reproductive Status." *Marine Mammals: Public Display and Research* 1, no. 1 (1994): 26–31.

Reeves, R. R., and J. G. Mead. "Marine Mammals in Captivity," 412–36. In J. R. Twiss Jr. and R. R. Reeves, eds., *Conservation of Marine Mammals.* Washington, D.C.: Smithsonian Institution Press, 1999.

Reijnders, P. J. H. "Reproductive Failure in Common Seals Feeding on Fish from Polluted Coastal Waters." *Nature* 324 (1986): 456–57.

Reyes, J. C. "A Possible Case of Hybridism in Wild Dolphins." *Marine Mammal Science* 12, no.2 (1996): 301–7.

Reynolds, J. E., III. "Evaluation of the Nature and Magnitude of Interactions between Bottlenose Dolphins, *Tursiops truncatus,* and Fisheries and Other Human Activities in the Coastal Waters of the Southeastern United States." Final Report to Marine Mammal Commission, Order Number MM291082-5. U.S. Department of Commerce, *National Technical Information Service Publication* PB86–162203, 1986.

———. "Efforts to Conserve the Manatees." In J. R. Twiss and R. R. Reeves, eds., *Conservation of Marine Mammals.* Washington, D.C.: Smithsonian Institution Press, 1999.

Reynolds, J. E., III, and C. J. Gluckman. "Protection of West Indian Manatees (*Trichechus manatus*) in Florida." Final Report to Marine Mammal Commission. National Technical Information Service. Report PB88–222922, 1988.

Reynolds, J. E., III, and K. D. Haddad, eds. "Report of the Workshop on Geographic Information Systems as an Aid to Managing Habitat for West Indian Manatees in Florida and Georgia." *Florida Marine Research Publication* no. 49, 1990.

Reynolds, J. E., III, and D. K. Odell. *Manatees and Dugongs.* New York: Facts on File, 1991.

————, eds. *Marine Mammal Strandings in the United States.* Proceedings of the Second Marine Mammal Stranding Workshop, Miami, Fla., December 3–5, 1987. NOAA Technical Report NMFS 98, 1991.

Reynolds, J. E., III, and S. A. Rommel, eds. *Biology of Marine Mammals.* Washington, D.C.: Smithsonian Institution Press, 1999.

Reynolds, J. E., III, S. A. Rommel, and D. K. Odell. "Marine Mammals of the World," 1–14. In J. E. Reynolds III and S. A. Rommel, eds., *Biology of Marine Mammals.* Washington, D.C.: Smithsonian Institution Press, 1999.

Richardson, W. J. "Documented Disturbance Reactions," 241–324. In W. J. Richardson et al., eds., *Marine Mammals and Noise.* San Diego, Calif.: Academic Press, 1995.

Richardson, W. J., and B. Würsig. "Significance of Responses and Noise Impacts," 387–424. In W. J. Richardson et al., eds., *Marine Mammals and Noise.* San Diego, Calif.: Academic Press, 1995.

————. "Influences of Man-Made Noise and Other Human Actions on Cetacean Behavior." *Marine and Freshwater Behavior and Physiology* 29 (1997): 183–209.

Ricklefs, R. E. *Ecology.* 3d ed. New York: W. H. Freeman and Co., 1990.

Ridgway, S. H. "Buoyancy Regulation in Deep Diving Whales." *Nature* 232 (1971): 133–34.

————. *Mammals of the Sea: Biology and Medicine.* Springfield, Ill.: C. C. Thomas, 1972.

————. *The Dolphin Doctor.* New York: Fawcett, 1988.

————. "The Central Nervous System of the Bottlenose Dolphin," 69–97. In S. Leatherwood and R. R. Reeves, eds., *The Bottlenose Dolphin.* New York: Academic Press, 1990.

Ridgway, S. H. and R. H. Brownson. "Relative Brain Sizes and Cortical Surface Areas of Odontocetes." *Acta Zoologica Fennica* 172 (1984): 149–52.

Ridgway, S. H., and D. A. Carder. "Tactile Sensitivity, Somatosensory Responses, Skin Vibrations, and the Skin Surface Ridges of the Bottlenose Dolphin, *Tursiops truncatus,*" 163–79. In J. A. Thomas and R. A. Kastelein, eds., *Sensory Abilities of Cetaceans: Laboratory and Field Evidence.* New York: Plenum Press, 1990.

Ridgway, S. H., and C. A. Fenner. "Weight-Length Relationships of Wild-Caught and Captive Atlantic Bottlenose Dolphins. *Journal of the American Veterinary Medicine Association* 181 (1982): 1310–15.

Ridgway, S. H., and R. Howard. "Dolphin Lung Collapse and Intramuscular Circulation during Free Diving: Evidence from Nitrogen Washout." *Science* 206 (1979): 1182–83.

Ridgway, S. H., and D. G. Johnston. "Blood Oxygen and Ecology of Porpoises of Three Genera." *Science* 151 (1966): 456–58.

Ridgway, S. H., T. Kamolnick, M. Reddy, C. Curry, and R. J. Tarpley. "Orphan-Induced Lactation in *Tursiops* and Analysis of Collected Milk." *Marine Mammal Science* 11, no. 2 (1995): 172–82.

Ridgway, S. H., and M. Reddy. "Residue Levels of Several Organochlorines in *Tursiops truncatus* Milk Collected at Varied Stages of Lactation." *Marine Pollution Bulletin* 30, no. 9 (1995): 609–14.

Ridgway, S. H., B. L. Scronce, and J. Kanwisher. "Respiration and Deep Diving in the Bottlenose Porpoise." *Science* 166 (1969): 1651–54.

Robeck, T. R., B. E. Curry, J. F. McBain, and D. C. Kraemer. "Reproductive Biology of the Bottlenose Dolphin (*Tursiops truncatus*) and the Potential Application of Advanced Reproductive Technologies." *Journal of Zoo and Wildlife Medicine* 25, no. 3 (1994): 321–36.

Rommel, S. A. "Osteology of the Bottlenose Dolphin," 29–49. In S. Leatherwood and R. R. Reeves, eds., *The Bottlenose Dolphin.* New York: Academic Press, 1990.

Rommel, S. A., D. A. Pabst, and W. A. McLellan. "Functional Morphology of the Vascular Plexuses Associated with the Cetacean Uterus." *Anatomical Record* 237 (1993): 538–46.

———. "Reproductive Thermoregulation in Marine Mammals." *American Scientist* 86 (1998): 440–48.

Rommel, S. A., D. A. Pabst, W. A. McLellan, J. G. Mead, and C. W. Potter. "Anatomical Evidence for a Countercurrent Heat Exchanger Associated with Dolphin Testes." *Anatomical Record* 232 (1992): 150–56.

Rommel, S. A., D. A. Pabst, W. A. McLellan, T. M. Williams, and W. A. Friedl. "Temperature Regulation of the Testes of the Bottlenose Dolphin (*Tursiops truncatus*): Evidence from Colonic Temperatures." *Journal of Comparative Physiology, B* 164 (1994): 130–34.

Ross, G. J. B. "The Taxonomy of Bottlenosed Dolphins *Tursiops* Species in South African Waters, with Notes on Their Biology." *Annals of the Cape Provincial Museums. Natural History* 11 (1977): 135–94.

Ross, G. J. B., and V. G. Cockcroft. "Comments on Australian Bottlenose Dolphins and the Taxonomic Status of *Tursiops aduncus* (Ehrenberg, 1832)," 101–28. In S. Leatherwood and R. R. Reeves, eds., *The Bottlenose Dolphin.* New York: Academic Press, 1990.

Ross, G. J. B., V. G. Cockcroft, D. A. Melton, and D. S. Butterworth. "Population Estimates for Bottlenose Dolphins *Tursiops truncatus* in Natal and Transkei Waters." *South African Journal of Marine Science* 8 (1989): 119–29.

Ross, H. M., and B. Wilson. "Violent Interactions between Bottlenose Dolphins and Harbour Porpoises." *Proceedings of the Royal Society of London B* 263 (1996): 283–86.

Ross, P. S., R. L. De Swart, R. F. Addison, H. Van Loveren, J. G. Vos, and A. D. M. E. Osterhaus. "Contaminant-Induced Immunotoxicology in Harbour Seals: Wildlife at Risk?" *Toxicology* 112 (1996): 157–69.

Rossbach, K. A., and D. L. Herzing. "Underwater Observations of Benthic-Feeding Bottlenose Dolphins (*Tursiops truncatus*) near Grand Bahama Island, Bahamas." *Marine Mammal Science* 13, no. 3 (1997): 498–504.

Saayman, G. S., and C. K. Tayler. "The Socioecology of Humpback Dolphins (*Sousa* Sp.)," 165–226. In H. E. Winn and B. L. Olla, eds., *Behavior of Marine Animals.* Vol. 3, *Cetacean.* New York: Plenum Press, 1979.

Saayman, G. S., C. K. Tayler, and D. Bower. "Diurnal Activity Cycles in Captive and Free-

Ranging Indian Ocean Bottlenose Dolphins (*Tursiops aduncus* Ehrenburg)." *Behaviour* 44 (1973): 212–33.

Safe, S. "Polychlorinated Biphenyls (PCBs) and Polybrominated Biphenyls (PBBs): Biochemistry, Toxicology, and Mechanisms of Action." *CRC Critical Reviews of Toxicology* 13 (1984): 319–95.

Samuels, A., and T. Gifford. "A Quantitative Assessment of Dominance Relations among Bottlenose Dolphins." *Marine Mammal Science* 13, no. 1 (1997): 70–99.

Samuels, A., M. Sevenich, T. Gifford, T. Sullivan, and J. Sustman. "Gentle Rubbing among Bottlenose Dolphins." Proceedings of the Eighth Biennial Conference on the Biology of Marine Mammals, Pacific Grove, Calif., December 1989.

Samuels, A., and T. Spradlin. "Quantitative Behavioral Study of Bottlenose Dolphins in Swim-with-the-Dolphin Programs in the United States." *Marine Mammal Science* 11, no. 4 (1995): 520–44.

Sayigh, L. S., P. L. Tyack, R. S. Wells, and M. D. Scott. "Signature Whistles of Free-Ranging Bottlenose Dolphins, *Tursiops truncatus:* Stability and Mother-Offspring Comparisons." *Behavioral Ecology and Sociobiology* 26 (1990): 247–60.

Sayigh, L. S., P. L. Tyack, R. S. Wells, M. D. Scott, and A. B. Irvine. "Sex Differences in Whistle Production in Free-Ranging Bottlenose Dolphins, *Tursiops truncatus.*" *Behavioral Ecology and Sociobiology* 36 (1995): 171–77.

Sayigh, L. S., P. L. Tyack, R. S. Wells, A. R. Solow, M. D. Scott, and A. B. Irvine. "Individual Recognition in Wild Bottlenose Dolphins: A Field Test Using Playback Experiments." *Animal Behaviour* 57 (1999): 41–50.

Schmidt-Nielsen, K. *Animal Physiology: Adaptation and Environment.* 5th ed. Cambridge: Cambridge University Press, 1997.

Schroeder, J. P., and K. V. Keller. "Artificial Insemination in Bottlenose Dolphins," 435–46. In S. Leatherwood and R. R. Reeves, eds., *The Bottlenose Dolphin.* New York: Academic Press, 1990.

Schulman, F. Y., T. P. Lipscomb, D. Moffett, A. E. Krafft, J. H. Licjy, M. M. Tsai, J. K. Taubenberger, and S. Kennedy. "Histologic, Immunohistochemical, and Polymerase Chain Reaction Studies of Bottlenose Dolphins from the 1987–1988 United States Atlantic Coast Epizootic." *Veterinary Pathology* 34 (1997): 288–95.

Schusterman, R. J. "Cognition and Intelligence of Dolphins," 137–40. In R. J. Schusterman, J. A. Thomas, and F. G. Wood, eds., *Dolphin Cognition and Behavior: A Comparative Approach.* Hillsdale, N.J.: Lawrence Erlbaum Associates, 1986.

Schusterman, R. J., and R. Gisiner. "Please Parse the Sentence: Animal Cognition in the Procrustean Bed of Linguistics." *Psychological Record* 39 (1989): 3–18.

Schusterman, R. J., J. A. Thomas and F. G. Wood, eds. *Dolphin Cognition and Behavior: A Comparative Approach.* Hillsdale, N.J.: Lawrence Erlbaum Associates, 1986.

Scott, G. P. "Management-Oriented Research on Bottlenose Dolphins by the Southeast Fisheries Center," 623–39. In S. Leatherwood and R. R. Reeves, eds., *The Bottlenose Dolphin.* New York: Academic Press, 1990.

Scott, G. P., D. M. Burn, and L. J. Hansen. "The Dolphin Die-Off: Long-Term Effects and Recovery of the Population." *Proceedings of the Oceans '88 Conference* (1988): 819–23.

Scott, M. D., and S. J. Chivers. "Distribution and Herd Structure of Bottlenose Dolphins in the Eastern Tropical Pacific Ocean," 387–402. In S. Leatherwood and R. R. Reeves, eds., *The Bottlenose Dolphin.* New York: Academic Press, 1990.

Scott, M. D., R. S. Wells, and A. B. Irvine. "A Long-Term Study of Bottlenose Dolphins on the West Coast of Florida," 235–44. In S. Leatherwood and R. R. Reeves, eds., *The Bottlenose Dolphin.* New York: Academic Press, 1990.

———. "Long-Term Studies of Bottlenose Dolphins in Florida." *IBI Reports* 6 (1996): 73–80.

Scott, M. D., R. S. Wells, A. B. Irvine, and B. R. Mate. "Tagging and Marking Studies on Small Cetaceans," 489–514. In S. Leatherwood and R. R. Reeves, eds., *The Bottlenose Dolphin.* New York: Academic Press, 1990.

Shane, S. H. *The Bottlenose Dolphin in the Wild.* N.p., 1988.

———. "Behavior and Ecology of the Bottlenose Dolphin at Sanibel Island, Florida," 245–66. In S. Leatherwood and R. R. Reeves, eds., *The Bottlenose Dolphin.* New York: Academic Press, 1990.

Shane, S. H., L. Tepley, and L. Costello. "Life-Threatening Contact between a Woman and a Pilot Whale Captured on Film." *Marine Mammal Science* 9, no. 3 (1993): 331–36.

Shane, S. H., R. S. Wells, and B. Würsig. "Ecology, Behavior, and Social Organization of the Bottlenose Dolphin: A Review." *Marine Mammal Science* 2, no. 1 (1986): 34–63.

Shimamura, M., H. Yasue, K. Ohshima, H. Abe, H. Kato, T. Kishiro, M. Goto, I. Munechika, and N. Okada. "Molecular Evidence from Retroposons That Whales Form a Clade within Even-Toed Ungulates." *Nature* 388, no. 6643 (1997): 666–70.

Simons, D., and M. Huigen. "Analysis of an Experiment on Colour Vision in Dolphins." *Aquatic Mammals* 5 (1977): 27–33.

Slijper, E. J. *Whales.* Ithaca, N.Y.: Cornell University Press, 1979.

Small, R. J., and D. P. Demaster. "Survival of Five Species of Captive Marine Mammals." *Marine Mammal Science* 11, no. 2 (1995): 209–26.

———. "Acclimation to Captivity: A Quantitative Estimate Based on Survival of Bottlenose Dolphins and California Sea Lions." *Marine Mammal Science* 11, no. 4 (1995): 510–19.

Smayda, T. "Novel and Nuisance Phytoplankton Blooms in the Sea: Evidence for a Global Epidemic," 29–40. In E. Graneli, B. Sundstrom, L. Edler, and D. M. Anderson, eds., *Toxic Marine Phytoplankton.* New York: Elsevier, 1990.

Smedley, K., and J. Mann. "Maternal Investment in Bottlenose Dolphins." Proceedings of the Seventh Annual Atlantic Coastal Dolphin Conference, Virginia Beach, Va., March 19–21, 1999.

Smolker, R. A., A. Richards, R. Connor, J. Mann, and P. Berggren. "Sponge-Carrying by Dolphins (Delphinidae, *Tursiops* sp.): A Foraging Specialization Involving Tool Use?" *Ethology* 103 (1997): 454–65.

Smolker, R. A., A. F. Richards, R. C. Connor, and J. W. Pepper. "Sex Differences in Patterns of Association among Indian Ocean Bottlenose Dolphins." *Behaviour* 123 (1992): 38–69.

Sokoloff, L. "Circulation and Energy Metabolism of the Brain." In G. J. Siegel, ed., *Basic Neurochemistry.* Boston, Mass.: Little Brown, 1972.

South Africa Government Gazette. "Marine Living Resources Act (Act no. 18 of 1998)." Pretoria, South Africa (Regulation Gazette no. 6284), 399, no. 19205, September 2, 1998.

St. Aubin, D. J., J. R. Geraci, and V. J. Lounsbury, eds. "Rescue, Rehabilitation and Release of Marine Mammals: An Analysis of Current Views and Practices. Workshop Summary and Recommendations." NOAA Technical Memorandum NMFS-OPR-8 (1996), 1–27.

Stedman's Medical Dictionary. 23d ed. Baltimore, Md.: Williams and Wilkins Co., 1976.

Stern, G. A., D. C. G. Muir, M. D. Segstro, R. Dietz, and M. P. Heide-Jørgensen. "PCBs and Other Organochlorine Contaminants in White Whales (*Delphinapterus leucas*) from West Greenland: Variations with Age and Sex." *Meddr Grønland, Bioscience* 39 (1994): 245–59.

Subramanian, A. N., S. Tanabe, R. Tatsukawa, S. Saito, and N. Myazaki. "Reductions in the Testosterone Levels by PCBs and DDE in Dall's Porpoises of Northwestern North Pacific." *Marine Pollution Bulletin* 18 (1987): 643–46.

Swartzman, G. L., and R. J. Hofman. "Uncertainties and Research Needs Regarding the Bering Sea and Antarctic Marine Ecosystems." U.S. Department of Commerce, National Technical Information Service Publication PB91–201731, 1991.

Szalay, F. S. "Origin and Evolution of Function of the Mesonychid Condylarth Feeding Mechanism." *Evolution* 23 (1969): 703–20.

Tayler, C. K., and G. S. Saayman. "The Social Organization and Behaviour of Dolphins (*Tursiops aduncus*) and Baboons (*Papio ursinus*): Some Comparisons and Assessments." *Annals of the Cape Provincial Museum (Natural History)* 9, no. 2 (1972): 11–43.

———. "Imitative Behaviour by Indian Ocean Bottlenose Dolphins (*Tursiops aduncus*) in Captivity." *Behaviour* 44 (1973): 286–98.

Terry, R. P. "Intergeneric Behavior between *Sotalia fluviatilis guianensis* and *Tursiops truncatus* in Captivity." *Zeitschrift fur saugetierkunde* 49 (1984): 290–99.

Thayer, V. G., and K. A. Rittmaster. "Marine Mammal Strandings in North Carolina," 50–52. In K. R. Wang, P. M. Payne, and V. G. Thayer (Compilers), "Coastal Stock(s) of Atlantic Bottlenose Dolphin: Status Review and Management." Proceedings and Recommendations from a Workshop Held in Beaufort, North Carolina, September 13–14, 1993. NOAA Technical Memorandum NMFS-OPR-4, 1994.

Thewissen, J. G. M., ed. *The Emergence of Whales: Evolutionary Patterns in the Origin of Cetacea.* New York: Plenum Press, 1998.

Thewissen, J. G. M., and F. E. Fish. "Locomotor Evolution in the Earliest Cetaceans: Functional Model, Modern Analogues, and Paleontological Evidence." *Paleobiology* 23, no. 4 (1997): 482–90.

Thewissen, J. G. M., and S. T. Hussain. "Origin of Underwater Hearing in Whales." *Nature* 361 (1993): 444–45.

————. "Why All the Blubbering?" *BISON Brookfield Zoo* 7, no. 2 (1993): 12–17.

Wells, R. S., K. Bassos-Hull, and K. S. Norris. "Experimental Return to the Wild of Two Bottlenose Dolphins." *Marine Mammal Science* 14, no. 1 (1998): 51–71.

Wells, R. S., D. J. Boness, and G. B. Rathbun. "Behavior," 324–422. In J. E. Reynolds III and S. A. Rommel, eds., *Biology of Marine Mammals*. Washington, D.C.: Smithsonian Institution Press, 1999.

Wells, R. S., L. J. Hansen, A. Baldridge, T. P. Dohl, D. L. Kelly, and R. H. Defran. "Northward Extension of the Range of Bottlenose Dolphins along the California Coast," 421–31. In S. Leatherwood and R. R. Reeves, eds., *The Bottlenose Dolphin*. New York: Academic Press, 1990.

Wells, R. S., S. Hofmann, and T. L. Moors. "Entanglement and Mortality of Bottlenose Dolphins, *Tursiops truncatus*, in Recreational Fishing Gear." *Fishery Bulletin* 96 (1998): 647–50.

Wells, R. S., A. B. Irvine, and M. D. Scott. "The Social Ecology of Inshore Odontocetes," 263–318. In L. M. Herman, ed., *Cetacean Behavior: Mechanisms and Processes*. New York: Wiley and Sons, 1980.

Wells, R. S., and M. D. Scott. "Estimating Bottlenose Dolphin Population Parameters from Individual Identification and Capture-Release Techniques," 407–15. In P. S. Hammond, S. Mizroch, and G. P. Donovan, eds., *Individual Recognition of Cetaceans: Use of Photo-Identification and Other Techniques to Estimate Population Parameters*. Report of the International Whaling Commission, Special Issue No. 12, 1990.

————. "Incidence of Gear Entanglement for Resident Inshore Bottlenose Dolphins Near Sarasota, Florida." 629. In W. F. Perrin, G. P. Donovan, and J. Barlow, eds., *Gillnets and Cetaceans*. Report of the International Whaling Commission, Special Issue 15, 1994.

————. "Seasonal Incidence of Boat Strikes on Bottlenose Dolphins Near Sarasota, Florida." *Marine Mammal Science* 13, no. 3 (1997): 475–80.

————. "Bottlenose Dolphin *Tursiops truncatus* Montagu, 1821," 137–82. In S. H. Ridgway and R. J. Harrison, eds., *Handbook of Marine Mammals*. Vol. 6, *The Second Book of Dolphins and Porpoises*. New York: Academic Press, 1999.

Wells, R. S., M. D. Scott, and A. B. Irvine. "The Social Structure of Free-Ranging Bottlenose Dolphins," 247–305. In H. H. Genoways, ed., *Current Mammalogy*. Vol. 1. New York: Plenum Press, 1987.

Williams, T. M., W. A. Friedl, M. L. Fong, R. M. Yamada, P. Sedivy, and J. E. Haun. "Travel at Low Energetic Cost by Swimming and Wave-Riding Bottlenose Dolphins." *Nature* 355 (1992): 821–23.

Williams, T. M., W. A. Friedl, and J. E. Haun. "The Physiology of Bottlenose Dolphins (*Tursiops truncatus*): Heart Rate, Metabolic Rate, and Plasma Lactate Concentration during Exercise." *Journal of Experimental Biology* 179 (1993): 31–46.

Williams, T. M., B. Le Boeuf, R. Davis, D. Crocker, and R. Skrovan. "Integrating Behavior and Energetics in Diving Marine Mammals: New Views Using Video Technology." Fifth European Conference on Wildlife Telemetry, Strasbourg, France, August 25–30, 1996.

Wilson, B. "Review of Dolphin Management at Monkey Mia." Unpublished Report Submitted to Executive Director, Department of Conservation and Land Management, Western Australia, 1994.

Wilson, B. "The Ecology of Bottlenose Dolphins in the Moray Firth, Scotland: A Population at the Northern Extreme of the Species' Range." Ph.D. thesis, University of Aberdeen, 1995.

Wilson, B., P. M. Thompson, and P. S. Hammond. "Skin Lesions and Physical Deformities in Bottlenose Dolphins in the Moray Firth: Population Prevalence and Age-Sex Differences." *Ambio* 26, no. 4 (1997): 243–47.

———. "Habitat Use by Bottlenose Dolphins: Seasonal Distribution and Stratified Movement Patterns in the Moray Firth, Scotland." *Journal of Applied Ecology* 34 (1997): 1365–74.

Wilson, E. O. *Sociobiology: The New Synthesis.* Cambridge, Mass.: Belknap Press of Harvard University Press, 1975.

Wood, C. J. "Movement of Bottlenose Dolphins around the South-West Coast of Britain." *Journal of Zoology, London* 246 (1999): 155–63.

Wood, F. G., Jr., D. K. Caldwell, and M. C. Caldwell. "Behavioral Interaction between Porpoises and Sharks." *Investigations on Cetacea* 2 (1970): 264–77.

Woodcock, A. H., and A. F. McBride. "Wave-Riding Dolphins." *Journal of Experimental Biology* 28 (1951): 215–17.

Worthy, G. A. J., and E. F. Edwards. "Morphometric and Biochemical Factors Affecting Heat Loss in a Small Temperate Cetacean (*Phocoena phocoena*) and a Small Tropical Cetacean (*Stenella attenuata*)." *Physiological Zoology* 63, no. 2 (1990): 432–42.

Worthy, G. A. J., and J. P. Hickie. "Relative Brain Sizes in Marine Mammals." *American Naturalist* 128 (1986): 445–59.

Würsig, B. "Occurrence and Group Organization of Atlantic Bottlenose Porpoises (*Tursiops truncatus*) in an Argentine Bay." *Biological Bulletin* 154, no. 2 (1978): 348–59.

Würsig, B., and M. Würsig. "Behavior and Ecology of Bottlenose Porpoises, *Tursiops truncatus*, in the South Atlantic." *Fishery Bulletin* 77, no. 2 (1979): 399–412.

———. "Day and Night of the Dolphin." *Natural History* 88 (1979): 60–68.

Year of the Ocean Discussion Papers. Prepared by the U.S. Federal Agencies with Ocean-Related Programs, 1998. Copies available from Office of the Chief Scientist, NOAA, Washington, D.C.

Zagaeski, M. "Some Observations on the Prey Stunning Hypothesis." *Marine Mammal Science* 3, no. 3 (1987): 275–79.

Zimmer, C. "The Dolphin Strategy." *Discover,* March 1997, 72–83.

Index

APHIS. *See* Animal and Plant Health Inspection Service

Aquariums, 2, 152. *See also* Captivity; Education of the public

Archeocetes, 28

Archeoceti, 25

Art, dolphins in, 18, 19

Arteriovenous anastomoses (AVA), 58

Artiodactyls, 25–27, 28, 57–58, 63

Atlantic croaker. *See Micropogonias undulatus*

Atlantic spotted dolphin. *See Stenella frontalis*

Atlantis Marine Park, 2–3

Australia: Environment Protection and Biodiversity Conservation Bill of 1998, 198

Australia: National Parks and Wildlife Conservation Act, 199

Australia: Wildlife Conservation Act of 1975, 198

Autonomic nervous system, 138

AVA. *See* Arteriovenous anastomoses

"Babysitting." *See* Allomaternal care

Baiji. *See Lipotes vexillifer*

Bairdiella chrysoura, 128

Balaena mysticetus, 30*t*, 87*f*

Balaenidae, 30*t*

Balaenoptera musculus, 30*t*

Balaenoptera physalus, 30*t*, 37, 93–94

Baleen whale, 28, 30*t*, 169. *See also Balaenoptera physalus*

Basilosauridae, 28

Basilosaurinae, 28

Basking, 72

Beaching. *See* Die-offs

Beaked whales, 29, 30*t*, 211n.3

Behavior, 23; accomplishment of goals, 20; altruism (*see* Altruism); in captivity, relevance to the wild, 157; copulatory (*see* Copulatory behavior); diurnal, 132–33, 134*f*, 135; ecological aspects of, 105, 106;

effects of human contact on, 164–65; epimeletic, 121–22, 211n.11; feeding (*see* Feeding behavior); nurturing, 18, 120–21, 172; play, 122–23, 133, 134*f*; reproductive, 97*f*, 116, 117–19, 124; research methodology, 109–12; seasonal, 133–36; territoriality, 124–25; for thermoregulation, 72; use of tactile cues, 83

Beluga whale. *See Delphinapterus leucas*

Bends, 54, 65, 203, 217n.65

Berardius bairdii, 29, 30*t*, 69

Best-use plan. *See* Optimum sustainable population

Bioaccumulation: in blubber, 6, 46–47, 215–16n.41; in breastmilk, 5, 174

Bioconcentration, 5, 6

Birth, 97*f*, 152, 156*f*, 206, 222n.21

Birth defects, 4

Birth rate, 100–101

Birth size, 10, 98

Blood. *See* Circulatory system

Blowhole, 38, 38*f*, 180*f*; anatomy of, 54; sense of smell and the, 82; in sound production, 55*f*

Blubber: anatomy of, 42, 42*f*; buoyancy of, 46; composition of, 43–44; energy storage in, 37, 44; heat conduction by, 44; hydrodynamic efficiency and, 44, 45; lipophilic toxicants, 6, 46–47, 215–16n.41; as protection against predation, 46; seasonal changes in, 72, 134

Blue whale. *See Balaenoptera musculus*

Boats, effects on dolphins, 166, 168, 173, 174–75, 175*f*

Body heat. *See* Thermoregulation

Body length: dolphins, 32, 39, 94, 96, 98; other marine mammals, 95*t*

Body postures, 116

Body shape, 38, 43, 44

Body size, 40*f*; as an adaptation to the marine environment, 37; at birth, 10, 98; intraspecific variation, 32; life history strategy and, 89*t*

Body weight, 39, 137

Bootstrap analysis, 33

Bottlenose dolphin. *See Tursiops truncatus*

Bottlenose whale. *See Berardius bairdii*

Bowhead whale. *See Balaena mysticetus*

Bow riding, 50, 68*f*, 135, 166

Bradycardia, 66, 203

Brain, 20, 23; acoustic regions of, 75; anatomy of, 138–41, 138*f*; blood supply in, 58; encephalization quotient of, 142–44, 204, 233nn.33, 34; human, 137; lack of olfactory bulbs in, 82; magnetite in the, 82; in other marine mammals, 143*f*; as percent of body weight, 137, 143*f*; size of, 137, 142–44, 143*f*; tolerance to anaerobiosis of, 67

Breeding: in captivity, 125–26, 152, 156*f*, 160; episodes per lifespan, 89*t*; hybridization, 2, 125–26, 158–59. *See also* Reproductive status; Reproductive success

Brevetoxin, 7, 9

Brevoortia spp., 7

Bull shark. *See Carcharinus leucas*

Buoyancy: from blubber, 46; energy dynamics of diving, 68; lung volume and, 53–54, 65; from oil within bones, 51

Bycatch. *See* Fishing industry, dolphins as incidental take

Caldwell, David and Melba, 21, 112, 154

California sea lion. *See Zalophus californianus*

Calves: age at weaning, 95*t*, 98, 120, 227n.49; development of signature whistle, 77; discipline of, 124; and infanticide, 124; ingestion of toxicants in breastmilk by, 5, 174; interbirth interval fir, 91–92, 95*t*, 208n.21; mother carrying deceased, 99, 121, 223n.34; per lifetime for dolphins, 93, 95*t*, 96; per lifetime for other marine mammals, 93, 95*t*; rearing behavior (*see* Parental care); swimming with mother, 86*f*, 98*f*, 99*f*

Cancer, 6–7

Caperea marginata, 30*t*

Captivity, 151–64; breeding in, 125–26, 152, 156*f*, 160; breeding with other species in, 125–26; capture and release for research, 103*f*, 111, 157–58; ethical issues of, 2, 160, 161, 169; number of bottlenose dolphins in, 2, 207n.5; for rehabilitation, 155*f*, 158; and research issues, 156–59, 200; role in conservation of, 158–59, 200; survival rates in, 2; swim-with-the-dolphin programs, 161–64, 161*f*, 162*f*, 164*f*. *See also* Release

Carcharinus leucas, 102

Carcharinus obscurus, 102

Carcharinus plumbeus, 126

Carcharodon carcharias, 102

Carrying capacity, 87, 93, 104, 177, 178*f*, 203

"Cat's eyes," 173

Cerebellum, 138*f*, 139, 140*f*, 204

Cerebral cortex, 139–40

Cerebrum, 138*f*, 139*f*, 204

Cetacea, 14, 25, 27

Chemoreception, 82

Circulatory system: anatomy of, 58–59; blood volume in, 64; countercurrent heat exchangers in, 59, 60*f*, 61; thermoregulation by the, 44, 58–59, 60*f*

CITES, 197

Climate and life history strategy, 89*t*

Cognition, 145–49

Colonizing ability and life history strategy, 89*t*

Coloration. *See* Markings and coloration

Committee of Scientific Advisors on Marine Mammals, 167

Common dolphin. *See Delphinus delphis*

Communication, 21, 116; effects of noise pollution on, 175–76; of identity (*see* Sound production, signature whistle); "language-like," 145; response to hand signals, 146; role in conservation, 191;

Communication—*continued*
syntactic ability in, 146–47; telescoping
and, 52. *See also* Sound production
Conflict resolution, 190
Conservation, 185–201; definition of, 187–
88; development of the ethic of, 153,
153f, 154, 156, 163; dynamics of
stakeholders, 190; general approaches to,
189–92; life history strategy and, 93;
reasons for, 188–89; role of captivity in,
158–59, 200; three fundamental
principles of, 191; truisms of, 191–92.
See also Wildlife management
Conservation plans, 182, 194, 199, 243n.23
Contaminants. *See* Toxicants
Convergent evolution, 24
Copulatory behavior, 97f, 116, 118, 135
Corpora albicantia, 91
Corpora lutea, 91
Corpus callosum, 140
Countercurrent heat exchangers, 59, 60f, 61
Cranial nerves. *See* Nervous system, cranial
nerves
Crater feeding, 130, 131f
Cynoscion nebulosis, 128
Cytochrome B sequences, 33

Daily activity budget, 133–34, 134f, 135
Dall's porpoise. *See Phocoenoides dalli*
DDT and metabolites, 5
Death. *See* Diseases; Mortality
Delphinapterus leucas, 5, 6, 30t
Delphinidae, 29, 30, 30t, 40f, 212n.28,
213n.3
Delphinoidea, 29, 30
Delphinus delphis, 33, 63
Dentition. *See* Teeth
Deodenum, 57
Depleted stocks, 181–82, 194, 243n.28
Dermis, 42, 42f
Developmental toxicity, 4
Die-offs: algal toxins and, 7–9; of manatees,
7, 209n.35; of monk seals, 8, 9, 209n.50;

mortality rate from, 83; stock depletion
under the MMPA, 180–81, 194, 196,
243n.28; use of stranded dolphins for
research, 83, 91, 94
Diffusion, 218n.75
Digestive system, 56–58
Dinoflagellates, 7, 9
Diseases: common, 102, 156; group living
and, 106; introduction by human
contact, 165; introduction following
release, 158; morbillivirus, 8, 156, 180,
205; opportunistic, 8; susceptibility to
cancer (*see* Immunosuppression);
tumors, 4, 6–7, 159
Distribution, 31, 31f, 32, 178–79
Diurnal behavior, 132–33, 134f, 135
Diving: adaptations for, 51, 54, 58, 63, 64–
70; efficient movement during, 68; lung
volume and, 53–54, 65; time limit in,
68; training for, 68, 69f; "triad of
asphyxia," 64
DNA analyses, 27, 111, 119, 183
Dolphin Human Therapy, 163
Dolphin watching and dolphin feeding,
164–66, 165f, 188, 238n.63
Dominance. *See* Social aspects, dominance
hierarchies
Dorsal fin: anatomy of, 38, 38f, 39; use of,
in identification, 109, 110f
Dorudontinae, 28
Drag, 37, 46f; integument characteristics
which minimize, 41, 43, 45; pressure
(inertial), 45; viscous (frictional), 44;
wave, 45–46, 49
Dugong dugon, 51
Dusky shark. *See Carcharinus obscurus*

Ear: anatomy of, 52, 75–76, 80; of terrestrial
mammals, 76. *See also* Hearing
Echo (dolphin), 3
Echolocation, 54, 204; acoustic regions of
the brain, 75; anatomy of "equipment,"
79; ear anatomy and, 76; extrapolation of

Flukes, 38, 38*f*; circulatory system of, 70; fish whacking with the, 129*f*, 130; hydrodynamics of, 49; kerplunking with the, 130

Food: absorption of nutrients from, 57; energetics of eating and foraging, 37, 73; fresh water from, 64; simultaneous swallowing and breathing, 55*f*; sources of, 127, 128. *See also* Feeding behavior; Predator/prey relationships

Food supply, 128–29; effects of fishing industry on, 9, 10; effects on home range, 123; effects on sexual maturity, 93

Food web. *See* Bioconcentration; Predator/prey relationships

Foraging strategies, 37, 73, 127–32, 148

Forestomach, 57

Fossil record, 24, 25, 26, 28–31

Freeway (dolphin), 50, 158

Freeze brands, 111, 183

Function and structure, 35, 83–84

Galeocerdo cuvieri, 102

Gas exchange, 54, 65, 203, 217n.65

Gastric ulcerations, 102, 156

Gastrointestinal system. *See* Digestive system

Genetic analyses, 27, 111, 119, 183, 215n.26

Genetic aspects: of discrete stocks, 184, 196; of gene pool benefits to humans, 188; of mixing, 2, 125–26, 158–59

Genome, 27, 33

Genotoxicity, 4

Geographic Information System (GIS), 194–95

Gestation, 61, 95*t*

Gill net fishery. *See* Fishing industry, dolphins as incidental take

GIS. *See* Geographic Information System

Global Conference on the Non-Consumptive Utilization of Cetacean Resources, 160

Global warming, 74

Globicephala spp., 8

Globicephala macrorhynchus, 95*t*, 126

"Goosebeak." *See* Larynx

Grampus griseus, 40, 40*f*, 126

Gray whale. *See Eschrichtius robustus*

Great Barrier Reef Marine Park Authority, 198

Great white shark. *See Carcharodon charcharias*

Group living, 76*t*, 106–8, 112–16, 127

Group size, 106–8, 117

Growth rate, 39, 94, 98, 100, 204

Gulliver (dolphin), 111*f*, 155*f*

Gustation. *See* Taste

Gymnodinium breve, 7

Gyration Index, 139

Habitat degradation, 4, 12, 93, 173–76, 186, 200

Harassment, 166, 168, 209n.55, 238n.75

Harbor porpoise. *See Phocoena phocoena*

Harbor seals. *See Phoca vitulina*

Harp seal. *See Phoca groenlandica*

Hawaiian monk seal. *See Monachus schauinslandi*

Heard Island experiments, 176

Hearing: directional, 79; effects of noise pollution on, 175–76; functional anatomy of, 75–76, 140*f*, 144; intramandibular fat bodies, 36, 52, 76, 79; listening for prey, 127–28; range of, 76

Heart rate, slowing of, 66, 203

Hemoglobin, 64, 67

Hepatic degenerative disease, 156

Hepatitis, 102, 156

Herman, Louis, 145–46

Historical background: in ancient Greece, 17, 18, 19, 151; dolphins as directed take, 169–70; dolphins in captivity, 152, 159–60; mythological reference to, 18, 19, 21; population status of, 169–70

Home range, 3, 118, 123–24, 204

Hormone system: and ovulation, 61; and role of the pancreas, 57; and testosterone levels for determination of sexual maturity, 91

Human interactions with dolphins, 17–23, 150; associated with fishing (*see* Fishing; Fishing industry); boat collisions, 173; cognition research on, 145–48, 156; dolphin watching and dolphin feeding, 164–66, 165*f*, 188, 238n.63; environmental impact (*see* Habitat degradation; Toxicants); injuries due to, 162; killing dolphins with guns, 22, 176; for scientific research (*see* Research); swim-with-the-dolphin programs, 161–64, 161*f*, 162*f*, 164*f*; veterinary activities, 155*f*, 158

Humans: body size of, 137, 214n.5; brain of, 137; as components of ecosystems, 190; diving time limit of, 68–69; dolphins in therapy programs for, 163; hearing range of, 76; perception of dolphins as special by, 17–20, 22–23; photoreceptors in the eye of, 80; population growth of, 185, 189; and similarities to dolphins, 22, 41, 70; skull of, 52*f*; sperm production of, 226–27n.38

Humility principle, 191

Humpback dolphin. *See Sousa chinensis*

Humpback whale. *See Megaptera novaeangliae*

Hybridization, 2, 125–26, 158–59

Hydrodynamics, 49–50, 204. *See also* Buoyancy

Hypercapnia, 64

Hypodermis, 42, 42*f*

Hypothalamus, 138

Hypoxia, 64

Identification methodologies, 109, 110*f*, 111, 183

Idling, 132

Immunosuppression, 4–5, 6–7, 8, 174, 208n.25

Incidental take. *See* Fishing industry, dolphins as incidental take

Indicator species, 22

Indus river dolphin. *See Platanista indi*

Infanticide, 124

Infants. *See* Calves

Infections. *See* Diseases; Immunosuppresssion

Iniidae, 29, 30*t*

Insulation. *See* Blubber

Integument, 41, 43, 45

Intelligence, 20–22, 137–49

Interbirth interval, 91–92, 95*t*, 208n.21

Interbreeding with other species, 125–26

Interleukin-2 gene, 27

International Year of the Ocean, 185–86

Intramandibular fat bodies, 36, 52, 76, 79

Intraspecific variation, 32, 96

Ischemia, 67

Jaw, 35–36, 51–52, 79

Juveniles. *See* Calves

Kentriodontidae, 30

Kerplunking, 130

Kid, The (dolphin), 114–15, 114*f*

Kidney: anatomy of, 62, 62*f*, 63*f*; concentration of urine by the, 62, 63–64, 218–19n.83; reniculate, 62–63, 206

Killer whale. *See Orcinus orca*

Kogiidae, 30*t*

K-strategists. *See* Life history, K-strategists

Lactation: age at weaning, 95*t*, 98, 120, 227n.49; energetics of, 92; milk collection for research, 120*f*; nutritional cost of, 119; precipitated, 120; transfer of lipophilic toxicants to calves, 5, 174

Lagodon rhomboides, 128

Language, 147–48. *See also* Cognition; Communication; Sound production

Larynx, 54, 55*f*, 56

Legislation, worldwide, 198–99

Length. *See* Body length

Lesions, 4, 159

Life cycle, stages of the, 85

Life history: definitions, 85–86; of dolphins, 86–87, 94–104, 95*t*; K-strategists, 87–88, 89*t*, 98, 101*f*, 104, 192, 205; of manatee, 87*f*, 88, 90, 91–93; r-strategists, 87–88, 89*t*, 101*f*, 194, 205

Lifespan: age determination, 90*f*; breeding episodes per, 89*t*; of dolphins, 22, 86, 88, 100; of other marine mammals, 88, 95*t*

Lilly, Dr. John, 20, 137, 145

Limbs. *See* Pectoral appendages; Pelvic limb

Lipophilic toxicants, 5, 6, 46–47, 215–16n.41

Lipotes vexillifer, 159, 200

Liver disease, 156

Locomotion: hydrodynamics of, 41, 43, 44–45, 46*f*; minimization of drag (*see* Drag); swimming, 16, 38–39

Lung volume, 53–54, 65

Magnetic reception, 82

Magnetite, 82, 205, 221n.145

Mammalian features of dolphins, 16, 27, 41, 53, 210n.4

Mammals, terrestrial: digestive system of, 57; ear anatomy of, 79; life history strategy of, 87*f*, 88; musculoskeletal system of, 48*f*; phylogeny of, 25–28, 29*f*; sound production by, 55*f*; urinary system of, 62, 63*f*; vision of, 80. *See also* Humans

Mammary glands, 61. *See also* Lactation

Management. *See* Conservation; Marine Mammal Protection Act of 1972; Wildlife management

Manatee. *See* Trichechus manatus latirostris

Marine environment. *See* Adaptations, to the marine environment

Marine Mammal Commission, 167, 205, 238n.63

Marine Mammal Protection Act of 1972 (MMPA), 205; bycatch of dolphins under the, 170–71; collection limitations (*see* Permits); conservation plans in, 182,

194, 199, 243n.23; education requirements in, 154; as a global standard, 153; harassment under the, 166, 168, 209n.55, 238n.75; management strategy in, 93, 177, 178*f*, 180, 192, 194–97; swim-with-the-dolphin programs under, 163–64; "take" under the, 159, 209n.55; three issues addressed by, 170

Mariposia, 62, 63–64

Markings and coloration, 39; predator/prey relationships and, 40; in stock analysis, 183; thermoregulation by, 72; use in behavioral research, 109, 110*f*, 111

Mating. *See* Copulatory behavior

Maximum net productivity level (MNPL), 177, 178*f*

Maximum sustainable yield (MSY), 93, 179*f*, 192, 194–95

Media, dolphins in the, 2, 4, 201

Medulla oblongata, 138

Megaptera novaeangliae, 8–9, 30*f*

Melon, 38*f*, 40, 55*f*, 79

Mesencephalon, 138

Metabolic rate, 37

Metabolism: aerobic, 67, 203, 216n.54; anaerobic, 67, 216n.54; during a dive, 66–67; during thermal stress, 70

Micropogonias undulatus, 128

Migration, 123–24; of coastal migratory stock, 181, 196; effects of human contact on, 165; and magnetic reception, 82; seasonality of, 133–34, 135; traveling as percent of daily activity, 134*f*

Military uses of dolphins, 168–69. *See also* U.S. Navy research

Milk. *See* Lactation

Milling, 132, 134*f*

Mind of the Dolphin: A Nonhuman Intelligence, The, 137

Mirounga angustirostris, 69

Mirounga leonina, 64

Misha (dolphin), 3

MMPA. *See* Marine Mammal Protection Act of 1972

MNPL. *See* Maximum net productivity level

Molecular systematics, 24, 25, 26–28, 33, 183

Monachus monachus, 8, 9, 209n.50

Monachus schauinslandi, 11

Monitoring, 190

Monk seal. *See Monachus monachus*

Monodontidae, 29, 30, 30*t*

Morbillivirus, 8, 156, 180, 205

Morphometrics, 183

Mortality: in boat collisions, 173, 175*f*; during captivity, 160; capture in nets, 9, 170, 171, 171*f*, 183; data collection for MMPA, 182; gender ratio, 100; by gunshot, 22, 176; life history strategy and, 89*t*; mother carrying deceased calf, 99, 121, 223n.34; from predation by killer whales, 102; from predation by sharks, 11–12, 46, 100, 102; rates of, 83, 100–101; from sting ray spines, 11–12, 102; from toxicants, 7–9, 174; by trauma from other dolphins, 124. *See also* Die-offs

Ms. Mayhem (dolphin), 11*f*, 113, 114*f*

MSY. *See* Maximum sustainable yield

Mugil spp., 10

Mugil cephalus, 128, 129

Mullet. *See Mugil* spp.; *Mugil cephalus*

Musculoskeletal system, 42*f*, 50; anatomy of, 47–53; of the eye, 82; force generated by muscle contraction, 47–48, 48*f*; thermoregulation of the spinal cord, 61

Myelin, 139

Myoglobin, 42*f*, 64, 67, 205

Mysticeti, 14, 25, 29*f*, 30*t*, 205, 211n.3

Mythology, 18, 19, 21

Nasal passages, 54, 55*f*, 56, 79, 141

Nat (dolphin), 114*f*, 115

National Marine Fisheries Service (NMFS),

205; captivity permits by, 152, 153, 159, 167, 238n.74; dolphin rescue by, 3; listing of fisheries by category, 171; management responsibilities of, 182–83, 238n.73; overview of tour operators by, 166; public education program of, 197; swim-with-the-dolphins regulation by, 163

Navigation, 82

Neobalaenidae, 30*t*

Nephron, 62

Nervous system: acoustic nerves, 140*f*; adaptation to diving, 67; autonomic, 138; cranial nerves, 76, 140, 141, 232n.7; meninges, 221n.145. *See also* Brain

NMFS. *See* National Marine Fisheries Service

Noise pollution, 175–76

Norris, Dr. Kenneth, 1, 35, 116, 154*f*

Northern elephant seals. *See Mirounga angustirostris*

Notty (dolphin), 168

Nursery groups, 113, 120–21

Oceanaria. *See* Captivity

Odobenus spp., 51, 238n.73

Odontoceti: brain anatomy of, 139; definition of, 205; diving adaptations of, 67; phylogeny of, 28, 29, 29*f*; taxonomy of, 14, 25, 30*t*; telescoping of the skull in, 51

Offspring. *See* Birth; Calves; Parental care

Oil industry, 175, 186

Olfaction. *See* Smell, sense of

Opo (dolphin), 19

Optimality theory, 106, 107

Optimum sustainable population (OSP), 177, 178*f*, 192, 194–95, 205

Orcinus orca, 2, 12, 102

Organochlorine pesticides, 5, 6, 205, 208n.16

Origin of Species, The, 24

Osmoregulation, 62–63

OSP. *See* Optimum sustainable population
Ospanus tau, 128
Ovaries, 61, 91
Overharvest: life history strategy and
    recovery, 93; overfishing, 9, 10–11, 12;
    in wildlife management theory, 178,
    179*f*
Ovulation, 61, 91
Oxygen stores, 64–65, 67, 218n.75
Oyster toadfish. *See Ospanus tau*

Pakicetus spp., 28
Paleontological evidence. *See* Fossil record
Pancreas, 57
Pancreatitis, 102, 156
Pan-tropical spotted dolphin. *See Stenella
    attenuata*
Parasites, 102
Parental care, 119–22; allomaternal, 120–
    21; energetics of, 92; life history strategy
    and, 89*t*, 92, 93, 98, 119; low calf
    mortality and, 101; "playpens," 121;
    timespan with calves, 98–99, 113;
    training in parental skills, 121
Paternity testing, 111, 119
PBB. *See* Polybrominated biphenyls
PBR. *See* Potential biological removal
PCB. *See* Polychlorinated biphenyls
Pectoral appendages: anatomy of, 38, 38*f*,
    39; countercurrent circulation in, 59, 70;
    crater feeding with, 130, 131*f*; skeleton of
    the, 53
Pelvic bone, vestigal, 38, 53
Pelvic limb, 53
Penaeus duorarum, 86, 87
Penis, 39, 61
Perissodactyls, 26
Permits, 152, 153, 159, 167, 238n.74
Pesticides. *See* DDT and metabolites;
    Organochlorine pesticides
Phoca groenlandica, 170
Phoca vitulina, 6
Phocoena phocoena, 32, 44, 95*t*

Phocoenidae, 29, 30, 30*t*, 212n.28
Phocoenoides dalli, 6, 32
"Photo identification," 109
Photoreceptor cells, 80
Phylogeny, 25–34, 212n.28; definition of,
    206; evolutionary convergence in, 24;
    revision of, 213n.29; of the urinary
    system, 62, 63*f*
Physeter catodon: brain size of, 137–38, 144;
    diving by, 69; phylogeny of, 28; skull of,
    51; taxonomy of, 29; whaling of, 169
Physeteridae, 28, 30*t*
Physeteroidea, 29
Pilot whale. *See Globicephala* spp.;
    Globicephala macrorhynchus
Pinfish. *See Lagodon rhomboides*
Platanista indi, 144
Platanistidae, 29, 30*t*
Platanistoidea, 29
Play, 122–23, 133, 134*f*
Pneumonia, bacterial, 102, 156
Pod, definition, 112
Pollutants. *See* Toxicants; Toxins
Polybrominated biphenyls (PBB), 6
Polychlorinated biphenyls (PCB), 5, 6
Polymerase chain reaction (PCR), 24
Polymorphism, 32
Pons, 138
Pontoporiidae, 29, 30*t*
Population dynamics: energetics and, 74;
    life history strategy and, 86, 89*t*
Population status: current estimates of,
    178–79, 182; historical overview of, 169–
    70; human, 185, 189
Population stocks. *See* Stocks
Porpoises, 29, 30*t*, 212–13n.28
Porpoise Watcher, The, 35, 214n.3
"Porpoising" (leaping), 49, 50*f*, 206
Potential biological removal (PBR), 183,
    243n.28
Pox virus, 102, 156
Precautionary principle, 190–91
Predator/prey relationships, 40. *See also*

Feeding behavior; attunement to cues, 75; blubber, 46; coloration, 40; diversity of prey, 41; echolocation to stun prey, 78, 79*f*, 131; foraging strategies, 37, 73, 127–32, 148, 151; killer whales, 102; nursery groups, 121; patchiness of prey, 108; sharks, 11–12, 46, 100, 102, 126–27, 229n.102; social aspects, 106, 107–8, 121; sting rays, 11–12, 102, 127

Pressure drag, 45

Prey. *See* Predator/prey relationships

Primiparous, 5

Prosencephalon, 138

Protocetidae, 28

Pseudorca crassidens, 126

Public display. *See* Captivity

Pumpkin (dolphin), 113, 114*f*, 115*f*

Purse seine nets. *See* Fishing industry, dolphins as incidental take

Pygmy right whale. *See Caperea marginata*

Pyloric stomach chamber, 57

Queensland Department of the Environment, 199

Radioimmunoassay, 61

Radio tags, 111

Rake marks, 116, 124

Range, 31, 31*f*, 32, 182

Rearing of young. *See* Parental care

Recovery, from overharvest, 93

Recovery Plans, 243n.23

"Red tide," 7–8, 9

Reintroduction. *See* Release

Release: into degraded "natural" habitat, 12–13; impromptu or illegal, 3, 207n.9; programs for, 3–4; survival skills following, 2–4. *See also* Captivity

Renal function, 62–63

Reniculate kidney, 62–63, 206

Reproduction potential. *See* Fecundity

Reproductive behavior, 97*f*, 116, 117–19, 124

Reproductive organs: female, 61, 91, 111;

internal, 39, 91; male, 39, 59, 60*f*, 61, 90–91, 111; urogenital opening, 38*f*, 61

Reproductive status: assessment of, 90–91; synchronized, in nursery groups, 113

Reproductive success, 5, 10, 152

Reproductive toxicity, 6

Research: behavioral, 109–12; and captivity issues, 156–59, 167; capture and release for, 103*f*, 111, 157–58; and cognition, 145–48, 156; collection of dolphins for (*see* Permits); eyecups used in, 78*f*; milk collection for, 120*f*; by the U.S. Navy, 65*f*, 66*f*, 71*f*, 72*f*, 92*f*, 168–69; use of stranded dolphins for, 91, 94; *vs.* harassment by the public, 167–68

Respiration: fresh water from, 64; gas exchange in, 54, 65, 203, 217n.65; separation of swallowing and breathing, 55*f*, 56; surfacing to breathe, 37

Rete, 58, 206, 217–18n.72

Retina, 80, 81, 81*f*

Reversibility principle, 191

Rhombencephalon, 138

Ridgeway, Dr. Sam, 154*f*

Right whales, 30*t*

Risso's dolphin. *See Grampus griseus*

River dolphin, 29, 30*t*. *See also Lipotes vexillifer; Platanista indi*

Rorquals, 30*t*

Rostrum, 40, 121, 130

Rototags, 111, 111*f*

Rough-toothed dolphins. *See Steno bredanensis*

r-strategists. *See* Life history, r-strategists

Sandbar shark. *See Carcharinus plumbeus*

Satellite tags, 111, 111*f*

Saxitoxin, 7, 8, 9

Scientific Review Groups, 197

Scomberomorus cavalla, 211n.21

Scrotum, 59

Seal: bone density, 51; reproductive toxicity, 6. See also Mirounga angustirostris;

Seal—*continued*
  Mirounga leonina; Monachus monachus;
  Monachus schauinslandi; Phoca
  groenlandica; Phoca vitulina
Sea lion, 51, 238n.73. *See also Eumetopias*
  jubatus; Zalophus californianus
Sea otter. *See Enhydra lutris*
Seasonal behavior, 133–36
Sensory biology, 74–83
Serology, antibodies from past viral
  infections, 8
Sexual maturity, 10; age at onset of,
  dolphins, 5, 91, 94, 95*t*, 96, 222–23n.23;
  age at onset of, other marine mammals,
  91, 95*t*; determination of, 90–91, 111; life
  history strategy and, 89*t*; male-female
  dimorphism, 39, 94, 96
Sharks. *See* Predator/prey relationships,
  sharks
Shrimp, pink. *See Penaeus duorarum*
Sight. *See* Vision
Signature whistle. *See* Sound production,
  signature whistle
Silver perch. *See Bairdiella chrysoura*
Size. *See* Birth size; Body size; Group size
Skeleton. *See* Musculoskeletal system;
  Skull
Skin. *See* Integument; Markings and
  coloration
Skull: anatomy of, 51–52, 52*f*; evolution of
  the, 38; fatty deposit for hearing, 36, 52,
  76, 79; phylogeny of, 28, 30; telescoping
  of the, 38, 51, 52, 206
Sleep patterns, 141
Smell, sense of, 82, 141
Social aspects: of allomaternal care, 120–
  21; attunement to cues, 75; of brain
  size, 143–44; of daily socializing, 133,
  134*f*; of dominance hierarchies, 116,
  124–25; effects of the environment on,
  106, 135; of group living, 76*t*, 106–8,
  112–16, 127; of interactions with other
  species, 125–32; life history strategy

and, 89*t*; of long-term bonds, 92, 95*t*,
  99, 101, 136; of male pair bonds, 114–
  15, 126; of play, 122–23, 133, 134*f*; of
  signature whistles, 77, 113, 115; of
  social maturity, 222–23n.23; of sound
  production for group cohesion, 76*t*,
  112; of use of tactile cues, 83. *See also*
  Altruism
Sonar reflectors, 173
Sotalia fluviatilis, 125
Sound, speed in seawater, 75
Sound production, 76*t*; for echolocation,
  76, 76*t*, 78–80; by fishing nets, 173;
  imitation in, 148; popping, 118; by prey,
  127–28; signature whistle, 76–78, 77*f*,
  113, 115, 206; social aspects of, 76*t*, 112,
  116; structures involved in, 54, 55*f*. *See*
  also Hearing
Sousa chinensis, 125
South Africa: Marine Living Resources Act
  of 1998, 199
Sperm production. *See* Testes, sperm
  production
Sperm whale. *See Physeter catodon*
Spine, 49, 61, 82. *See also* Musculoskeletal
  system
Spinner dolphin. *See Stenella longirostris*
Spiritual aspects, 17, 188
Spotted dolphin. *See Stenella* spp.; *Stenella*
  attenuata; Stenella frontalis
Spotted sea trout. *See Cynoscion nebulosis*
Squalodontoidea, 29
Stellar sea lion. *See Eumetopias jubatus*
Stenella spp., 33
Stenella attenuata, 43–44, 140
Stenella coeruleoalba, 8
Stenella frontalis, 125
Stenella longirostris, 39–40, 40*f*, 116
Steno bredanensis, 126
Stewardship, 189
Sting rays. *See* Predator/prey relationships,
  sting rays
Stock assessments, 196

Stocks, 159; definitions of, 177, 180, 206; depleted, 181–82, 194, 243n.28; discreteness of, 184, 196; endangered, 180; geographic designations of, 181; identification and monitoring of, 183–84; and management considerations, 177–79, 192; potential biological removal from, 183; strategic, 196

Stomach compartments, 57–58

Strandings. *See* Die-offs

Striped dolphin. *See Stenella coeruleoalba*

Striped mullet. *See Mugil cephalus*

Strong v. United States, 238n.63

Structure and function, 35, 83–84

Sturgeon. *See Acipenser oxyrhynchus*

Subdermal sheath, 42–43, 47, 49

Subgroup, 206

Surface-area-to-volume ratio, 37, 43, 70

Survivorship, 89*t*, 101*f*, 160, 174

Sustainability, 187

Swimming, 16; adaptations for efficiency in, 49–50, 204; burst-and-glide, 68; flanking, 118; musculature for, 48–49; parallel, 117*f*; "porpoising" (leaping), 49, 50*f*; speed of, 38–39; wave or bow riding, 50, 68*f*, 135, 166

Swim-with-the-dolphin programs, 161–64, 161*f*, 162*f*, 164*f*

Syntactic ability, 146–47

Tactile sensation, 82–83, 116

Tagging, 111, 111*f*

Take, definition, 209n.55

Take reduction planning process, 196–97

Tapetum lucidum, 80

Taste, sense of, 82, 116, 141

Taxonomy, 25, 212n.28

Teeth, 15*f*, 51–52; age determination by, 90*f*; design of, 56; nondeciduous, 217n.61; number of, 39–40, 52; in taxonomy, 14, 28; of whales, 211n.3

Telencephalon, 138, 139

Telescoping. *See* Skull, telescoping of the

Terrestrial mammals. *See* Humans; Mammals, terrestrial

Territoriality, 124–25

Testes: anatomy of, 59, 60*f*, 61; determination of sexual maturity by, 90–91; and sperm production, 118, 222nn.10, 11, 226–27n.38

Testosterone. *See* Hormone system

Thalamus, 138

Thermoneutral zone, 70–71, 72, 73*f*

Thermoregulation, 70–73, 206; body size and, 37; by the circulatory system, 58–59, 60*f*, 70; energetics of, 37; role of blubber in, 37, 44, 47

Thunnus albacares, 10

Tidal state, 125

Tiger shark. *See Galeocerdo cuvieri*

Tongue, 82

Touch, sense of. *See* Tactile sensation

Tourism. *See* Dolphin watching and dolphin feeding; Swim-with-the-dolphin programs

Toxicants: in blubber, 6, 46–47; in breastmilk, 5, 174; DDT and metabolites, 5; definitions of, 206, 208n.15; deposition in the body (*see* Bioaccumulation); fertilizer, 9; lesions due to, 4, 159; lipophilic, 5, 6, 46–47, 215–16n.41; polybrominated biphenyls, 6; polychlorinated biphenyls, 5, 6; sewage, 174

Toxins, 7–8, 9, 206, 208n.15

Traveling. *See* Migration

Trichechus manatus latirostris: body weightof , 88; die-offs by, 7, 209n.35; life history strategy of, 87*f*, 88, 90, 91–93; management strategy for, 194; skeleton of, 51

Trophic levels. *See* Bioconcentration; Predator/prey relationships

True dolphins. *See* Delphinidae

Tucuxi. *See Sotalia fluviatilis*

Tuffy (dolphin), 68, 69*f*

Tursiops aduncus, 33

John E. Reynolds III is professor of marine science and biology at Eckerd College in St. Petersburg, Florida. He also holds a presidential appointment as chair of the U.S. Marine Mammal Commission. His research involves anatomy, behavior, life history, and population biology of manatees and dolphins.

Randall S. Wells is a behavioral ecologist with the Conservation Biology Department of the Chicago Zoological Society. He also serves as director of the Center for Marine Mammal and Sea Turtle Research at Mote Marine Laboratory in Sarasota, Florida, where his three-decade bottlenose dolphin research program is based. He has worked with a variety of dolphin and whale species, as well as with manatees.

Samantha D. Eide has worked for the past five years on the Eckerd College Dolphin Project. She graduated from Eckerd College in 1998 and is working toward her master's degree in marine science at University of South Florida. Her thesis involves behavioral ecology of bottlenose dolphins in Boca Ciega Bay.